D0973366

THE
BRAND
CALLED
YOU

Create a Personal Brand That Wins Attention and Grows Your Business

PETER MONTOYA with TIM VANDEHEY

New York   Chicago   San Francisco
Lisbon   London   Madrid   Mexico City   Milan
New Delhi   San Juan   Seoul   Singapore
Sydney   Toronto

The McGraw·Hill Companies

Copyright © 2009 by Peter Montoya. All rights reserved. Printed in the United States of America. Except as permitted under the United States Copyright Act of 1976, no part of this publication may be reproduced or distributed in any form or by any means, or stored in a data base or retrieval system, without the prior written permission of the publisher.

7 8 9 0   QFR/QFR   1 5 4

ISBN   978-0-07-159750-0
MHID   0-07-159750-6

McGraw-Hill books are available at special quantity discounts to use as premiums and sales promotions, or for use in corporate training programs. To contact a representative please visit the Contact Us pages at www.mhprofessional.com.

This book is printed on acid-free paper.

Library of Congress Cataloging-in-Publication Data

Montoya, Peter.
   The brand called you / by Peter Montoya with Tim Vandehey.
     p. cm.
   Includes bibliographical references and index.
   ISBN   0-07-159750-6 (alk. paper)
1. Success in business. 2. Brand name products. 3. Career development.
   I. Title.
HF5386.M746 2008
650.1—dc22

2008017053

CONTENTS

Introduction: Theory, Schmeory, I've Got a Business to Run   v

PART I: The DNA of a Personal Brand   1

CHAPTER 1—Why Brand Yourself?   3

CHAPTER 2—How Personal Branding Works   17

CHAPTER 3—Getting and Keeping the Cream of the Crop   31

PART II: The Brand with Three Brains   47

CHAPTER 4—Specialize or Spend   49

CHAPTER 5—Branding Channels   67

CHAPTER 6—Creating Customer Delight   96

PART III: Anatomy of a Personal Brand   109

CHAPTER 7—Brand Identity   111

CHAPTER 8—Personal Brochure and Personal Postcard   126

CHAPTER 9—The Internet   144

CHAPTER 10—Public Relations and Community Outreach   164

CHAPTER 11—Networking and Referrals 182

CHAPTER 12—Advertising 201

PART IV: It's Alive! Bringing Your Brand to Life in 12 Months 217

CHAPTER 13—Create Your Branding Strategy 219

CHAPTER 14—Launch Your One-Year Branding Plan 237

CHAPTER 15—Maintaining and Defending Your Brand 250

Resources 264

Index 267

INTRODUCTION: THEORY, SCHMEORY, I'VE GOT A BUSINESS TO RUN

Politics and Personal Branding go together like baseball and hot dogs, so let's talk politics for a second. Back in early 2007, it looked as if the long career of Senator John McCain was over. He seemed to be an also-ran for the 2008 Republican presidential nomination, far behind such glamorous candidates as former mayor of New York Rudy Giuliani, former Massachusetts governor Mitt Romney, and even former senator and TV actor Fred Thompson, whom some dubbed the heir to Ronald Reagan. By contrast, McCain was a maverick who angered conservatives with his refusal to adhere to party lines, hadn't raised much money, and wasn't getting much press coverage. Even former Arkansas governor Mike Huckabee began to steal his thunder, especially after "the Huck" won the Iowa caucuses.

But McCain did a very wise thing: he remained John McCain. He stayed on board his Straight Talk Express, didn't pander to anyone, and remained his authentic, cantankerous self. Compared with Romney, who seemed to flip-flop between liberal and conservative positions, Giuliani, who couldn't utter five words without saying, "9/11," and Thompson, who seemed to be asleep, McCain began to look pretty good. He seemed authentic: a genuine war hero who had been taking the same positions for decades and wouldn't back down from them. He was real. Voters responded, and you know the rest of the story. McCain wound up with the 2008 GOP nomination. From our perspective, he did a very smart thing: he established a Personal Brand and stuck to it despite what conventional wisdom dictated.

THE CURE FOR CONVENTIONAL WISDOM

Conventional wisdom says that when you're in a competitive situation, you should copy what the other guy is doing, only try to do it better. Don't go against the grain or stand out, because you might alienate someone, somewhere. Fit everyone else's mold. Like him or dislike him, that's precisely what McCain didn't do, and it worked wonders for him. Conventional wisdom is surprisingly stupid. I'd go so far as to say that following it is the surest way to end up on the sidelines, watching the more daring thinkers pass you by and wondering what in hell happened.

Do you ever find yourself asking these questions about your professional life?

- Why am I flush with cash one month and struggling the next?

- Why do competitors with less ability consistently get more business than I do?

- Why am I so dependent on a few clients?

- Why do I never seem to reach my income goals?

- When does it get easier?

If you do, you're not alone. Millions of self-employed professionals ask themselves those very same questions every year. They ask those questions because they find that making the living they aspire to means working more hours than they ever anticipated and having less time for enjoying life. They find that they spend far too much time scraping by, servicing unpleasant clients, and selling. They're not enjoying their lives, and they should be. *You* should be. Because things can be different, and I'm going to show you how to make them different.

I'm going to show you how to thumb your nose at conventional wisdom and do something that every successful professional in every industry has done to get rich:

Create an irresistible, dominant Personal Brand.

TWO DELUSIONS

What does that mean? I'll get to that as we go along, but right now, let's start by blowing a couple of pieces of conventional wisdom out of the water. Actually, these ideas are so ridiculous and so damaging to individual businesses that I'm going to call them what they are: *delusions*. You may have been running your business according to one or both of these delusions; the vast majority of professionals do. So to prepare for our dive into Personal Branding, I'm going to turn these two sacred cows into beef and make us some burgers.

> *Delusion 1:*
> *The public cares about your business.*
> *Reality:*
> *The public doesn't know you exist.*

Have you ever seen restaurants or stores in your community that open their doors with no fanfare or advertising, seemingly expecting people to know by telepathy that they're open? There's something very narcissistic about opening a business or professional practice; it's the center of your world, so it's easy to kid yourself that it's the center of other people's worlds as well. But it's not. We all have a thousand different entities clamoring for our attention every day—businesses, schools, civic organizations, churches, family, friends, doctors, and so on. If we don't know you personally, we don't care about your business unless you make us care. Businesses that don't find a way to make other people care about them aren't around very long.

> *Delusion 2:*
> *You're offering something different from and superior to your competitors' offerings.*
> *Reality:*
> *You're offering pretty much the same services.*

OK, you're good enough and smart enough, and, doggone it, people like you. I know this one is hard to swallow. We all want to feel that we do what we do better than anyone else. But while you have your strengths and certain skills that may be superior to those offered by others, you're probably not offering a service that's all that different from what your competition is offering. If you're a family physician, you're offering physicals and vaccinations and prescriptions. If you're a tax lawyer, you're offering tax planning and tax shelters and negotiations with the IRS. And so on. There will be variations here and there, but there's not much new under the sun.

This all means that what many professionals are relying on to grow their businesses—being better than the other guy and somehow using a business card and a Yellow Pages ad to make people care about them—isn't going to work. Ever. Sure, you'll get some business using those methods, but you didn't go to med school or law school or architecture school or get your stockbroker's license to get "some business." You've worked hard to make a great living and build a great lifestyle, and if that's not happening, it's probably because you've been buying into that delusional conventional wisdom.

WHAT IS PERSONAL BRANDING?

Personal Branding is the key to changing all that. Quite simply, it's the most potent tool for building a million-dollar professional practice that's ever been devised. Used properly, with creativity, planning, and consistency, a Personal Brand will help you do three things:

1. Turn your name and persona into a distinctive "product" that has desirable qualities associated with it.

2. Attract a more elite, more profitable type of clientele.

3. Help you retain more of those top-quality clients even when business is slow for everybody else.

We've established that you can't win by talking about how much better you are than your competition, and that you can't expect people to simply walk in your door and hand you their money. Your only advantage is yourself. What you do may not be unique, but *you* are. So instead of focusing on services or price, you're going to focus on yourself, to reach out to your target market and shape how they think about you and how they see you—to connect with them personally. That's what a Personal Brand does for you. If that sounds counterintuitive and scary, good. Defying conventional wisdom is always scary. It's also effective.

But we're talking a lot about business-this and professional-that, so who is this book really for? Ideally, it's for anyone running a professional practice:

- Health-care providers (physicians, dentists, therapists)

- Attorneys

- Financial advisors

- Real estate agents

- Insurance and mortgage brokers

- Architects

- Personal trainers

- Consultants / Coaches

But in reality, it's completely applicable to anyone running a personal-service business whose name is on the business card: contractors, caterers, graphic designers, owners of advertising agencies, clothing designers, interior designers, and professional speakers, to name a few. If you're the star of the show, you need a powerful Personal Brand.

You are your business. Clients choose you not because you have a cool business card or a snazzy office, but because something about you makes them trust you and decide that you can give them something that they value. Clients choose to work with *you*. The problem with that, of course, is that it means that the growth of your business is entirely dependent on you. You end up putting in long hours, spending a fortune acquiring new clients, and neglecting the other parts of your life that you really enjoy. Your business ends up running you instead of the other way around.

A Personal Brand becomes your "proxy self." It is you in the minds of prospects, and it's out there working for you, attracting new business, while you're on the beach in Maui. A great brand gives you the power to escape the cage of profits earned = hours worked. Professionals with the strongest Personal Brands (and the best systems to run and grow them) actually work fewer hours than their competitors and make many times more money each year!

THE DOCTOR IS IN

Sounds pretty good, doesn't it? In *The Brand Called You*, I'm going to walk you through every real-world step you need to take in order to build, launch, and maintain your own money-making, business-changing Personal Brand. I'm also going to do it with a minimum of psychobabble. There's a whole school of study about how branding works on the mind, and while I find it fascinating, I suspect you won't. Let's face it, you're out there every day trying to make a living, fend off competition, deal with government regulation, and somehow, some way, grow your company or practice. So this book will deliver a treasure trove of practical branding advice—things you can do today, tomorrow, next week, and next month to start turning yourself into a winning brand and building your business around that brand.

To do this, I'm going to take a page right out of Dr. Frankenstein: I'm going to build our Personal Brand part by part. I'll start with some information about the basic principles that make branding work, then move on to the essential components, the most important being specialization. Then I'll start sewing the parts together with the help of my hunchbacked lab assistant, and finally, I'll bring the brand to life, no atmospheric electrical storm required. By the time we're done, you'll have the equivalent of a master's degree in Personal Branding . . . and a huge edge over your competitors.

But since this is a book about practical advice, let's not waste any time. Here's your first real-world recommendation:

Name your business after yourself.

You may have already done this, and if so, great. Don't change a thing. But if you've given in to the temptation to name your practice Alliance Capital Investment or ThinkWell Marketing and Design or some other dreadful thing, stop what you're doing and pay attention.

You must name your business after yourself. Period. No one calls to talk to Alliance Capital; they call to talk to you. No one refers ThinkWell; they give your name and number to their colleagues who need advertising. You create the value, not your company name. Let's face it, the only reason you chose that silly name in the first place was so that people would think you're larger than you are. But trust me, you're not fooling anyone.

Corporations are the enemy in today's popular culture. They're faceless, uncaring, monolithic, and corrupt. They have a terrible image. Why would anyone choose a health-care provider who sounded like a corporation when she could choose to trust an individual human being who has the same basic concerns as she does? When you're looking to brand yourself, giving yourself a name that sounds like one of the Fortune 500 is the kiss of death.

Still doubtful? You're not alone. In my Personal Branding seminars, I run into more resistance on this issue than on almost any other. So let's try an exercise. On a piece of paper, write down 15 to 20 luxury brand names. They can be in any industry: clothing, shoes, cars, watches, wine, jewelry, and so on. If you're like me, you have a list that looks something like this:

Ferragamo

Versace

Mercedes-Benz

Dom Perignon

Rolex

Rolls-Royce

Prada

Reidel

Kohler

Lauren

Bang & Olufsen

BMW

Bentley

Yves Saint Laurent

L'Oréal

Cartier

Armani

Take a look at your list. How many of the luxury brands you listed are someone's name? On my list, the only ones that aren't are Rolex and BMW. Every other one began as a person who started a company, built it over time, developed a reputation for excellence, and along the way crafted a stellar Personal Brand. That's the power your name can have if you support it with the right message, the right marketing, and, above all, consistency and persistence.

So there's your first piece of practical counsel. There's a lot more to come. Let's get started.

Peter Montoya
June 2008

PART I

THE DNA OF A PERSONAL BRAND

CHAPTER

$$\boxed{1}$$

WHY BRAND YOURSELF?

Developing a strong personal brand can be the key to rising above the competition. It serves as shorthand to convey your skill set and style—whether you're a coordinator looking beyond your current job responsibilities or a midlevel network executive aiming for the presidency. Branding gives you an exceptionally effective way to broadcast who you are to your target market quickly and efficiently.

—Rick Haskins, Multichannel News

You know the names. Tiger. Oprah. Trump. Schwab. Madonna. They're among the few elite celebrities who can be instantly identified by a single set of syllables. More to the point, their names bring to mind an overpowering set of qualities—positive and negative—for almost anyone who hears them. That's the very definition of a world-class Personal Brand. You're not in that class; you probably don't have aspirations to be world-famous and have your picture in the supermarket tabloids. But you can be like these celebrities in one important way: you can have a public persona that stands for something clear, powerful, and compelling in the minds of the people you come into contact with.

WHAT IS A PERSONAL BRAND?

A clear, powerful, compelling public image—that's the very definition of a Personal Brand. There's a lot of talk about corporate and personal brands these days, and as a result, there's a great deal of confusion. When you hear about Nike or Anheuser-Busch spending $30 million on a brand-development campaign, it can be easy to conclude—incorrectly—that this branding stuff isn't for you. So let's cut through the clutter and talk about the three things that a Personal Brand is.

THINGS YOU CAN DO TODAY

1. Quit using your cheap brochures and promotional items.

2. Begin the process of changing the name of your business to your name.

3. If you haven't done it already, reserve the Web domain name www.yourname.com. It costs about $8.99 a year.

4. Write down the qualities that make you unique.

5. Write down your goals for income earned and hours worked 1 year, 5 years, and 10 years from now.

6. Write a description of your ideal client. This is the person you're going to target with your brand.

First of all, your Personal Brand is *you*, enhanced and expressed using polished, well-crafted communication methods. It is designed to convey two vital pieces of information to your target market:

1. Who you are as a person

2. What you specialize in doing

Your Personal Brand is the mental picture your prospects get when they think about you. It represents your values, your personality, your expertise, and the qualities that make you unique among your competitors. That's why it's so important to remain authentic to yourself as you create your brand. People want to work with you, not with some slick marketing creation.

Second, a Personal Brand is a *promise*. It tells prospects what they can expect when they deal with you. It's an implied covenant between a service provider and a client that makes the client believe, "Every time I see this person, I will receive a certain quality of service and care." You see this all the time with consumer product companies such as Apple Inc. Apple's customers are among the most fiercely loyal in the world; they hang on every new product release and line up for blocks to get new gadgets like the iPhone. They expect a certain set of valuable qualities from Apple: beautiful design, intuitive functionality, and innovative features. That's Apple's brand promise, and as long as the company continues to deliver on that promise, its brand will remain strong.

A Personal Brand creates expectations in the minds of others of what they'll get when they work with you. If you can figure out what your target market values and create a brand that promises to deliver that value again and again, prospects will beat down your door and burn up your phone lines. The catch: you've got to deliver on that promise 100 percent of the time. More on that later in the book.

A great example of a Personal Brand promise is Charles Schwab. Once upon a time, he was a lone financial professional, but now he's CEO of one of the world's largest discount brokerage houses. But his Personal Brand still carries a powerful promise: when we invest through his company, we'll be treated as if we're wealthy.

Finally a Personal Brand is a *relationship* that wields influence over prospects and clients. The attributes of your brand will determine how much influence you have. For example, if your best friend the carpenter tells you that you need to stop smoking and lose weight, you're probably going to scoff, but if your personal physician tells you the same thing, you're going to take it more seriously. The attributes of the relationship give the physician more authority in his or her area of specialization. In this book, you're going to learn how to create a brand that will help you build a relationship with your clients that casts you as a key influencer. This will help you reach three important goals:

1. Attract more new clients more easily

2. Increase your prices or fees to increase your income

3. Create client delight and generate a steady flow of referrals

WHAT A PERSONAL BRAND DOES

Linguist and anthropologist Gregory Bateson said, "The processes of perception are inaccessible; only the products are conscious and, of course, it is the products that are necessary." Personal Branding is all about perception—how other people perceive you. Try asking yourself this question: who is the "you" that people know? Sure, people who have become your clients or patients know you as a person, but what about the majority who've never worked with you? Do they know you, or do they know a *perception* of you constructed from ads in the telephone directory, maybe your name on a sign, and a newspaper ad or two, plus maybe some hearsay?

It's an interesting thing to ponder, isn't it? The "you" who's working in your office every day is not the same "you" that other people perceive before they have a personal, one-to-one relationship with you. That "you" is a perception made up of a hundred randomly assembled parts over which you have very little control.

Personal Branding is about taking control of how other people perceive you before they come into direct contact with you. Believe it or not, you already have a Personal Brand. People already have a perception of you, even if it's "just another accountant" or "that lawyer over on State Street." That's a brand you've built accidentally without even being aware of it. But here and now, you're going to start taking conscious control of that process and taking control of public perception.

Doing so will allow you to achieve three goals that are critical to making more money and building the lifestyle you want:

1. *Making people see that you're different.* Specialization—the perception that you're a specialist in an area of business that's

valuable to your audience—is the most important part of a successful Personal Brand.

2. *Helping people see you as being "like them."* We all want to work with people we like, people who "get us," who we feel share our values, and who are real and authentic. Your brand helps people relate to you on a personal level.

3. *Getting prospects in the door.* We live in a society that's saturated in sales and marketing, and we've come to be resentful of it. According to *USA Today*, consumers see an average of 3,500 to 5,000 marketing messages on a typical day. Our sales resistance is sky-high. You only have to look at the incredible popularity of the Do Not Call list to see that Americans hate to be sold to. So how do you get people into your office where you can use your charm and sales skills to turn them into clients? Your Personal Brand gives them a comfort level so that they'll prequalify themselves and make the appointment.

THINGS YOU CAN DO IN A WEEK

1. Decide on a new tagline that reflects who you are and what you do in the most precise way possible.

2. Break down all your clients/patients into three categories: A (most desirable), B (moderately desirable), and C (clients you'd rather not keep).

3. Make appointments to sit down with a cross section of your best clients and ask them why they keep coming back to you.

4. Look at your fees versus the industry average and your competitors' fees. Are you charging too much or too little?

5. Contact the companies that run your phone directory ads and any other advertising and either renegotiate your rates or pull your ads until you've built your new brand.

6. Talk to your staff about Personal Branding and get their opinions.

FEWER CLIENTS, BETTER CLIENTS

A great Personal Brand is your ticket to get off the treadmill of selling, spending money on marketing tools that don't work, and constantly chasing after every potential client who comes within striking distance. To return to politics for a second, one of the keys in political campaign strategy is said to be "define yourself before your opponent can define you." If you don't get your message out fast and firm, your opponent may call you a "flip-flopper," and you'll find yourself playing defense when you should be on offense.

By defining yourself in the minds of your prospects instead of letting them define you, your brand *attracts* new business to your door, so you spend less time doing business development and more time servicing clients. But a great brand does something else that's just as vital: it improves the *quality* of your clients. Let's say you're a CPA who specializes in tax preparation for other professionals—doctors, lawyers, and the like. If your only means of bringing in new business is a Yellow Pages ad, a few bus bench ads, and some cold calling, what type of new clients are you likely to attract? Clients who shop based primarily on price. You're going to get mostly people who are looking for the cheapest tax preparation service they can get, but who are going to want quality as well. So you're likely to end up with a bunch of demanding new clients who eat up your time and bring you minimal income . . . and some of them will probably complain about your fees anyway.

When you have a Personal Brand that positions you as a specialist and communicates who you are and what you stand for, you're going to attract a different type of client. If your branding materials (brochures, ads, signage, and so on) are polished and expensive-looking, you're automatically going to chase away some of the price-centric lookyloos. Instead, you're more likely to get calls from professionals who think, "He's like me; he's among the elite in his profession. I'd like to work with him." These will be people who will see your work not as a commodity but as a valuable expert service. They'll pay more for what you can offer, and because of that, you'll be able to turn away a lot of the budget business. The right brand leads to fewer but more lucrative clients, fewer hours worked, more money earned per hour, and a less stressful, more enjoyable business.

Who in his or her right mind wouldn't want that?

BRAND SURGERY
THE PATIENT: YOUR COMPANY BRAND

- Do not create a company brand that's separate from your Personal Brand. You are your company.

- If you have employees, pass along to them the personal values that make you love your business. They help spread your brand in everything they do, and if they understand your passions, most of them will reflect those passions. Get rid of the ones who don't.

- Design your workspace to reflect your Personal Brand. This doesn't have to mean renovating your building (let's be realistic), but it can be as simple as small changes in décor, signage, or furniture.

- Be specific in communicating the benefits underlying your brand and how they are reflected in your company. Everyone offers "great customer service" or "the lowest prices." Use your brand to communicate the unique things you do that create value, from creativity to specialized experience to comfortable chairs.

- Don't make your brand dependent on your direct involvement. If you do, you'll be a slave to your business, with everything being dependent on your hands-on participation. Part of being a successful Personal Brander is creating brand maintenance systems that keep things humming along while you're on vacation.

BRAND CASE STUDY

The Brand: David Bach

Specialization: Commonsense financial information for people who want to "finish rich"

Location: New York, NY

Channels: Books, seminars, Web, radio, television, motivational seminars and speaking

(continued)

Highlights: Bestsellers including *The Automatic Millionaire; Smart Women Finish Rich; Smart Couples Finish Rich; Start Late, Finish Rich;* and *Go Green, Finish Rich*—more than six million copies in print in 15 languages distributed in more than 40 countries

Online: www.davidbach.com, www.finishrich.com, and www.green green.com

The Story: David Bach was a senior vice president at Morgan Stanley and a partner of the Bach Group, which during his tenure managed over half a billion dollars for individual investors and still operates, run by his sister. Sensing demand, Bach began offering a series of Finish Rich seminars and eventually wrote his first book, *Smart Women Finish Rich.* Since then, his philosophy—values first, money second—has become a national movement that is revolutionizing how people save for the future and use their money to create the lifestyle they crave. Today, Bach has had nine consecutive bestsellers, including *Start Late, Finish Rich; The Automatic Millionaire Homeowner;* and *The Automatic Millionaire Workbook.* His latest bestselling book is on the environment and titled *Go Green, Live Rich.*

How It All Started: Bach came into his niche with passion and purpose. His first series of seminars, on money and investing for women, was a huge success; 200 women attended where he had expected 20 or 30. He realized that there was a tremendous need for what he could offer. "I was raised by a grandmother who taught herself how to invest," he says. "I thought all women were in charge of the money, but many were not. So, I started meeting with widows whose husbands had been managing the money. I taught that first class to bring our own clients up to speed."

As so often happens, the title of the seminar helped drive its popularity. "'Smart Women Finish Rich' has an emotional impact on people that drives them to the seminars," Bach says. "The title was a very important decision. When I wrote a book based on the seminar, the material I had been teaching for five years, I used the same title. I applied the knowledge that I had been teaching for years and packaged it to reach millions. Many people think that you package your knowledge to make money. The truth is, you package your knowledge to help more people. The more people you successfully help, however, the more you succeed. It's a wonderful circle of life, where you live and finish rich. After the initial success of the first seminars, I realized there was a national need for this information, and ultimately a global demand."

What This Brand Stands For:

- *A simple, friendly approach to explaining the dizzying world of finance.* Bach somehow manages to make subjects like exchange-traded mutual funds understandable, and his advice is always expressed in normal language without talking down to his reader.

- *The Latte Factor.* Bach came up with this shorthand label for the idea of daily spending that we don't even think about but that adds up to big money over a long period. It's become nationally known and a source of instant recognition for his personal brand.

- *Longevity.* "I've stood the test of time," Bach says. "I've been referred to as the John Grisham of personal finance. I've not written one book and gone away; I've written nine books in nine years. I did a tour with Trump and Tony Robbins, which was a cue that my brand had reached a new level—to be sharing the stage with those two was a sign that my brand had reached a new stage. Over a million people attend my seminars throughout North America. I am now using my trusted status with consumers and the media to talk about the need to act on the issue of global warming. My book launch has impacted over a hundred million people, and it is the most fulfilling campaign of my life."

- *Caring.* Bach is truly passionate about his subject and is willing to go to the mat to bring his passions to American readers. He tells the story of how *Go Green, Live Rich* came about:

  I got separated, moved with my son into an environmentally friendly building, and my son's asthma and my allergies improved overnight. I realized how important it is to live in an environmentally clean building. A lot of the changes I was making in my life were not only improving my health and my son's health but were also saving me

  (*continued*)

money. Some people may assume that this was a smart marketing effort, but in reality my publisher originally didn't want to publish the book, feeling the market wasn't big enough for a book on the environment. It took me three months to sell them on Go Green. I wrote the book for no advance and told them, "This is really important to me, please support me," and they have. It was the hardest book I've ever done. I had to learn a new topic, but this is something I'm really passionate about. I think what's happening with my brand is that I've really become a consumer advocate. My next book will be called Fight for Your Money, *about all the ways that Americans are being ripped off financially and how to fight for your money.*

X-Factor: A woman named Oprah. In January 2004, Bach launched *The Automatic Millionaire* on *The Oprah Winfrey Show,* and the result was galvanic: not only was the book a number one bestseller within two weeks, but Bach's backlist books all hit the bestseller list as well. Bach is grateful: "It took me almost five years to sell a million books, and on Oprah I reached tens of millions of readers in a week, and we sold a million more books in the next six months," he says. "They had such amazing feedback that they immediately booked me to do another show, a couples show. All my books were on the bestseller list. In 2005 I had six books on the bestseller list for the year, a record for the publishing industry."

Branding Wisdom: "A lot of people look at me and think everything has been strategic, that I have some master plan. And there has been a plan, but the main thing has been to keep things simple. I listened to my readers. When I was a financial advisor, people said, 'This is what's great about what you do, but I need it simpler.'

"I didn't set out to brand myself. None of my books have my picture on the front. They are books about my audience, not about me. But when you go on TV shows and on stage in front of 10,000 people, your brand gets elevated. I haven't been out there trying to be famous. I stay focused on a mission in terms of delivering a message that changes peoples' lives. My brand is about making a difference; it is what I have dedicated my life to."

EVERYTHING IS BRANDING

In Chapters 2 and 3, we're going to talk in greater detail about how Personal Branding works and what kind of bottom-line results it can deliver for your business. But before we go on, I've got to make a critical point about branding and what it means for your future:

Once you create a Personal Brand, there's no turning back.

Sounds harsh, doesn't it? Well, business can be harsh. The fact is, once you establish and launch a brand, you're committed. Everything you do in your professional life—and even some of the things you do publicly in your personal life—affects your Personal Brand. You see, every brand is kind of like a ship under sail, constantly in a state of equilibrium between the force of the wind that moves it forward and that same force that wants to tear out the masts and sink the ship. Make the wrong decision at the helm or misread the weather and you're calling Mayday and breaking out the life rafts.

A Personal Brand also exists in a delicate equilibrium between the promise you make to your market and your daily actions. Once you've established your brand, everything you do will either confirm that promise or contradict it. If your brand pledges an incredible customer service experience, you've got to deliver that experience at least 90 percent of the time. Every time you fail, you dent your brand slightly. Enough failures—enough contradictions of your promise—and you'll wreck your brand. People will start to assume that your promise is a lie and that you're a phony. Then you're sunk. Mayday.

That's why once you create a Personal Brand, everything you do is branding. What do I mean by everything? Consider this list:

- What you drive
- What you wear
- Where you dine
- What charities you give to
- Where you attend church

- How clean the exterior of your building is

- How your home looks

- How you shake hands

I could go on for a while. It seems ridiculous, doesn't it? What does your choice of restaurant have to do with the public perception of you as a lawyer? Well, what if you've branded yourself as a champion advocate for the Latino community, but you never, ever eat in the authentic *taquerias* in your neighborhood? Mightn't the locals think your talk about being a Latino champion is hot air? It's not rational, but consumers aren't rational. We make buying decisions based on emotion just as much as on intellect.

When you commit to creating a Personal Brand, you're really committed. That's why it's so essential that your brand reflect who you really are—what you care about, what you enjoy, and how you live. If it's not authentically you, you won't be able to support it in the long run.

THINGS YOU CAN DO IN A MONTH

1. Start searching for copywriters, designers, and Web developers to assist you in creating your branding tools.

2. Start attending networking events and making important referral contacts.

3. Redesign your entire "look"—your office, your attire, and your physical appearance—to suit your brand. For example, if you're branding yourself as a dentist who's also a sailor, you need to look the part.

4. Create a one-year branding budget. We'll cover this in great detail later on.

5. Implement suggestions from your staff on how to support your Personal Brand at each client interaction.

6. Decide on the characteristics that will define your Personal Brand.

PERSONAL BRANDING TRUTHS

We're almost ready to move on to look at the components that make a Personal Brand get results in the marketplace, but before we do, I want to share some hard, cold truths about branding that you need to know. There are plenty of misconceptions about Personal Branding, and if you're going to become a branding expert, you need the facts. So, without further ado:

1. *Branding takes time.* A smart brander can put the elements of a great brand in place, but it's going to grow at its own pace. Brands are about trust, and trust comes with time. You can't manufacture it. Oprah Winfrey is a perfect example of growing a brand over time with exposure, sincerity, and accomplishment. She spent years acting, doing her talk show, and working to help other women before she became a world-famous media mogul. Even the best Personal Branding campaigns take six months to a year to show measurable results. It's important to temper your expectations, because if you think you're going to get a flood of new business in a week, you're going to get discouraged and give up too soon.

2. *Brands grow organically.* The best Personal Brands develop at the grassroots level, in the community, based on relationships and the person behind the brand staying consistent and on message. With the help of judicious PR and consistent public exposure, people start to perceive that you're someone they can trust and relate to. You can't force a Personal Brand down someone's throat in this skeptical age; they'll spit it back in your face. You have to plant your brand, tend it, and let it grow.

3. *Brands are not rational.* Imagine the meeting when ad agency Wieden+Kennedy pitched the slogan "Just do it" to Nike. The tagline had nothing to do with shoes, but it's become a classic. Why? Because branding is about emotion. People will not choose to work with you because you went to the best dental college or because you offer the widest range of investment advisory services. They'll choose you because you "feel" right. You must account for the irrational nature of decision making when you build your brand.

4. *Brands demand absolute commitment.* David Bach, whom you met earlier in a personal brand case study, says that he built his brand primarily by staying on the road constantly pitching his "finish rich" message and by publishing nine books in nine years. Most great brands are built through sheer persistence and repetition. There's no magic bullet, just a lot of work and smart decision making.

5. *Branding always has an effect.* You hear a lot these days about how branding doesn't work. Nonsense. Branding always works. The thing is, it can work for you or against you. But it always has an effect. A strong, appealing Personal Brand will enhance your business and increase your profits; an artificial or poorly supported brand will waste your money and harm your business. Branding always works. The question is, how will it work for you?

BY NOW YOU SHOULD BE . . .

- Questioning your business model

- Looking around at what your most successful competitors are doing

- Assessing your life and career goals

- Thinking about how you're perceived

- Tossing any cheap brochures, flyers, business cards, or Yellow Pages ads you've been using in the trash

---

HOW PERSONAL BRANDING WORKS

A Personal Brand is a positive expectation, a promise to your market. It is the preferred position in your client's mind. A personal brand owns the equity stake, the mindshare on which no one else can compete.

— Joe Heller, president, Heller International

You went to college. You may have earned a graduate degree, or even a doctorate. Congratulations. You pride yourself on having a strong intellect, being driven by reason and analysis, being a researcher and a person who makes decisions based on the data. You're not prone to hazy thinking or tear-jerky responses. Then you go shopping for a new car, and what do you do when you get into the showroom?

You sit in the driver's seat and inhale. You sink into the leather seats and count the cup holders. You listen to how the doors sound when they close. A solid clunk? Must be a good car. But wait, where's your sheaf of notes about fuel economy, safety and rollover ratings, reliability, and resale value? Whoops, you must have left them on your desk.

Bryan Eisenberg, cofounder of the marketing consulting firm Future Now and author of *Call to Action*, makes the issue crystal clear when he writes, "People rationalize buying decisions based on facts, but they make buying decisions based on feelings." That's true even for the most educated, scientific, and rational people in society, even if we may not want to admit it. We're driven by our emotions to buy the things that satisfy a visceral need for something shiny, for power, for cool design, or to feel sexy. That's what I call the "I want" factor. We let the "I want" guide us to our purchase, and then we let what I call the "I should" factor kick in. That's the rationalizing side that uses facts and figures to justify the buying decision that we've already made based on our gut.

So when you stroll through the showroom at the auto dealership, you might convince yourself that you're shopping for the best balance of ride, gas mileage, reliability ratings, features, and cargo space. But in reality, you're probably looking for the car that feels the coolest and most fun to drive. The Cadillac Escalade, the beast of an SUV that resurrected the moribund Cadillac brand when it came on the market in 1999, is a perfect example of this phenomenon. In 2006, Escalade sales were skyrocketing even though average national gasoline prices for that same year went up as much as 34 percent. So why were people snapping up this huge, gas-guzzling SUV when gas prices were off the charts? Because the car was cool. Rappers drove them. Shaquille O'Neal drove one. They were plush and macho and came with sound systems that caused brain hemorrhages. The desire to buy a "'Slade" had nothing to do with logic or fuel economy. It was all about "I want."

THINGS YOU CAN DO TODAY

1. Write a survey to send to your clients or patients asking what they like about working with you and what you could improve upon.

2. Contact the company Constant Contact (www.constantcontact.com) about creating an e-mail newsletter.

3. Look at the sales process you use when you've got people in your office and identify its strengths and weaknesses.

4. Contact local advertising outlets (newspapers, magazines, billboards, cable TV stations) and ask for a "media kit" that tells you their ad rates.

5. Write down your lifestyle goals for the next one, three, and five years.

6. Designate one of your staff as client relationship manager.

WE DO BUSINESS WITH PEOPLE WE FEEL COMFORTABLE WITH

What does this have to do with Personal Branding? Everything. Like it or not, people will choose to do business with you for the same kinds of emotional reasons that drive them to pick a certain car. They might rationalize their decision by citing your experience, your location, or your education—and in fact, those might be the ultimate reasons that they decide to become your client or patient. But what gets them in the door to find out more about you is how they feel about you. Emotion is what turns prospects into leads.

We do business with people we feel comfortable with. Someone doesn't have to want to have a beer with you to decide to hire you as his lawyer, but he does need to feel that you understand him, that you share some common values, that you're "the same" as he is in some way. Basically, he wants to see if your doors make that comforting "clunk" sound when they close. At the stage where prospects are deciding whether or not they want to call you and learn more about what you do, their decision making is all about irrational, emotional cues. This is where your Personal Brand has tremendous power.

The purpose of a Personal Brand is to convey that all-important promise in a way that is in sync with the values of the people you want as your clients. This is why knowing everything you can about your target market is vital. If you're a financial advisor and you know that your ideal client (more on that concept later) is an affluent recent retiree from the entertainment industry, you can tailor your Personal Brand to communicate those qualities that you possess that are likely to appeal to that kind of person: progressive values, creativity, probably

19

some knowledge of how the entertainment industry works. Your brand makes your perfect potential client say, "Wow, he's got a lot in common with me. I think I'll give him a call."

This is why all the informative brochures and information packages in the world, no matter how much they tell prospects about your education, certification, and experience, will never get people through your door as effectively as a Personal Brand that creates a level of comfort and familiarity. The hard, cold facts might sell people once you get the meeting, but to get past people's sales resistance, you've got to meet their need for you to be someone they can trust and relate to.

THE FOUR LEVELS OF BRAND RESPONSE

You may be finding all this hard to accept. After all, you're proud of your credentials, your degrees, and your experience, and you should be. However, from a business development perspective, they're fairly insignificant. If you're like most of the professionals I've counseled, this is a hard pill to swallow. It becomes easier once you pull back the curtain and see the psychological process each consumer goes through when he or she comes into contact with a branding message. Keep in mind that this process applies whether we're talking about shopping for graphic design services, picking someone to clean your house, or buying a home theater system. Everyone who ends up in your office asking questions will pass through this quartet of steps:

1. *Awareness.* This is when your prospects first come into contact with your brand and your message. Up to this point, they have no idea that you exist, who you are, or what you stand for. So the first job of any brand and any branding campaign is to get the attention of your prospects and tell them who you are, what you do, that you're in the area, and that you're actively seeking business.

2. *Affinity.* If you've done your branding work right, after repeated exposures to your message and your persona, prospects begin to have a positive feeling about you, even if they don't know much about what you do and how you do it. This is where a brand creates a feeling that "this person is like me." Affinity takes time, which is why it's so critical that you be persistent in your marketing, even if you see no short-term results. You don't know where and how

affinity is growing in your market, because it's silent, like flower bulbs growing under the soil. The plants are there even if you don't see them for a while longer.

3. *Understanding*. Eventually, affinity leads to greater investigation. At this point, either prospects have developed a positive enough feeling about you to override their natural sales resistance, or some urgent need has compelled them to make a decision. At this point, they will start checking you out—going to your Web site, calling to have a brochure or other material sent to them, or scheduling an in-person appointment. This is the stage where information about your background, experience, and so on can be very useful. Now you're appealing to the intellect as well as the emotions, giving prospects what they need to know in order to find out if you're the right service provider for them.

4. *Decision threshold*. If everything goes right, your prospect has enough relevant information and enough positive feeling about you to step over the decision threshold and choose you as his dentist, accountant, or productivity consultant. He has reached what psychologists call a *gestalt*—he has made up his mind about you and attached to you a set of permanent qualities. This is the good part, where you get the business.

But why go through all this branding business in the first place? Can't you just get out there, sell people on yourself, and bring them in the door? Sure, if you have all the time in the world, which you don't. There's a good reason why branding has become the gold standard for building a personal service business or professional practice: it beats selling and marketing seven ways to Sunday.

THINGS YOU CAN DO IN A WEEK

1. Write down everything you know about the people in your target market: their needs, their tastes, what they care about, how liberal or conservative they are, and so on. Create a detailed dossier on them, including geographic location, age, and other such characteristics.

(continued)

2. Start identifying your best professional referral sources, such as doctors, accountants, or other professionals whose work complements your own.

3. Send out inquiries to friends and contacts about printers. Start getting sample kits from them, because eventually you'll need printing services.

4. Send e-mail to your current database informing them of your name change, your new emphasis on customer service, and anything else that you think will create affinity.

5. Begin thinking about what you want your specialization to be.

6. Have a designer create your new business cards and identity package (logo, letterhead, envelopes, mailing labels, and note cards) based on your tagline and specialization.

OUR EIGHT-STEP PROGRAM

Before this gets too abstract, why don't we take a detour down Practicality Lane and check out how all this plays out in the real world of your business?

Step 1. You craft a Personal Brand based on the attributes that create a sense of value for your target market.

Step 2. Your brand determines the design of your business card, the style of your Web site, the target markets you pursue—all your business development and promotion decisions.

Step 3. You launch your brand, creating a new collateral piece, redesigning your office, retraining your staff, publishing articles in the local paper, sending out some direct mail, and putting up a new, interactive Web site.

Step 4. You continue this over a period of months, gradually letting your brand establish itself organically as prospects become aware of you. Even when you don't see new business right away, you stick with it.

Step 5. You see the first benefit of your Personal Branding: longtime clients respond to your brand positively and start sending you more referrals.

Step 6. You see the second benefit, as quality prospects who have "heard of you" begin to appear from nowhere, contacting you for appointments.

Step 7. You begin meeting with and closing new clients. You find this process is easier because they are coming to you looking for reasons *not* to work with you, instead of needing to be sold. You begin to refer out clients who don't fit your ideal profile.

Step 8. You start charging more and working only with those clients who bring you a blend of great income and personal enjoyment.

That's the final goal: more money and more fun. You deserve to enjoy your work and the lifestyle that it makes possible, rather than spending all your time chasing after new clients. You should be attracting people who share your passion for what you do, who can appreciate not only that you're among the best in your specialty, but that you love what you do. When you can get that much enjoyment out of your career, that's wealth.

THINGS YOU CAN DO IN A MONTH

1. Order new business cards and identity materials.

2. Have one of your staff check with the regulatory body that governs legal matters for your profession to see if it's OK for you to give incentives to colleagues for referrals. In some industries, it's forbidden.

3. Begin physical changes to your office.

4. Start identifying colleagues to whom you could refer clients you don't want in return for some kind of finder's fee (again, make sure this is legal in your profession).

5. Begin creating a client handbook that will direct all client interactions from the first impression to handling crises.

(continued)

6. Break down client feedback and determine those things that clients love about you and the areas where you need the most improvement.

BRAND CASE STUDY

The Brand: Wally Amos

Specialization: Goodies: cookies and muffins

Location: Kailua, Hawaii

Channels: Retail, Web, speaking, books

Highlights: Starting Famous Amos cookies, losing the rights to his name, launching Aunt Della's Cookies and Uncle Wally's Muffins

Online: www.wallyamos.com, www.unclewallys.com, and www.chipandcookie.com

The Story: Wally Amos was an agent at the William Morris Agency in New York City, representing the likes of Simon & Garfunkel, Marvin Gaye, and the Supremes. Then in 1975, a colleague suggested over dinner that they go into business selling the chocolate chip cookies that Amos made. The company, Famous Amos, was huge when Mrs. Fields was still single. Amos appeared on the TV show *Taxi*, sold cookies to Hollywood celebrities, and spread the Famous Amos logo everywhere. However, in the late 1980s, he lost control of the company—including the right to use his name in a business venture. No problem. Always a lover of great baked goods, as well as the owner of an irrepressible spirit, Amos launched a series of new companies from his Hawaii base: Aunt Della's Cookies, Uncle Wally's Muffins, and now, Chip & Cookie. Along the way, he's written eight books and become a charming, exuberant motivational speaker. Today, he sells Chip & Cookie cookie dough through Costco and other mainland retailers.

How It All Started: "I wanted to open a store selling only chocolate chip cookies," Amos says. "I'd been eating them since I was 12. For years, people had suggested it. But I always said that it didn't make sense, that I couldn't make a living doing that." But in 1974, at dinner with B. J. Gilmore, personal secretary to Quincy Jones, that changed. "We were eating cookies I had made, talking about how my life wasn't fulfilling, and she said we should go into business together selling cookies. She said she had a friend she could get to put up the money. I walked into her office the next morning ready to make the commitment and said, 'Let's go!'" Amos started off on the right foot by naming his company Famous Amos: research has shown that names and slogans that contain rhymes or alliteration are recalled more easily.

What This Brand Stands For:

- *Charisma*. Amos is one of the most naturally positive, enthusiastic guys you'll ever meet. He's famous for wearing a watermelon top hat and a huge grin, and he's a tireless promoter, a spry older gentleman with a candid manner who loves to tell stories and can laugh at anything . . . especially himself.

- *Focus*. To anyone who knows Amos, this attribute is almost laughable, but the fact is that in recent years, he's set aside some of his many prior pursuits—speaking, fund-raising, and other business lines like Uncle Noname's—and focused on what's given him the greatest satisfaction and prosperity. "Two years ago, I launched Chip & Cookie, two chocolate chip cookie dolls created by my wife, Christine, in Kailua on Oahu, and soon we'll have a second store in Waikiki. That is what I expect to propel me into another arena, like franchising. All this keeps me busy. I'm more focused than I was in 2003. My primary focuses are Uncle Wally and Chip & Cookie. I don't have time to do anything other than what I'm doing right now. People call me to do endorsements, but I can't. I've had to resign from boards I was on. It's all-consuming."

- *Giving*. For years, Amos has been a devoted activist for literacy and for programs to keep kids in school. "My wife and I started the Read It LOUD! Foundation (www.readitloudfoundation.org). We have a campaign going in Savannah and partnered with the Library of Congress to launch a national campaign to promote awareness of the importance of reading aloud to children. The idea is to create a marketing movement in the United States that *(continued)* promotes the values, benefits, and rewards of having parents read aloud to their children, from birth to six years old, at least 10 minutes a day."

- *Authenticity*. One reason Amos was so in demand as a fund-raiser, spokesperson, and author is that he's easy to reach and easy to talk to. The "cookie king" is a regular Joe who loves making cookies, loves giving them out, and loves to talk to everyone.

X-Factor: Sticking around and just trying to do good. Few deposed business leaders are as beloved as Amos; his personal brand is built on a bedrock of love and service. He has stayed "Famous Amos" by bursting with spirit and positive energy and always reaching out to help others. "Being around so long has just made me more famous," he says. "Some people have said that I'm an icon, but if someone believes it, that's fine. My goal was to open one store and have it be successful. I never set out to be famous. It just rhymes with Amos. Thirty-three years later, I'm still famous because I haven't tried to be famous. I'm just Wally."

Branding Wisdom: "Retirement is a flawed concept. Retire to what? It's a speedy trip to the grave. I think when people retire from their careers, they should move to a life of service, because if you don't use your body and your mind, they will vanish. A friend who was VP of human resources for a large company said the average length of time they sent a retirement check was 15 months. Another friend spent two years on the road with his wife after retirement, then came home and said, 'What do we do now?'

"You have to do something that benefits society as a whole and gives you satisfaction. Everything I've done was important in building Famous Amos, Uncle Wally, and Chip & Cookie. It's a combination of many things, and you must mix all of them up, just like mixing cookies. There's no one ingredient that's more important than another if you want to have the cookies come out exactly as you want them to. They are all important. Life is like that: all the ingredients must be applied diligently every day. If there's one piece of advice I have, it's do everything you have to do and do it diligently every day. Don't give up. Always give everything you do the best you've got. Above all else, be positive, regardless!"

THE KEYS TO A WINNING BRAND

Not all Personal Brands are created equal. There are certainly service providers and professionals out there (probably in your community) who've created brands but done it poorly. This is worse than having no branding at all, because you're wasting money to send the wrong message. You'll avoid the same fate by knowing the essential elements of any winning brand.

1. *Clarity.* If it does nothing else, your brand must tell your audience who you are and what you do. It's fine to package that information with beautiful photos, glossy brochures on expensive paper, and a fantastic Web site. But that's just the wrapping; keep the message simple and clear. Don't convolute it by trying to tell your prospects all the factual reasons that they should choose you. People should come away from any exposure to your brand knowing who you are (your name, what you stand for) and what you do (the specific service you provide, and for whom). That's it.

2. *Specialization.* Key number two is pure common sense: you've got to be different from your competitors to get noticed. Though many professionals claim to know this, I'm appalled at how few practice it. How many times have you looked through the phone directory for insurance brokers and found page after page of identical ads making the same promises? You may as well stick the pages to a wall and throw darts. That's not the way I'd go about getting my new business.

   Specialization means that you stake out a very precise "position" in the marketplace that sets you apart from your competition. For example, if you're a Realtor and your main competitors are all marketing themselves as specializing in selling condominiums, the last thing you want to do is position yourself the same way. Instead, choose to become the "oceanfront home seller." The point is, be different and you'll stand out. I've devoted Chapter 4 entirely to the importance of specialization.

3. *Consistency.* People have a lot of things vying for their attention. Typically, they will begin to notice and appreciate your brand only after multiple exposures. That means that it's critical that you put

your Personal Brand in front of people again and again over a long period of time. Keep the basic message the same and keep plugging away. You never know when you're on the cusp of a flood of new business, so it's essential to stay consistent.

BRAND SURGERY
THE PATIENT: YOUR BUDGET

- Don't waste big bucks on advertising in large-circulation publications that appeal to a wide target market. You'll get more bang for your buck with smaller, tightly focused publications.

- Beware of buying mailing lists. They're often full of dead addresses and errors. *good info*

- Invest in professional apparel unless you're in a profession where appearance doesn't count. This usually means dressing more professionally than your clients. If they tend toward jeans, dress in Dockers. If they prefer khakis, wear a casual suit, and so on.

- Do not hire your brother's friend's cousin to design your Web site.

- Don't get talked into printing your stationery in expensive full color (also known as four-color). It's not always necessary, and the right designer can make two colors look spectacular.

- Resist the temptation to jump the gun and send out direct mail or run ads "just to do something." You'll waste money to little effect, and you might damage your brand. Always remember that bad branding is worse than no branding at all.

- Resist the temptation to buy marketing products or premiums based on a "deal." Just because you can get a really great rate on a quarter page of advertising in the local business journal does not mean that this is the right tool for building your brand.

- Do as much PR as possible: writing articles for local publications, being interviewed as an expert source, sponsoring public events, and so on. It's effective and cheap.

WE "DO KNOW WHY" SHE'S A SUPERSTAR

Jazzy chanteuse Norah Jones is a perfect example of a superstar with a Personal Brand who's done everything right. Jones burst on the scene in 2002 with her album *Come Away with Me*. Since then, she's remained at the top of the charts in defiance of the "pop tart" trend of scantily dressed, hip-hop-dancing female singers. Jones's music is quiet, smoky, and very personal. She's shy and low-key and matter of fact about her extraordinary success. How has she done it?

The best way to explain it is that Jones has remained true to herself and therefore to her Personal Brand. She's created music that pleases her first, and her passion for jazz, country, and folk has grabbed her fans emotionally. She's kept things clear and simple: clean, soft, beautifully crafted songs that defy the blaring beat-box tunes that crowd the charts around her. And she's been both specialized and consistent, sticking to her mellow, introspective style despite detractors who call her "Snorah Jones." She's never been anything but herself, and that, combined with spectacular talent and natural charm, explains why she's a multi-platinum star as well as, by all accounts, a very normal, well-adjusted young woman whom people adore.

Norah Jones has mastered the final crucial element of a winning Personal Brand: *authenticity*. You have to be real. With so much marketing swirling around consumers at all times, we all have extremely powerful B.S. detectors. We despise phonies. We assume that anyone who's patently not real about who and what he or she is is trying to manipulate us, and nobody wants to feel manipulated. Be yourself. Do not try to be all things to all people. Do not pander and pretend you're something you're not. That's a ticket to failure.

YOU'LL HATE THIS

Finally, a bit of branding truth that every professional I work with despises. But it's true and it's important for you to understand, so here goes:

> *Your visibility is more important than your ability.*

I told you you'd hate it. Everyone does, because we're all proud of our talents and skills. If you weren't, you wouldn't be in the business you're in. Despite that, if you're not seen in the right way by the right people, over and over again, you will lose business to lower-quality competitors who are more visible. When you're trying to get business, the first step is to be considered, to get into the "decision set." That doesn't happen because you're wonderful at what you do; prospects have no way of knowing that. It defies logic, but visibility increases your credibility.

When people see your name or face consistently, they assume you must be more successful—and therefore better—than the service providers they never see. They'll say, "If I haven't heard of her, she can't be very good." Your visibility affects people's perception of your competence. Those businesses that are highly visible will get the calls. Visibility becomes a self-fulfilling prophecy.

Your Personal Brand is your weapon in the visibility battle. It keeps you visible to prospects and constantly reminds them of who you are and what you do. That's why it's so important that you constantly promote your brand. If you're not keeping your brand in front of the members of your target market, they'll assume you're out of business. It's astonishing how quickly people forget.

Ability does matter, of course. Once you get the business, your ability to perform and provide value helps you keep it and turn it into referrals. Visibility gets prospects in the door. Ability keeps them with you for many years. Like love and marriage, you can't have one without the other.

[handwritten note in left margin: very good]

BY NOW YOU SHOULD BE . . .

- Talking to graphic designers and copywriters
- Calling local newspapers and magazines to get their ad rates
- Deciding what personal qualities you want to build your Personal Brand around
- Talking to your staff and your spouse about Personal Branding and what it means to them
- Thinking about the type of client you like to work with most
- Thinking about how you can specialize

[handwritten note at bottom of page: what can I do to have people talk about NVT?]

GETTING AND KEEPING THE CREAM OF THE CROP

Messaging skills separate those with million-dollar Personal Brands from their peers walking the corporate corridors today.
—Meredith Fischer, vice president, Marketing Communications,
Pitney Bowes Inc.

Let's be honest. You're in your profession to help people and to be stimulated intellectually and emotionally, but you're also in it to make a great living. If you could, you'd love to get rich doing what you do, or at least have a comfortable lifestyle that you can really enjoy without spending 80 hours a week at the office.

The final building block in the DNA of a Personal Brand is a clear understanding of how creating a brand around yourself translates into bottom-line benefits. Why would you spend the time and money to launch and maintain a brand if you weren't going to earn more money in less time? In more than 10 years of working with thousands of financial advisors and other professionals on their brands, I've heard one question more than any other: "What can I do right now to earn more and grow my practice?" So, what kind of tangible benefits can a Personal Brand deliver for your business in the next 12 months?

THINGS YOU CAN DO TODAY

1. Compose the sample letter that you'll send to clients when you cut them loose or refer them to other providers.

2. Begin compiling all your client e-mails into a single database.

3. Reach out to newspaper and magazine editors in your area about their willingness to run original articles with your byline.

4. Make an appointment to have new photos taken of you and your business.

5. Calculate the percentages of your income provided by your A, B, and C clients.

6. Call local colleges to find a journalism student who can ghostwrite articles for you.

DO YOU WANT TO DOUBLE YOUR EARNINGS?

Based on my more than ten years working to help professionals build and maintain their Personal Brands, I would say that a well-built, well-supported, well-maintained brand is worth at least 100 percent of the value of your business over five years. That is, if you follow the advice you're going to find later in this book to the letter and follow through consistently, you should be able to at least double your revenues in five years. But I've seen clients who did much more, such as doubling revenues in less than one year. It all depends on four factors:

1. How fully you're willing to embrace the concept that shaping perception is the key to bringing you the best prospects

2. How thoroughly you integrate your Personal Brand into every aspect of your business and your life

3. How consistently you follow up your initial effort with communications, marketing, and outreach

4. How well you support your brand promise with excellent performance and customer service

If you do those four things, you will earn more money and enjoy your work more. You could do a lot more and become like Omaha, Nebraska–based financial advisor Ron Carson, who developed a sterling client service program and today is ranked as the number one independent financial advisor in the country by *Registered Rep* magazine. Ron produces more than $7 million in commission and fee revenue per year and manages more than $1 billion in assets . . . and he takes three months off each year to travel with his family! When was the last time you did that? Have you ever done that? I haven't. But Ron has, and he makes money while he's hiking through Yosemite. That's branding success.

IT'S ALL ABOUT THE CLIENTS

However, in order to follow in the storied footsteps of Ron Carson, you must make attracting and keeping a better quality of clients the heart and soul of your business. That's the success equation we're talking about:

A better brand = better clients = a better, more profitable business

To turn a world-class brand into big success, bringing in the best possible clients is everything. To make this a reality, I focus on the concept of the "ideal client." Every professional and service provider has an ideal client, and the ideal client is different for each individual. For some people, the ideal client is simply the most affluent individual possible, someone who can pay an exorbitant fee. For others, it's a person who blends high net worth with discriminating taste, a sense of humor, a willingness to take risks, and a strong sense of loyalty. Your ideal client will not be the same as anyone else's, but right now you need to figure out who your ideal client is and build your entire business around corralling these clients and holding on to them.

You already know who your ideal client is. The problem is, you're trying to service everybody who comes along because you're afraid to turn away business. See if this sounds familiar: for every great client or patient you have, you have at least two or three who take up a ton of your time, complain about your fees, and really don't produce that much income. But you don't cut them loose because you're nervous about replacing even the meager revenue that they bring in. You're making one of the most common and most devastating mistakes of entrepreneurs and professionals:

You're trying to be all things to all people.

To paraphrase my mother, knock it off! Specialists are the people in this world who make the big bucks. If you're a general dentist, you might make a good living, but the real money is in pediatric orthodontics. Specialists who zero in on a market with specific needs can charge more for their services, work with fewer clients, spend less time servicing those clients, and work shorter hours while increasing their per-hour income. So if you want to become more successful, I have a very simple, terrifying piece of advice:

Cut your number of clients in half.

You're going to do that by determining who your ideal client is and then, over the next year, slowly peeling away the layers of non-ideal clients while adding more ideal clients through your Personal Branding.

BRAND SURGERY
THE PATIENT: SELLING AND MARKETING

- Don't start your quest for new business by selling. If people don't know anything about you, why would they buy from you?

- Don't spend the majority of your time on sales calls. Let the prospects be attracted to you through your branding. It's a better use of your time.

- Teach your sales staff about Personal Branding. All members of your staff should have their own Personal Brands for the people they come into contact with.

- Make sure your sales techniques and those of your staff fit your brand. Personal Branding gets prospects in the door, but when they're in your office, it's time to sell and close the deal.

- Don't copy. If a competitor launches a branding campaign, don't emulate it. You don't want to be the follower in a category; you want to lead your own category.

WHO'S YOUR IDEAL CLIENT?

To answer this question, start by separating your clients into three groups (I suggested this in an earlier "Things You Can Do" sidebar): A, B, and C.

- "A" clients are the people who can afford to pay premium fees, who appreciate that you're an elite professional, who are easy and enjoyable to work with, and who are willing to give you referrals. They might total 15 percent of your client base but provide 50 percent of your revenue. These are the clients you want to keep.

- "B" clients are less able to pay big dollars, are more likely to waste your time with complaints or silly requests, and are generally more stressful. They're not bad, but you don't want to build your business around them. They're probably about 35 percent of your clients and produce 30 percent of your income. You'd like to jettison them from your practice in the next six to nine months.

- "C" clients are cheap and stressful, and you spend 50 percent of your time keeping them happy. They're a pain in the neck, and even though they're 50 percent of your clients and take up 60 percent of your time, they generate maybe 20 percent of your revenues. You want to kick them to the curb in the next three months. Good riddance.

By identifying the qualities that make your A clients your best clients, you will tailor your Personal Brand to attract more of them. At the same time, by cutting loose your B and C clients, either by referring them to colleagues or simply by no longer servicing them, you're going to have more time to care for your best clients. But because your A clients deliver much more income, you'll be able to increase your revenue while servicing fewer clients who are easier to work with and don't demand as much of your time.

Most professionals will be able to identify their ideal clients based on the following characteristics:

- They're educated and understand what you're telling them, even when it's complex.

- They appreciate the importance of working with a highly qualified professional.

- They've got the money to pay higher fees for premium service, and they know that what you offer them is worth the money.

- They're self-starters who educate themselves and don't waste your time with silly questions and panicked complaints.

- You have something in common with them and enjoy their company.

- They're more than willing to refer you to people who are like them.

- When you tell them you're becoming more exclusive, they appreciate and understand what you're trying to do.

Identify the clients who meet all these criteria; they are your ideal clients. Your mission is to clone these people and bring in more of them. For example, let's say you're a physician who's sick of dealing with insurance companies, Medicare billing, and all the rest. You decide you want to start a "concierge" practice, in which you have a small group of affluent clients who are willing to pay $10,000 a year for exclusive access to your practice and a package of premium services. So you identify the 25 patients you currently see who can afford to do this, start referring all your other patients out, and launch a branding campaign to attract more ideal patients. The transition takes a year, but at the end of that year, you have a base of 100 affluent concierge patients who generate $1 million in gross revenues. You're spending less on billing and bureaucracy, so your net income is higher and you can spend more time actually practicing medicine and more time with your family.

THINGS YOU CAN DO IN A WEEK

1. Begin scheduling meetings with colleagues to whom you might refer the clients you no longer want.

2. Send your new business cards and letterhead out to your current A and B client base.

3. Have one of your staff contact local sports teams, schools, youth sports leagues, and so on to ask about sponsorship opportunities.

4. If you don't have a staff or an assistant, consider a virtual assistant at www.ivaa.org.

5. Work with your Web developer to create a new structure and content map for your new online presence.

6. If you have profiles on social networking Web sites like LinkedIn, delete them and replace them with new profiles that reflect your Personal Brand.

BRAND CASE STUDY

The Brand: Wyland

Specialization: The world's leading environmental artist

Location: Laguna Beach, California

Channels: Art, music, Whaling Walls, marine activism, education

Highlights: Painting nearly 100 marine life murals all over the world, starting his own record label, becoming the bestselling environmental artist in the world

Online: www.wyland.com, www.wylandfoundation.org

The Story: Wyland is the world's foremost marine environmental artist. Based in his spectacular Laguna Beach studio/bachelor pad with a 180-degree view of the Pacific, this midwestern transplant has built one of the art world's most powerful personal brands and

(continued)

franchises with his evocative, soulful paintings and sculptures of whales, sea lions, and other marine life. But the friendly, laid-back Wyland is much more than his paintings and his famous paint-signature logo: He has built a brand on goodwill, global eco-awareness, education, and his latest passion, his own jazz label. With 2008 the thirtieth anniversary of the Wyland Studio and the fifteenth anniversary of the Wyland Foundation, the artist has a lot to celebrate.

How It Started: "The first thing I did when I came out here was starve," says Wyland from his oceanfront deck, adjacent to the hotel parking lot where he painted his first whale mural. "As it turns out, I was in the right place at the right time, as Greenpeace and Jacques Cousteau were coming on. That's when I started working on my goal of being a marine-life artist."

As it turned out, Wyland exploited one of the critical principles of personal branding by accident: first-mover advantage. "The art that was done before was marine art, but what I do is marine life art, a celebration of the life in the sea, not man's conquest of it," he says. "So it was really a new art form that was evolving at the time." Pioneering a new type of marine art gave him an exclusive brand identity in his field, fueling public perception that Wyland was "the" marine artist.

Without any real intent to turn himself into a franchise, Wyland sensed that to promote his art, he needed to promote his love for the sea and its inhabitants. He proved to be a natural. "I didn't have anybody to mentor me, but by being friendly to people and using my personality, I became well known," he says. "A lot of artists are introverted, but not me. I love people. I love the response I get to my art. I've always been hands-on and very involved, and my brand just started evolving very slowly from that."

What This Brand Stands For:

- *A lifestyle.* With his cool beach crib, his travels, and his aquatic ways, Wyland has created a lifestyle brand reminiscent of this singer who lives in someplace called . . . Margaritaville? "My brand is more of a lifestyle, sharing the art and the vision, getting people excited and involved," he says. "It feels like a Jimmy Buffett thing; kind of contagious for people. Doing good things and giving back, people want to be involved in something like that. We have nearly a million Wyland collectors over the last 30 years. But we've only touched the tip of the iceberg as far as what it can be. It's globally recognized now. But it's still grassroots—one person can make a difference."

- *Passion.* Wyland tells anyone who will listen that at this point in his career, when he's sold millions of paintings, sculptures, and other works, it's all about what he cares about: educating kids about preserving the ocean ecosystem and spreading international goodwill through his many Whaling Walls (huge aquatic murals that are part public art creation, part media circus). If he doesn't love it, Wyland doesn't do it. "You always want to stay excited when you're an artist," he says. "It's nice to be able to do things on your terms, because you have only so much time. It elevates the whole thing. Everybody has to do what they have to do to get by, but once you get beyond that, it's an amazing transformation."

- *Constantly evolving.* Art, activism, and conservation aren't enough. This guy's also into music. "I started a record company, Wyland Records, and we just produced our first jazz CD, *Rhythms of the Sea,*" he says. "Art and music are so powerful, I wanted to try to get the message out that way. The music business was so dysfunctional, I decided to start my own record company with no obstacles and create a new paradigm for distribution. I also needed music for the films I've been creating for my film and video company. The theme was the ocean and the art and the message. We're already working on the second record, which will be the blues. I put together the greatest musicians on the planet, write the melodies and the words, and put it all together. The next one will tell the story of water through the blues: the Mississippi Delta, Memphis soul, all that."

- *Giving back.* Wyland's Wyland Foundation and other charitable work promotes and funds environmental education programs to teach children about protecting and appreciating the ocean ecosystem. It's one of the central reasons he gets up in the morning: to preserve what he loves.

- *Business savvy.* Wyland and his team have built a sophisticated licensing strategy and a worldwide distribution network for his art,
(continued)

which is reproduced in dozens of different forms. They maintain tight control of his personal brand, right down to his distinctive signature and his name, which is always "Wyland." Never a first name. His brand is consistent and is always tied to the same ideas: the ocean, marine life, and clean water conservation.

X-Factor: The Whaling Walls. Wyland might have remained a successful but regional personality had it not been for his Whaling Walls. These enormous murals, each depicting an underwater scene of great whales and dolphins, began in 1981 with the Laguna Beach wall. They have become Wyland's signature, adorning 95 public walls and buildings around the world. Now, with the end in sight, he's got some big plans for 100—and beyond.

"I'll be painting my last four walls in Cape Town, Abu Dhabi, Singapore, and Beijing for the 'Green Olympics,'" he says (he's the official American artist for the 2008 Olympic Games in China). "It will be called 'Hands Across the Oceans,' and there will be more than a mile of canvases. But it can't be about me, so I'm inviting kids from 204 countries to paint with me on 204 canvases. We're going to inspire these kids to take the inspiration home to their countries and get them involved in clean oceans and clean water—to get these kids to take a leadership role in conservation through the arts. It's really exciting to do it on a world stage. I will also dedicate the first sculpture I did for the Olympics, three dolphins.

"That's a great way to finish my quest to do 100 aquatic murals. And for the next 25 years, I want to do 100 monumental sculptures in cities around the world." Gee, is that all?

Branding Wisdom: "The core message of the brand is not, 'Buy this painting!' It's to learn everything we can about our environment and use art to educate and inspire people to get involved. At the end of the day, it's a brand for conservation. Of course it's pure art, but it's art with a message. The idea was that people would see the art and the beauty and see the message. I dive in it, take photos of it, write about it, paint it, sculpt it, paint it on the sides of buildings, and now I'm writing songs about it. The investments you make, they eventually bear fruit. I'm like Johnny Appleseed."

DITCH THE LOSERS

Not a bad scenario, is it? The biggest barrier to reaching this promised land, sadly, is *fear*: fear of cutting business loose and not being able to replace the income. That's something that I can't help you with other than to present the logic of going after your ideal client. But I won't deny that waving good-bye to three-quarters of your client base can be very scary. That's why it's important for you to focus not just on how great your A clients are, but on how bad your worst clients are.

After you identify your best clients, find the clients who meet only half of the A-client qualifications. These are your B clients. They're not bad, but they take up a lot of your time and don't bring in a major chunk of money. They might be educated and even rich, but maybe they're chronic complainers who waste your staff's time and make everyone angry. Or they're nice as pie but never, ever pay their bills on time. Phase them out slowly.

C clients are not fun to work with, they think you charge too much, and they bury you in complaints. When you look at the hours you spend servicing them, they're money losers. Send them a letter telling them that you're changing your practice and will no longer be able to service their needs, but that you've enjoyed working with them over the past few years and you wish them luck. Try not to cackle with glee as you mail the letters. It's tacky.

TAKE THE A TRAIN

So now you have that golden list of ideal A clients in front of you. Great. Now repeat after me:

I will no longer accept any new clients/patients who do not fit my ideal requirements.

You may want to post that on your office wall for about six months and say it every day as a sort of mantra. Because you're going to be tempted. New deadbeats will call or come into your office, and your reflex is going to be to process them and turn them into clients. But unless they're A quality, say no. The fact is, at the outset of your

Personal Branding campaign, few new ideal clients will come off the street at random. Most will come via referral from your current clients. Why? Because your brand won't have had time to make everyone perceive you as an elite service provider. That takes a while. So you'll still get some bottom-feeders for a while. Have a system in place to refer them elsewhere. (More on that later.)

The other thing you're going to do is use your A list as your template for creating your Personal Brand and the marketing tools that communicate it. You want to attract more and more ideal clients, so take the time to deconstruct those ideal clients and write down the qualities that they share. Those are the qualities you want your brand to appeal to. For example, let's say that your ideal clients turn out to share six common qualities:

1. They have an average household income of over $200,000.

2. They average 53 years old.

3. They own businesses.

4. They are politically conservative.

5. They live in the same 10-mile-radius area around several premium golf courses.

6. They are not technology-savvy.

Your Personal Brand must push those six buttons in order to attract both referrals from your existing client base and new ideal clients off the street. Since your ideal client is quite affluent and conservative, you'll want to create a gorgeous, high-end brochure about yourself that features images of golf and family. That's what your ideal client will expect to see from you. You'll still have a Web site, but because your ideal clients aren't tech wizards, you won't send an e-mail newsletter or send content to their wireless phones. You'll stick to old-fashioned snail mail. And your in-office experience will be as elegant as the Ritz-Carlton.

Once you know what makes your A clients lucrative and enjoyable to work with, and what they have in common with you, you can tailor your Personal Brand to attract people with those qualities. That's branding in a nutshell.

THINGS YOU CAN DO IN A MONTH

1. Hire a graphic designer to begin work on your new collateral materials.

2. If you work from home, begin searching for an affordable office. You need to convey a certain image with your brand, and it's likely that your home doesn't do it.

3. Apply for a bulk-rate mailing permit from the post office.

4. Pick up a copy of the *Lifestyle Market Analyst* (about $500), a huge, indispensable book that breaks down detailed demographic information for every metro area in the United States. It's invaluable for developing your target market.

5. Put together your basic press kit.

6. Attend your first professional networking events with your new business cards in hand.

BOTTOM-LINE BENEFITS

It's time to cut to the chase. These are the ways you will benefit from creating a brand that draws a steady flow of new A clients:

- *Higher fees.* By limiting your services to a more select group of people, you create what economists call *scarcity*. The demand for your services exceeds supply, and prices rise. By becoming exclusive, you can justify raising your fees. The message to your clients: you're limiting your practice to a select group of top people and offering a premium level of service, so you must raise your fees accordingly. But be prepared to deliver that premium-quality service, not just lip service.

- *Greater income.* It's not much of a leap to see that higher fees lead to more money in your pocket. If 20 percent of your clients generate 50 percent of your income now, if you cut the other clients loose and double your number of A clients, then increase your fees by 50 percent, you're going to raise your overall income by 50 percent. But it gets better.

- *Lower costs.* With fewer clients to service, your staff won't need to spend as much time handling complaints. Maybe you can let some people go, or you can turn them toward marketing and bringing in new business or creating customer delight. In general, fewer clients means reduced costs, and that also raises your net income.

- *Fewer hours worked.* Fewer clients who are not wasting your hours with ridiculous requests translates into less time spent at the office. If you calculate your hourly wage, you'll quickly see that reducing your hours at work from 75 per week to 50 dramatically boosts your per-hour income.

- *Creating a referral channel.* In order to winnow your practice down to your ideal clients, you're going to create a referral system that sends your B clients to other people and automatically deflects new inquiries and sends them to alternative service providers. Doing that not only creates tremendous goodwill for you, but also creates a potential reverse referral channel that can bring you new ideal clients from time to time.

- *Building something you can sell.* This is a big deal. Right now, you're probably the sole asset in your business. Maybe your mailing list or client database has some resale value, but not much. But when you build a Personal Brand that attracts top-quality clients and gives you an elite reputation in the community and the industry, your brand becomes your biggest asset. You can open new locations and eventually sell your business when you retire early, because your brand has the value. Charles Schwab will go on long after its founder retires or dies because the brand is so strong. A great Personal Brand allows you to sell your business or pass it on to an heir.

- *More enjoyment.* You want to love what you do, don't you? Often this is an overlooked side of business, and it shouldn't be. Part of the reason you got your education and went into business for yourself was to control your time and enjoy being your own master. Well, when you're choosing whom you work with instead of letting them choose you, you'll enjoy each day more. You'll get real pleasure out of your business relationships.

- *A better lifestyle.* The purpose of launching any career is to fuel a lifestyle that gives you joy and meaning. It's really that simple. Unfortunately, many of us forget that in the rush to build a company and the headlong panic to stay ahead of expenses and grow. But think about it: better clients + more income + fewer hours worked + more enjoyment from your clients = a better lifestyle. You'll have more time to spend with your family and friends doing the other things you enjoy. When you have a system in place to maintain your Personal Brand and keep your client relationships strong even when you're away (an area I'll cover in detail later), you're free. You run the business. It doesn't run you. You can take vacations, go to your kids' soccer games, and live your life.

Of course, doing all this demands a financial investment. But how much, and what's the return on investment? I'll talk about that in detail when we look at Branding Channels in Chapter 5. For now, let's move along to the three brains of Personal Branding.

BY NOW YOU SHOULD BE . . .

- Settled in with the new name of your business, your name

- Looking at design drafts for your new logo, business cards, and stationery

- Planning your new Web site

- Talking to editors and radio program directors around your community about what it takes to get in print or on the air

- Redesigning your workspace to be a more client-centric environment

PART II

THE BRAND WITH THREE BRAINS

SPECIALIZE OR SPEND

*Long before "self-branding" became a business school buzz-
word, Ellas McDaniel developed the ultimate personal brand: Bo
Diddley. Bo Diddley is his professional name, "Bo Diddley" is the
title of his first record, and the "Bo Diddley beat" is the popular
term for the rhythmic juggernaut energizing his music.*
                                    —Joseph Tortelli, *Goldmine* Magazine

A great Personal Brand is a three-headed monster constructed, like
Victor Frankenstein's creation, out of parts from different places.
The first and most indispensable of these components is specialization. Why did the late, great Bo Diddley remain a familiar face and
name even though his music was more than 50 years old? Because he
was a specialist. He "owned" one small but powerful part of the audience's mind.

Specialization is the single most important Personal Branding
strategy in your arsenal. You simply cannot build an effective brand
without being a specialist. Specialization builds on the ideal client
you chose in the last chapter and uses that information to help you
narrow down the scope of your brand communication. When you
specialize, you run counter to the common business impulse to do
more for more people. In specialization, you do less for fewer people,
packaging yourself as an elite specialist in a smaller, more precise

range of services. Specialization lets you pick a few lucrative, in-demand areas of your business and build your brand around them.

Specialization offers many important benefits to any business:

- *Differentiation.* Instead of being a generalist who tries to be all things to all people, you set yourself apart from your competition by doing a few things very well. General ideas do not endure in the human mind; we don't remember jacks-of-all-trades. We remember those people who spark our interest with a precise talent, a precise field of knowledge, or a precise fact. Human beings remember what's unique.

- *Presumed expertise.* When you tell people that you're a specialist in something, they naturally presume that you're especially skilled in that area. They respect what you say and are more likely to pay more for your perceived special knowledge.

- *Clearer client understanding.* It's very difficult for people to appreciate the hard work you do and agree to pay you well for it if they don't understand what you do every day. For instance, clinical psychology or tax accounting can seem like an impenetrable mystery to laypersons, but if you position yourself as an "addictions counselor" or an "inheritance and estate tax planner," clients will be more likely to comprehend at least the basics of your profession.

- *A focus on your strengths.* Specialization should allow you to focus not only on the areas of your work that are more lucrative, but on the ones you're best at. So you get to enjoy your work and make more money. Bonus.

- *Clients prequalify themselves.* Have you ever spent an hour consulting with a prospect, only to find out that he's not right for your business? What a waste of your time. Specialization prevents this by telling prospects exactly what you do and whom you work with, so they know right away if you're for them or not. If you are, they call. If you're not, they stay away. Remember, you don't want everyone as your client, just your ideal clients.

But I think the best reason of all to specialize is that it makes your business more manageable. If you decide you're going to be the general insurance broker to your entire metropolitan area (50,000 population), you've got a massive task ahead of you. You've got to brand yourself as a generalist who can provide a huge range of insurance products and market your brand to a big geographic area while fending off dozens or hundreds of competitors. That costs a lot of money. You can build a thriving business as a generalist, but you'd better have a huge marketing budget.

This is why I say, "specialize or spend." Unless you have millions to pump into your brand marketing, specialization makes infinitely more sense. By restricting the scope of your business, you reduce your costs and your work. Instead of being the insurance broker for everyone under the sun, consider specializing in worker's comp and business liability insurance for about 1,000 small businesses in your metro area. Instantly, your work and your costs go down. You don't have to battle dozens of entrenched competitors. You don't have to send direct mail to 20,000 homes; instead, you send it to 1,000 companies. You can laser-focus your communications materials, sales presentation, signage, staff training, and Web site on this one small market. Life gets easier.

THINGS YOU CAN DO TODAY

1. Make a list of special events you could hold to reach out to your clients, such as ice cream socials, free classes, or fund-raisers.

2. Make a list of physical locations around your area where point-of-purchase displays might reach your ideal clients.

3. Search the Web for sites related to your business where you might run articles or place advertising.

4. Research possible venues for public seminars, such as conference centers or churches.

5. Check with any organizations you belong to—churches, political groups, or civic organizations (the Elks, for example)—about the possibility of making a presentation to the membership.

6. Decide on your new fee structure.

THE RISKS

Of course, there are risks to specialization, especially if you don't do it right. To be fair, most of these risks exist only in the minds of nervous professionals, but that doesn't make them less likely to inhibit successful branding. Most businesspeople—especially if they haven't been in business very long—are scared to death at the idea of turning away any business, no matter how small or troublesome. This is the major psychological risk of specialization: "What if I can't find new business to replace the clients I turn away?"

I see this as the entrepreneurial equivalent of the girl who stays with the abusive boyfriend because she's afraid that if she breaks up with him, she'll never find anyone else. It's fear-based nonsense. If you're good at what you do and are able to communicate the human parts of you that make people want to work with you, you'll always find new clients. Let's leave fear behind and look at the real risks of specialization:

- You might turn away a segment of your market that's not profitable now but will become profitable in the future. But unless you're psychic, you can't predict this, so why worry about it?

- You alienate those members of your current client pool whom you refer out or simply turn away. This does happen, and it can poison your image a bit if former clients are left resentful. So it's important to "move clients along" with class, subtlety, and the impression that it's for their benefit. "I'm reorienting my practice, and I don't think I'll be able to continue to service your needs appropriately" and that sort of thing.

- Being too narrow and reducing your income. This is why it's so important to research your target market carefully and make sure there's enough room in your specialization to bring you all the clients you need to reach your income goals—and then some. It's always good to have some room to make mistakes and still earn the living you want. It is possible to be too specialized and therefore too limited in how big your business can get.

That's about it. As you can see, the benefits of specialization far outweigh the risks. Most of these risks can be managed with smart planning and good communications. So, since the downside of specialization is so small and the ceiling so high, let's get into how you become a specialist.

THE THREE STEPS OF SPECIALIZATION

It should be clear by now that Personal Branding is all about your clients. Without them, you have nothing. So you've got to learn everything you can about them, then tailor your business to make them love you passionately. Let's jump in and walk through the three steps involved in doing this. You're ready to start becoming a Personal Brander.

Step 1: Identify Your Target Market

Wait, didn't we already do this? No. We identified your ideal client, but your ideal client and your target market are not the same thing. Here's the difference:

- Your ideal client is a profile of the perfect prospect around whom you want to build your business.

- Your target market is the real-world pool of prospects to whom you're going to market in order to attract those ideal clients and get the meeting.

Your ideal client is just that: an ideal. But you've got to find those people and communicate with them, and that means picking a target market that will receive your mailings, see your advertisements, read your articles, and meet you at networking events. A target market is a group of prospects that can be defined by a broad range of possible characteristics, including geographic location, lifestyle and hobbies, income, gender, life stage, occupation, religious belief, or ethnicity. You could even have a target market consisting just of people working at a single company or attending a single megachurch. In any case, your job is to figure out what target market, defined by what characteristics, gives you the best odds of attracting the largest number of ideal clients.

This may seem daunting, but you probably already know a lot about what your perfect target market is. After all, you've already identified your ideal client. Well, what demographic group is most likely to include the largest number of those ideal clients? The best way to launch the target market discovery process is to write down your ideal client profile, then brainstorm possible demographics. As you do this, keep four questions in mind:

1. Is this target market big enough to allow me to reach my income goals?

2. Is there already entrenched competition?

3. Do I enjoy working with this type of person and in this area of my business?

4. Is there an unmet need that I can meet?

For example, let's say you're a residential architect in the San Francisco Bay area. You're trained in and enjoy doing eco-friendly architecture. You've decided that your ideal client is an upscale property owner, politically and socially liberal, who wants to build a new "green" home from the ground up and be involved in each stage of the process. Where are you most likely to find such people? Using your common sense and experience, along with resources like *Lifestyle Market Analyst* and Web sites like www.freedemographics.com and www.marketresearch.com, you come to the following conclusions:

- If you want people who want to participate in the design process, you need a college-educated audience.

- The more conservative areas of the East Bay are not ideal for you. Berkeley offers the liberal politics, education, and eco-awareness, but the college community doesn't have the affluence you need to bring you new residential projects.

- Silicon Valley does have the affluence, and while it's not the hotbed of liberalism that Berkeley is, it's young and progressive, full of high-tech geniuses who see themselves as being in the vanguard of new technologies and lifestyles.

- You recognize that most new homebuilders who want to "go green" are younger, so you decide to target an under-40 demographic.

In the end, you decide that your target market will be "under-40 executives and key personnel at Silicon Valley high-tech companies with a total household income of more than $200,000 per year." Some more digging reveals that there are between 3,000 and 4,000 individual ideal clients in this group. Now you ask the four questions:

1. Is this target market big enough to allow me to reach my income goals? Yes; if you assume you can capture 1 to 2 percent of these prospects as clients, that's plenty.

2. Is there already entrenched competition? Some, but no one has dominated the market.

3. Do I enjoy working with this type of person and in this area of my business? Yes, you're comfortable with technology and enjoy creative, tech-savvy people.

4. Is there an unmet need that I can meet? Yes, for green living.

Looks like this target market is a fit! This is the same process that you'll need to go through as you begin to develop your specialization. When you know your target market, you can create your specialization and design your entire business to appeal to that market.

BRAND CASE STUDY

The Brand: Dr. Laura Schlessinger

Specialization: No-nonsense family-values-first radio talk-show host

Location: Los Angeles, California

Channels: Radio, Web, books, one-woman shows, travel events

Highlights: Her latest book, *Stop Whining, Start Living,* debuted at number two on the *New York Times* bestseller list

Online: www.drlaura.com

The Story: She has a Ph.D. in physiology, but Dr. Laura is better known for her training as a marriage, family, and child therapist, leading her to dispense no-nonsense advice on traditional family and parenting values and to drive her detractors crazy with her uncompromising statements
(continued)

Her hard-edged, pull-no-punches style has given her more than 15 million regular listeners on more than 300 stations nationwide, multiple bestselling books, and something that most media personalities would kill for: a Personal Brand that no one is neutral about.

How It All Started: Schlessinger came out to California to teach at USC and discovered West Coast talk radio. "Radio in California was very different from radio in New York," she says. "People were actually on the air, taking calls. It was funny, entertaining, and charming." She called a talk show on KABC-AM to answer the question of the day, gave a fake name, and was "discovered." Later, when she appeared as a guest on KWIZ in Santa Ana, the host was rude and abusive to her, and she walked out. "People were calling into the show as I was driving home and giving this guy hell for being so rude to me," she says. "He got fired, and the next week, guess who was on the air with her own show?"

What This Brand Stands For:

- *Integrity.* For Schlessinger, integrity is her most prized possession. That really means defending traditional, conservative family values against modern cynicism, relativism, and political correctness. It also means candor. She is renowned (and in some quarters, reviled) for giving her unvarnished opinion about such topics as feminism, child rearing, sex, and pornography. Don't agree with her? Don't listen. Millions of others do. Her integrity and sense of moral values have also led her to support foundations that serve abused and neglected children and the families of fallen military heroes.

- *The guts to stay the course.* Schlessinger says that one of the secrets of her success is her longevity: she's been on the radio with a sincere mission for 30 years and has been syndicated since 1994. In all that time, she hasn't bent with the times so much as she has intensified her mission to protect kids and preserve families. Even when a scandal erupted in 1998 when a former boyfriend published nude photos of Schlessinger on the Internet, she did not cave. She went to court to prevent the release of the photos and explained her prior actions as a result of her once-feminist mentality . . . from which she had "recovered."

- *Consistency.* She calls herself "a fearless, tireless warrior for kids, families, personal responsibility and ethical behavior. I have consistency in my message, and I focus on getting it out through my Web site, radio show, and books. The consistency and focus of the message create the brand."

- *Channel savvy.* These days, she's about far more than radio. Besides her books, the good doctor has a huge (more than 170,000 members) online "family," a one-woman show appropriately titled *In My Never to Be Humble Opinion*, and a series of Dr. Laura–themed cruises. She knows how to work brand development.

X-Factor: Her "I'm my kids' mom" sign-on, which came off the cuff when she switched to a daytime show and introduced herself by what was most important to her. But that statement has become her trademark and a flashpoint for people who love to criticize her. That was her brand's watershed moment. Someone of national stature had come out of the feminist closet and stated that her family, not her career, was the focal point of her life. It made Schlessinger an icon.

Branding Wisdom: For all her success, Schlessinger doesn't consider herself a brand. In fact, she hates to be called one, because she feels that it makes her seem like her persona was created by a corporate marketing board. But she knows the power her brand has and always puts respect for her audience first. "If I'd tried to create a Dr. Laura persona so I could sell T-shirts, people would have rejected it immediately," she says. "When you're synthetically coming up with a brand concept to sell something, you're not going to make it, because you don't have trust. People see that I mean what I say and what I do.

"I think I am about integrity, honesty, morals, ethics . . . personal responsibility, and the guts to stay the course in spite of challenges from within and without. It's exactly my up-front, non-PC truthfulness that appeals to people. They're yearning for support for that beleaguered inner moral sense that's been beaten down by a 'whatever you want' culture. This approach has earned me my tenth *New York Times* bestseller status."

How Big Should Your Target Market Be?

That depends on three factors: your income goal, how much you earn from each ideal client, and what percentage of your total prospect pool you can expect to turn into paying clients. You should already have your income goal. Let's go back to our architect and say that his goal is to gross $200,000 in the first full year after launching his Personal Brand. Next, he looks at his list of A clients, the ideal clients that he wants more of. In the last fiscal year, he had 20 A clients who produced $100,000 of his gross income, so each A client was worth $5,000. So he needs 40 A clients to reach his goal, right?

Not necessarily. He also wants to raise his fees by 25 percent. If he does this, he'll need only 36 A clients to reach his $200,000 goal. That doesn't look like much of a difference, but if each client represents 50 hours of work, 4 clients represent 200 hours that he's not working. That's a week's vacation plus some time to recover. So 36 clients is the goal. Now the third factor: market penetration. What percentage of the prospects that see his marketing will actually become his clients? This is going to be different for each profession (people need their family physician and tax accountant pretty regularly, while they might need an architect or photographer once in five years), but the general guideline is that of all the people who come into contact with your brand marketing, you'll turn 1 to 4 percent of them into clients.

That includes people who are referred to you (though referral conversion rates tend to be quite high) as well as those who see your ads, brochures, direct mailers, and Web site, and people who encounter you through any sort of community outreach or public relations you might do. So our architect looks at his past marketing and takes his best guess: he's been converting about 2 percent of his prospects into clients. That means that to get 36 ideal clients per year, he needs to reach a total of 1,800 prospects with his Personal Brand. That's doable, since he's going after Silicon Valley companies that employ more than 250,000 people. Now he's got his target market:

1,800 executives of Silicon Valley tech companies with an annual household income of more than $200,000 and an unmet need for guidance in building a "green" home.

Follow the same process and you'll have your target market as well. The only remaining question to ask is if you can service the number of clients you'll need to reach your income goal without raising your fees out of sight. My answer is, probably, once you get rid of those time-wasting B and C clients.

THINGS YOU CAN DO IN A WEEK

1. Finish reinventing your physical office environment.

2. Create a "first impressions" program designed to dazzle new clients.

3. Begin developing a curriculum for seminars—coursework, a workbook, and so on.

4. Contact companies in your region about private seminars.

5. Start your own blog (if you have time to post to it at least four times a week) at blogger.com, typepad.com, or wordpress.com.

6. Surf the Web to remove anything that might be potentially embarrassing, e.g., MySpace photos from your Mexican vacation, angry comments on someone else's blog, and other such material.

Step 2: Design Your Service for Your Ideal Client

Once you know what prospects you're aiming for, you're ready to create your Personal Brand. The first step in that process is to redesign your service to position you as a specialist who can deliver products and services that meet your prospects' unmet needs.

Your service cannot be generic; it's got to be highly specialized and tailored to the nature of your target market. If you're an incorporation and patent lawyer who's been marketing herself up to now as offering "legal services for small businesses," stop. That's not going to work. You need to specialize your service for your target market. So maybe your new service needs to be "intellectual property protection for innovative small and medium-sized businesses." You get the picture. Be precise and anticipate what your market needs.

59

In redesigning your service offering, think not only about what kind of custom-tailored services you can offer, but what to strip away. If filing articles of incorporation is a small sliver of your law practice, get rid of it. The more focused you can be, the better. In specialization there is value.

Step 3: Reinvent Your Business Model

Reaching your goal depends entirely on connecting with this collection of prospects in such a way that they become ideal clients. So every aspect of your business must reinforce your Personal Brand and create the perception that you're someone whom they'll enjoy doing business with and who will give them what they need.

Deconstruct every aspect of your business:

- How you communicate with clients

- Your physical location and its design

- Your payment structure

- Your customer service and ongoing relationship maintenance protocols

- How you handle complaints and problems

- How technology affects your efficiency and communication

- Your hours and availability

Nothing is out of bounds here. You might end up leaving some aspects of your current business model alone while changing others radically. It all depends on what will make the people in your target market feel that you understand them and can give them what they need. Our architect is going to be going after Silicon Valley techno-geeks, so he knows he's got to run a high-tech shop. He plans to invest in handheld computers for all his people, a state-of-the-art laptop for showing 3D renderings, and a splendid Web site where clients can learn about the status of their project in seconds, 24/7.

Some key questions to ask here:

- Do I need additional products or services?

- Are my services priced right for the market?

- How can I construct my business to make it easier, faster, and more convenient for my clients to work with me?

BRAND SURGERY
THE PATIENT: YOUR BUSINESS
RELATIONSHIPS

- If you say you're going to do something, do it. No excuses, even if it's something small. Clients will base their opinion of your trustworthiness on the smallest of factors.

- Spell out what you do and don't do in your marketing materials, and again when you meet with prospects. Make it clear that if something is outside your area of expertise, your clients will have to find another vendor. Then have a list of possible vendors to offer them.

- Be open with prospects about your quirks. That will drive away some, but attract others. They'll be the people with whom you can form long-term alliances.

- Never believe the "If you do this for us at a lower price, there'll be a lot more work coming down the line" gambit. It's as old as the hills, and it's really just a ploy to save money. A quality prospect will pay you what you're worth, instead of trying to get you to discount by holding out the carrot of more work.

KEEP IT SIMPLE

Now you're ready to write your *specialization statement*. This states the territory in the marketplace that you're staking out for yourself, in exactly the same way that an old-time gold miner staked out a claim. Your specialization statement must tell your prospects:

1. Who you are

2. What you do

3. For whom you do it

After going through the three specialization steps, you should already know this stuff. You should have in mind a more precise description of who you are as a professional, a honed and razor-sharp service offering, and a clear idea of your target market. Mash these three things together and you've got your specialization statement. Some perfect examples:

- A Yale-educated financial advisor offering succession planning for Sarasota business owners

- A board-certified gerontologist offering longevity strategies for women 55 and over

- Boise's "Get me out of this DUI!" lawyer

Each brief statement tells potential clients or patients who the service provider is, what he or she does, and whom he or she does it for. Each element is precise and specific, not general. The gerontologist works only with women, the financial advisor appeals to Ivy League snobbery, and the lawyer handles only drunk-driving cases. Practice writing your specialization statement. Try to make it as concise and exact as the ones given here. Think about who your ideal clients are and write it for them, no one else.

Brainstorm and have fun with this. It should be fun, not a chore. But also keep in mind that your specialization statement is not a public document. It's for you and your staff to keep your branding efforts focused. You'll adapt your statement later on to create your slogan, but keep your main specialization statement to yourself.

THE BIG MISTAKES

You can see the proof of all this in our pop culture. The greatest Personal Brands today are specialists. Rachael Ray, who has become an industry unto herself with her multiple television shows, her books, and her *Every Day* magazine, has built her booming brand around one simple idea: 30-minute meals. Yes, she's got a girl-next-door image and all the rest, but everything starts from this idea of cooking something great in a half hour. Rather than try to be a general cuisine wizard, she staked out a position that she knew would appeal to busy women everywhere.

James "The Amazing" Randi was successful as a magician, but he became a cultural icon when he became the world's foremost crusader against the paranormal, quack medicine, and pseudoscience. Now over 80, grouchy and candid and intolerant of anything resembling "woo-woo," he's a polarizing figure who is seen as a hero by millions of skeptics who fight against things like intelligent design being taught alongside evolution, and as a villain by people who believe in homeopathy and psychic abilities. If Randi had stayed a magician, he would probably have been forgotten, but as an arch-skeptic, he's forged a lasting legacy.

Jim Cramer, host of the popular *Mad Money* cable TV program, has also built a thriving, growing Personal Brand based on a specialization, but his is more about style than about content. Cramer is the "hyperkinetic, crazy stock guy." There's no shortage of stock market experts advising people on how to pick the right companies to invest in, but only one of them is chewing the scenery, screaming, and bouncing off the walls while imparting some pretty solid Wall Street wisdom. His specialization is his personality, not the information he delivers.

The Personal Brands you don't hear about anymore are probably the ones that made specialization mistakes. You're susceptible to these, too, so don't get complacent.

Common Mistake Number One: Diversification

Some business owners specialize, then get tempted. If I can serve this one target market so well, they think, why not choose two or three more? That's faulty logic. You're doing so well because you're focused and your efforts aren't diluted by trying to be everyone's dentist or Realtor. Don't diversify.

Diversification creates confusion. It plants seeds of doubt in the minds of prospects. When you read an ad or brochure for a service provider and see a laundry list of services as long as your arm, it's natural to think to yourself, "If he does so many different things, he can't be very good at any of them."

THINGS YOU CAN DO IN A MONTH

1. Get competitive bids from mailing-list companies for lists that go to your target market.

2. Hire and train a telemarketing staff.

3. Send your letter to your C clients explaining that you are reengineering your practice and will no longer be able to service their needs, but will be happy to recommend other service providers.

4. Talk to local radio stations to see about the possibility of your getting your own radio show or being a regular guest on someone else's show.

5. Develop your time management system: mobile electronic calendar, e-mail alerts of upcoming meetings or events, a Web-based system for communicating with your clients, and whatever else works for you.

6. Work with a copywriter to craft your first set of direct-mail messages.

Common Mistake Number Two: Dilution

Dilution means that you've stopped being exclusive and started taking on clients who are outside of your ideal client range. When you do this, you're no longer creating scarcity, and you're diminishing the perception that you're an elite professional. Now you're becoming common.

A good example of the damage dilution can do is Calvin Klein. For decades, his brand of clean-lined, stylish attire set the standard for the industry. Then he made a critical error: he decided that if he was a specialist in mainstream retail, he could make even bigger profits in discount stores. Hence the appearance of Calvin Klein clothes at chains like Costco. Sure, he sells more of his low-end product. But in the long run, he's done damage to his Personal Brand by robbing it of any sense of exclusivity.

Stick to your exclusive circle of clients. If you want to increase your income, offer new, more costly services or add a partner. If you must take on more clients, stick to your ideal client core.

TIPS FOR BETTER SPECIALIZATION

1. *Be aware of emotional needs.* Sometimes the members of a target market don't need a service to fill an unmet need. They need a vendor with a sense of humor, or someone who's renowned for always meeting deadlines. You can specialize in such areas. One example is author Robert Bly, who saw an unfilled need in 1980s men seeking a path back to traditional masculine values after a decade of "sensitivity." His book, *Iron John*, filled this void and turned Bly into a phenomenon.

2. *Create something new.* If there's no void to fill, develop a Personal Brand that offers a novel product, service, or benefit. This can be risky if there's no demand for what you create. But if it works, you'll have *first-mover advantage*. If you're stumped for something new, look at what the competition is doing and do the opposite.

3. *Focus and get smaller.* Instead of constantly doing more, do less. If your branding isn't working as well as you'd like, become even more specialized. The trick: knowing exactly what your prospects would love to have in a service provider, providing that single gold-plated service, and having strategic partners who can give clients the other services they need without poaching them.

4. *Find partners.* Like I just said, find specialist partners who complement what you do. If you're a Realtor, these might be mortgage brokers, appraisers, home inspectors, and contractors. Become a resource, not just a service provider.

5. *Change as your needs change.* Maybe you don't have kids now. But in five years, you might, and if you do, your needs will change. You might need to cut back your hours, earn more money, or work closer to home. Be ready to change your specialization and business model to work with your life, not against it.

BY NOW YOU SHOULD BE . . .

- Deciding on the kind of specialist you want to be

- Reviewing drafts of brochure designs, Web site designs, and branding copy

- Drafting a client service manual

- Attending professional networking events to see what the professional referral possibilities are

- Winnowing down your client list to decide which ones you want to keep

- Telling the clients you want to keep about your plans and asking them for referrals

BRANDING CHANNELS

To nurture personal brand, the following advice needs to be followed: prepare messages; focus on perceptions, not reality; know yourself; explain capabilities; use simple language; use the 5Ws in discussions (who, what, where, when and why); avoid clichés; ask questions; and make an impact.

—Australasian Business Intelligence

Have you ever run a Yellow Pages ad? Sent a direct-mail postcard to clients? Done cold calling? Congratulations, you've used branding channels. Branding channels are the second brain of a Personal Brand. They're the roads to your prospects, the various marketing communications tools and methods that you use to convey your brand to your pool of prospects and turn them into ideal clients.

There are two categories of branding channels: *inclusive* and *exclusive*.

- *Inclusive channels.* With inclusive channels, you don't have much control over who sees the message, so you'll probably attract a larger response but lower-quality prospects. This works for building seminar attendance and a mailing list.

- *Exclusive channels.* With these channels, you can control who sees your message, but you reach fewer people. This is ideal for target marketing and times when you need to focus your message on converting a smaller group of ideal prospects.

I'll identify each of the 21 branding channels as either inclusive or exclusive. Ideally, your branding strategy should include a blend of both.

CHANNEL 1: BUZZ MARKETING

- Inclusive.

- Advantages: Grows organically and on its own when it captures the imagination; very low cost.

- Disadvantages: Impossible to control; hard to predict success; can have unpredictable consequences.

Buzz marketing involves doing provocative things to create a buzz about yourself in the community, such as supporting a political cause or making a very public donation to a charity. Anything that gets people talking about you is fair game in buzz marketing, but I don't recommend this channel because it's uncontrollable. Your ability to shape people's perception is quite limited because buzz marketing is very grassroots and tends to take on a life of its own.

CHANNEL 2: CANVASSING

- Exclusive.

- Advantages: Provides personal contact with prospects; offers the chance for give-and-take and direct questions.

- Disadvantages: Very, very time-consuming; inappropriate for some professions.

Canvassing means going from door to door. This is something that Realtors commonly do, but it can be used by those in other professions as well. There's something very personally appealing about meeting a potential service provider face-to-face. You get to ask questions and form an impression of his or her manner, clothing, and so on, and you can decide for yourself if you have a comfort level with the person. But canvassing is obviously very time-consuming, so I recommend it only for professionals whose business is so predicated on personal contacts and relationships that face-to-face branding is the only way to go: Realtors, midwives, landscapers, contractors, and so on.

Also, the more educated and perceived as elite your profession is, the more inappropriate canvassing is. I would never recommend it for doctors, lawyers, or therapists, as being seen as "common" would do serious harm to their brands. That said, if you decide to canvass, make sure you have three things: time, a great collateral piece as a leave-behind, and a brief, informal script to start a conversation. And be prepared to have doors closed in your face.

CHANNEL 3: CLIENT REFERRALS

- Exclusive.

- Advantages: There's nothing better to create trust in a new prospect than a referral from someone he or she has known for years. It's also cheap.

- Disadvantages: You have no control over the prospects clients refer to you or what people say about you. There's sometimes an expectation that you'll treat referrals like the emperor of Japan, so you can get roped into a service nightmare.

No ad or brochure will get you in the door with a new prospect faster than a referral. The thumbs-up from someone who's used you and experienced your good work is all the endorsement you need to get business. If you have a group of happy clients, it's wise to leverage them and turn them into a referral resource.

Nothing builds your Personal Brand better than a great story from someone who likes you, trusts you, and wants to help someone else get to know you. Some professionals get all their new business through referrals. That's how powerful this channel is. You turn your happy customers into an army of unpaid marketers. This is why it's so vital to work only with ideal clients. They're going to want to help you because they can fully appreciate the value you provide. I know professionals who get 75 to 80 percent of their new business from client referrals and pretty much do no other brand marketing at all.

The downside to client referrals is the lack of control you have, but this isn't a reason not to use them. There are so many advantages to client referrals—penetration into markets you might not know about, cheap advertising, instant rapport—that it's one of my gold-plated, recommended channels. There are three keys to making client referrals work:

1. Ask for the referral! Many professionals don't do this, and it drives me crazy. Clients won't know you need referrals unless you tell them. So ask, and odds are they'll be more than happy to help you.

2. Create a referral program. You'll need a system to ask for referrals regularly, give your clients materials that they can pass out to friends and family members, and a reward program to thank clients for great referrals.

3. Develop a special customer-service program to make sure that referred clients are treated better than gold.

I'll talk more about the specifics of these three components in Chapter 11, "Networking and Referrals."

THINGS YOU CAN DO TODAY

1. Choose the five channels that you think will work best for you.

2. Run your specialization statement by your staff and clients to get their feedback.

3. Start creating a manual that dictates how professional referral prospects are to be treated (*hint:* like royalty).

4. Finish re-creating your physical workspace with final decorating touches, books, kids' play areas, and other appropriate choices.

5. Write a press release about your relaunched business.

6. Get printing quotes for key collateral materials like your Personal Brochure and postcards.

CHANNEL 4: DIRECT MAIL

- Exclusive.

- Advantages: It gives you a tool to create a regular flow of branding and service information to your entire target market.

- Disadvantages: It can be expensive, and it's frequently misused, so you'll hear plenty of people claiming that direct mail doesn't work.

Direct mail can be the most strategically important channel for developing your brand. It can also be a money pit that costs you the hair you have left. It all depends on how you use it. Direct mail lets you customize your message and "drip" a regular stream of information to your prospect mailing list. You can use letters, brochures, postcards, boxes and other "dimensional mailers," newsletters, and other such items. For those who want to do direct mail, I recommend building your campaign around Personal Postcards that have a beautiful, classy design but a space for a customized message, and an equally gorgeous Personal Brochure that's your flagship Personal Branding piece. More on those collateral pieces later.

Direct mail can work for people in any profession, but there are a few keys to making it cost-effective:

- *It's got to be interesting.* Sales letters bore people to tears. If you're going to send a mailer a month to the people on your list, the messages should be personal, varied, and entertaining. Keep people guessing and forget the hard sell.

- *It's got to be profession-appropriate.* "Just Sold" postcards might be perfect for a Realtor, but "Cases I Just Won" postcards would be disastrous for a lawyer. A brief monthly newsletter containing easily scanned legal advice makes more sense.

- *It's got to be consistent.* People who claim that direct mail doesn't work are usually people who've sent out one piece, gotten zero response, and given up. Direct mail takes repetition and time. The average consumer needs 8 to 10 exposures to your message before registering that you're someone he or she might want to contact.

- *It's got to be high-quality.* Cheap flyers on canary paper from Kinko's are worse than no direct mail at all. If you're going to make direct mail part of your Personal Branding strategy, spend some dough on it. Make postcards and brochures glossy and beautiful. Send letters on expensive letterhead. Have newsletters professionally designed. The look and feel of what you send makes as strong an impression of your brand as what you say.

- *It's got to be targeted and maintained.* Make sure the company that provides your mailing list practices "list hygiene." That is, make sure it purges the names of people who have moved or died so that you're not wasting money and creating resentment by sending things to the wrong people.

CHANNEL 5: INDOOR ADVERTISING

- Inclusive.

- Advantages: It can create some public visibility for you.

- Disadvantages: It's costly and very difficult to target.

Indoor advertising includes things like airport signage, cinema advertising, and marquee advertising. I'm not a huge fan of this channel because it doesn't deliver much bang for your buck. You can't target it, and you have no control over who's going to see it. It's basically good for one thing: making your name and face more familiar to the public. But it's the individual professional's version of Budweiser running a Super Bowl ad: big bucks just so you'll be on people's lips for five seconds.

If you can get a great deal and you have other targeted brand marketing channels working, indoor advertising can be worth a shot. But like real estate, it's all about location, location, location.

CHANNEL 6: THE INTERNET

- Inclusive.

- Advantages: It reaches everyone 24/7; gives you a constant way to deliver information to your clients and communicate with prospects cheaply; can help you brand yourself as tech-savvy and innovative.

- Disadvantages: Developing an ambitious Web site can get expensive.

You have to have a great Web site. Period. It's simply not optional. If you don't have a strong online presence, you're handicapping your business in a huge way. Having an easy-to-use site with lots of useful information and features gives you a 24-hour information and branding center that your clients and prospects can access anytime. That's powerful stuff. You can control their user experience, publish articles, share useful resources, capture contact data, distribute private client data in password-protected areas, and drive home your Personal Brand with graphics and copy. Done right, your Web site is a powerful tool for building your brand with prospects, the media, and influencers in your profession.

But this goes beyond Web sites. Having a strong, well-thought-out Internet strategy (and an Internet marketing company as a strategic ally) can also mean sending regular direct e-mails to your prospect list, writing your own Weblog (or having someone ghostwrite it for you), sending a weekly or monthly e-newsletter filled with facts that your prospects can use, sending reminders of appointments to clients' wireless devices, and even creating your own audio podcasts, your personal radio show. The potential of the Internet is virtually limitless; it can be a marvelous tool for growing your company.

The only real downside to using the Web is that anyone can contact you and ask you about your services. But you can do a great deal with design and copy to discourage so-so prospects and bring in only the ones you want. Some tips on making the Internet work for you:

- Invest in it. The Net should be a major fraction of your Personal Branding budget. At the very least, you *must* have a good Web site.

- Hire a professional Web designer and programmer or a full-fledged Internet marketing firm that can assist you with strategy, programming, software, design, site maintenance, becoming more visible on search engines, e-mail, and beyond. Do *not* hire your cousin or your best friend's college-age son to create your Web site.

- Promote your site in all your marketing, from ads to your brochure and business card. Your Web address should be everywhere.

- Keep the information on the site fresh. New articles, blog postings, links to relevant news, and client testimonials are all good ways to keep a Web site interesting.

- Make sure your privacy policy is posted, so that users feel more comfortable about giving you their contact information.

- Don't get carried away with design tools like Flash or QuickTime video. They can be fun and useful, but solid design, strong copy, and ease of use are more important.

CHANNEL 7: NETWORKING

- Exclusive.

- Advantages: Allows you to forge new relationships with "key influencers" efficiently, at charity events or networking groups. Very personal, a great opportunity to distribute materials and explain what makes you different.

- Disadvantages: Time-consuming. Can be difficult for shy people or those who like to sell aggressively. Usually takes time to produce business.

You've networked. If you've ever gone to a professional conference, a charity auction, or a symposium where your colleagues were present, you've practiced networking. Networking involves making contacts with colleagues and influencers in your profession, most often at public gatherings and at professional get-togethers such as chamber of commerce meetings. The goal is to get people familiar with you, to lay the groundwork for productive relationships, and to hand out materials that people will keep, usually your Personal Brochure.

Networking takes place most often at two types of venues: formal settings such as conferences, conventions, networking groups, and charity gatherings; and informal settings like parties, sporting events, and arts events. Networking is all about letting people know you're out there, learn your name and what you do, and come to like and trust you. As we know, people do business with people they like, so networking can be a bonanza. It's about building relationships that slowly turn into business generators. Networking is a powerful tool for long-term growth because it's exclusive, letting you create relationships with only the people who you feel will help you succeed.

However, networking for the purpose of generating quick business is almost always a dismal failure. People don't want to be treated as resources for your business. The best networking, and therefore the best business relationships, involves mutual benefit and the building of trust. That takes time.

Good networking is a skill, and not everyone has it. If you're not comfortable talking off the cuff or if you're just plain shy, you might want to steer clear at least of formal networking events. However, anyone can learn to be more comfortable with networking, and there are some steps you can take to make it more effective:

- Join professional organizations where you'll meet people from all walks of life.

- Attend regularly so that people come to expect you.

- Always have first-class informational materials to give out (not business cards). I recommend handing out a Personal Brochure.

- Always get a card or something from each person you meet, and log the information into your database or address book within 24 hours.

- Avoid selling. Treat social occasions as what they are: chances to make friends and start dialogues. Everyone knows the subtext is business; there's no need to drive it into the ground.

- Have a follow-up plan for contacting people you meet who would be good prospects or referral sources. If nothing else, make sure you have a strong Web site to send them to.

- Have fun. Meeting others should be a good time, not a pressure situation.

CHANNEL 8: OUTDOOR ADVERTISING

- Inclusive.

- Advantages: Creates visibility for your face, name, and brand better than almost any other tool.

- Disadvantages: Expensive and hard to target. It's tough to motivate people who come into contact with your ad to make the leap to contact you.

Outdoor advertising can be billboards, building signage, transit advertising like bus benches or boards, lawn signs, posters and playbills, stickers and bumper stickers, flyers and banners. Just as with indoor advertising, I recommend this only for professionals who already have several very targeted brand marketing channels working and need a way to get their name and face known in the marketplace. Outdoor advertising is not going to make the phone ring; it's going to make people more receptive when they receive your postcard or brochure in the mail. Never use it as a stand-alone branding tool.

One tip: always, always negotiate rates. Most companies that sell outdoor ad space are eager to move inventory, and you can usually dicker for better prices, especially if you are willing to buy space in multiple locations. Never pay "rate card."

THINGS YOU CAN DO IN A WEEK

1. Review the first version of your new Web site and give your developer any needed redirection or revisions.

2. Compile a final list of local print media editors and radio and TV program directors.

3. Refine your first press release and send it to this list as part of a press kit.

4. Talk to your printer and order a custom Rolodex card to send to editors to position you as an interview resource.

5. If you'd like to do some radio or TV, Google "media training" and talk to some companies about working your on-camera or on-mic skills.

6. Send out your first e-mail announcement to the clients you're keeping about the new direction of your practice—and ask for referrals.

CHANNEL 9: POINT-OF-PURCHASE DISPLAY

- Inclusive.

- Advantages: Can get your materials into the hands of prospects with minimal work.

- Disadvantages: Impossible to control who will pick up your brochure and call you. Requires you to deliver materials to locations regularly.

Point-of-purchase (POP) displays are the brochures, flyers, or demonstration CD-ROMs often found in retail stores or at hotel desks and chambers of commerce. When you walk into a hotel, it's quite common to see a big rack of brochures from local attractions such as restaurants and theme parks, and from local Realtors, moving companies, and the like. This presents an opportunity for you if you're right for it.

POP displays aren't for everyone. Again, the elite nature of your profession comes into play. I wouldn't advise a physician, a lawyer, an architect, or a psychologist to do POP displays, because this would appear to cheapen their profession. But depending on the venue, some professions are ideal for POP. Realtors and mortgage brokers are a natural fit for chambers of commerce and visitor centers. Landscape designers and contractors make sense at home improvement stores. You get the picture.

The most important aspect of making POP work (other than choosing the right locations) is the quality of your leave-behind. It should always be a first-rate Personal Brochure that tells your story and does very little selling (more on that later). One more tip: some stores and other locations might charge you a fee to place your materials with them. Weigh each case individually; some locations might be worth it, especially if few or none of your competitors are there.

CHANNEL 10: PRINT ADVERTISING

- Inclusive.

- Advantages: A good way to be seen by many people; more targeted than outdoor advertising because you can choose the publication and the section of the publication; can make the phone ring.

- Disadvantages: Can be costly, and if the publication is cheesy or poorly produced, your ad will make a bad impression no matter how good it looks.

Print advertising means display advertising in a newspaper or magazine, classified advertising, Yellow Pages advertising, and inserts or circulars "blown in" to periodicals. It's great for reaching a large group of people without any effort on your part. You just place the ad, pay the fee, and wait. You can get your face, name, slogan, list of services, and contact information in front of 100,000 people in hours.

However, just like all other forms of advertising, print is weak on targeting. You don't have a lot of control over who sees your ad or who contacts you. Also, it's not easy to create ads that "pull." We're saturated with advertising, and it takes something extraordinary to get our attention. I know I never read the stacks of ads that fall out of my Sunday paper. Do you?

Yellow Pages advertisements tend to attract one-time customers who are price-sensitive. I don't recommend Yellow Pages ads for most high-end professional service providers, though you'll probably want to take one out just because all your competitors are doing it.

Tips for doing print advertising well:

- Make sure each ad has a "call to action," asking the reader to do something: call you for a brochure, go to your Web site, or take some other action.

- Include your Web address, phone number, logo, and slogan in all ads.

- Refresh your ads periodically—no less than once a year for ads that run continuously, such as Yellow Pages ads. New layouts and headlines attract attention.

- Make ads benefit-oriented—they should be about the customer, not about you and how wonderful you are.

- Include offers and incentives to encourage people to contact you.

- Run your ads for at least one year before you gauge their effectiveness. As with direct mail, repetition is critical.

CHANNEL 11: PROFESSIONAL REFERRALS

- Exclusive.

- Advantages: A fantastic way to create a regular flow of prequalified clients.

- Disadvantages: None, except that it requires an investment of time.

Professional referrals, how do I love thee, let me count the ways. Nothing is better for generating business than a referral. It's free, it's personal, and it has all the credibility of the person behind it. Along with a Web site and a Personal Brochure, I recommend that everyone create a professional referral channel.

Professional referrals occur when a colleague or someone in a field related to yours recommends you to his or her clients or customers. For example, if you're a real estate agent, sources of professional referrals are not just other Realtors, but "adjacent professionals"; mortgage brokers, appraisers, contractors, real estate attorneys, and escrow officers are ideal networking targets.

These people already have a high degree of credibility with their clients, so when they recommend you, you're almost certain to get a phone call. Do the math: since each of your professional contacts can have dozens or hundreds of clients, a few good professional referral sources can be your gateway to all the new business you can handle. Your goal is to build a network of professionals who are continually referring prescreened clients to you and for whom you are continually doing the same. Done right, this can position you and your referral partners as a powerful source of added value for your clients.

So why don't more professionals leverage this channel? They think referrals happen spontaneously. Wrong. You must cultivate a referral base. Ask for the referral, make it easy for the referring party to tell someone about you, and then reward the person providing the referral. Here's the process I recommend to my clients:

1. *Generate leads.* This can mean attending professional association events, contacting local professionals using cold calling, and even contacting the other professionals who service your current clients.

2. *Evaluation.* Look at how long each professional on your list has been in business. Experts are those who've been around for at least 10 years. Professionals are those who've had their shingle up for 5 to 10 years. Newbies have been in the business less than 5 years. I suggest going after only the experts.

3. *Take the meeting.* You'll contact each professional on your list and try to get a meeting. To this meeting, you'll bring a printed agenda, a detailed résumé, the details of your business model, the services you provide, and so on, and a proposal. The goal is to establish your credibility, then make your case for the value you can deliver to the professional's clients and why you should partner to cross-refer.

4. *Create and sign an agreement.* If all goes well, you'll create a formal document that will lay out the terms of your referral relationship. This should cover three major areas of concern:

   a. *Client service.* How will clients be serviced? How will clients be charged? How will angry clients be handled? What client information will be shared?

   b. *Marketing.* What joint marketing will you and your partner do? Seminars? Client events such as mixers? Direct-mail endorsements? Conference calls? Web links? PowerPoint presentations sent to clients? Spell out exactly what will be done and who will pay what share.

   c. *System.* What will be the system for screening possible referrals and sending them to each other? What will be the intake system for new clients? How will first impressions be handled? Will you give each other incentives or rewards?

All of this material, once agreed to and signed, should be shared with your key marketing and management personnel.

5. *Follow up.* Establish a system for staying in contact and monitoring how the agreement is working for both of you. This can be a monthly phone call or e-mail or a regular meeting. You should also establish and follow a reward system for bringing each other leads and new clients. It could be anything from a thank-you card to a dinner gift certificate to a points system that earns you something at the end of the year. *Hint:* If someone brings you $100,000 worth of new referrals in a year, buy him something that knocks his socks off.

A few tips:

- Make sure the people in your referral pool have copies of your Personal Brochure or other materials to hand out.

- Make sure you treat referral clients like royalty. Take better care of them than you do your other clients, because that's the only way you'll continue to get referrals.

- Be as selective in your professional referral partners as you are in your clients.

BRAND CASE STUDY

The Brand: Mike Parker, Mike Parker Landscape

Specialization: High-end, artistic landscaping for California's Gold Coast

Location: Santa Ana, California

Channels: His distinctive trucks, signage on his award-winning landscaping, word of mouth, connections with builders

Highlights: Designing several gardens for the Philharmonic Houses of Design, a program sponsored by the Philharmonic Society of Orange County and the American Society of Interior Designers (ASID)

Online: www.mikeparkerlandscape.com

(continued)

The Story: You can't miss the trucks with "Mike Parker Landscape" emblazoned on their sides. They wind their way through some of southern California's most idyllic, expensive neighborhoods like Laguna Beach, Newport Beach, and the Newport Coast. Follow them through the hills and you're likely to wind up parked in front of a home that's straight out of *Architectural Digest*, with a knockout lawn, terrace, or xeriscape. That's the work that's made Mike Parker the leading name in landscape design in this status-obsessed corner of the Southland.

Since 1976, Parker has presided over an empire built on landscape design, construction, and maintenance—and a strong personal brand. With his company now based in central Orange County (OC) (a move made for convenience and cost), the entrepreneur has corralled award-winning architects and landscape designers under the umbrella of Mike Parker Landscape and maintained a powerful brand through consistency and quality. Now he has a staff of around 90 and gross revenues of more than $7 million per year.

How It All Started: In 1976, Mike Parker Landscape was just one truck, one man, and a dream of making art and making a little money. The company began as more or less a landscape-maintenance business, one of hundreds in suburban southern California. But Parker brought a touch of artistry to his work, and that artistry became a leading attribute of his Personal Brand.

"I'd always been interested and involved in various artistic endeavors: ceramics, drawing, and painting," he says. "My clients recognized that I was doing more than just gardening, and began having me renovate their garden spaces. This allowed me an artistic outlet, and a way to pay the bills." Parker used his artistic ability to change the perceptions of his target audience and position himself not as a glorified gardener, but as a Picasso of the hedgerow and paving stone. Today, he specializes exclusively in high-end homes for affluent buyers in OC's most prestigious areas. "Rich people always have money," he says.

What This Brand Stands For:
- *Exclusivity.* Parker has deliberately turned down lower-end business as his brand has gravitated toward high-end landscaping. "We have become even more specialized by turning away homeowner's association business," he says. "The association business was not

supporting the core business. The associations had unrealistic expectations, and we spent a disproportionate amount of our management time for very little return. We were spending a lot of time trading dollars." By sticking to his ideal client, Parker grew the business with less hassle.

- *Quality.* In a status-conscious place like OC, no one wants his or her home to look second-best. Parker's company has thrived for one reason above all others: people know that when his team comes to the building site, the result will be a stunning piece of residential landscaping.

- *Loyalty.* "We still have 80 percent of the employees we had five years ago," says Parker. He takes good care of his people, so they take good care of him.

X-Factor: Mike Parker Landscape is a very visible company. It has designed some of the most picturesque residential landscapes in the region, landscapes that have been featured in newspaper and magazine articles. He's stayed on the cutting edge by recruiting the best in the business—scouting for landscape designers and architects who have built their reputations around a particular talent or style. "This helps keep our product fresh, and [it] has resulted in the networking of talents and projects," Parker says.

Branding Wisdom: "It never occurred to me *not* to put my name on what I do," he says. "Contractors in general face a challenge of overcoming the bad experiences people have often had with a contractor. Putting your name on what you do in conjunction with a good reputation makes the process of proving oneself that much easier."

CHANNEL 12: PUBLIC RELATIONS

- Inclusive.

- Advantages: A largely free, high-credibility way to get in front of prospects. PR can become "viral" and spread widely, especially thanks to the Internet.

- Disadvantages: Everyone and his brother is trying to get the same handful of newspapers and radio stations to pick up their story, so it's hard to get jaded editors to take notice of you. Also, there's no way to guarantee that people will perceive you the way you want them to.

PR involves working with the media to generate coverage of you, your business, and your outside activities, such as charity work and sponsorships. Local newspapers and magazines, local radio stations, cable TV stations, local network affiliates, online media, and even nonlocal trade publications that cover only your profession are all viable targets for your public relations effort.

The basic dynamic of PR is simple: you want to convince editors or program directors that you have something to say that will be unique and will interest their readers, listeners, or viewers. That's it. PR has to be focused on the end audience, not on you. If you can't capture the editor's imagination and make him or her believe that you can capture the audience's imagination, you're sunk.

For the most part, PR means sending professional press releases and using consistent follow-up to form mutually beneficial relationships with media decision makers. These are busy, deadline-driven professionals who receive hundreds of press kits and press releases each week; you've got to grab their attention and *make* them care about you. Get to know the print and broadcast editors and reporters you're targeting, learn about their audiences, and find creative ways to position yourself and speak to their audience.

PR is a fantastic credibility builder. Readers and listeners assume that if you're featured in an unbiased medium like the press (don't laugh), you must be good. The downside is that you can't guarantee the coverage you'll get from month to month. So PR is a complementary channel for most people, not a cornerstone.

The exception is when you can land a regular, high-profile gig producing published content. I'm talking about getting your own weekly column in the local daily newspaper, or landing your own Saturday morning radio call-in show. Those are huge opportunities, and you can make them the heart of your Personal Branding. Many professionals lack the time, the talent, or the media savvy to make those things happen, but if you can become a media personality in your own right, you'll reap major benefits.

Here are some good PR tips:

- Respect editors' time. Send them material and don't bombard them with calls. Consideration and professionalism go a long way in an industry where everyone wants something.

- Send a Rolodex card and a cover letter to editors, presenting yourself as an "expert source" in your field and offering to be interviewed at any time.

- Learn and follow standard press-release format. You can find excellent guidance at www.prwebdirect.com.

- Send a press release whenever you have news, even if it's just a new hire. Multiple exposures make editors remember you.

- Make news happen. Create events; publish a book; make yourself newsworthy.

- Find a good ghostwriter.

CHANNEL 13: PUBLISHING

- Inclusive.

- Advantages: Publishing a book in particular has a lot of prestige attached to it.

- Disadvantages: Cost, cost, cost.

I discourage most of my clients from publishing books or even paid newsletters. The reason not to publish a book is simple: it's really expensive. When you think about the cost of producing a 200-page hardcover book—paying for writing, editing, designing, printing, shipping, distributing, marketing—the whole enterprise can cost $30,000 to $40,000, or even more. That's beyond the reach of most professionals. Even doing a book that's available only via print-on-demand services (where books aren't printed until someone orders them—the In-N-Out Burger method of publishing) like Lulu.com or CreateSpace.com can run up five-figure bills.

Paid newsletters cost less but are more work. Let's say you've got 200 people who would pay $200 a year to get your monthly newsletter.

That's $40,000 a year, a no-brainer, right? Well, you've got to turn out a newsletter every 30 days, and that's a ton of work. I published a quarterly magazine a few years back, and it nearly killed me.

Publishing can work for one subclass of professional: the one who's been around for 20 years, is very accomplished, and either would like to either take his practice to the next level in order to sell it or would like to dial back his hours and make more money as a speaker. Books are great prestige vehicles; there's something about having a book that makes you instantly attractive to the media, speakers' bureaus, and so on. So if prestige is vital to your career plans, publishing may be worth a look. Otherwise, I'd avoid it. Having and trying to sell a book to recoup your investment can become a full-time job, and you've already got one of those.

CHANNEL 14: RADIO ADVERTISING

- Inclusive.

- Advantages: The same as other versions of advertising—it gets you in front of lots of people in a single shot, creates brand awareness, and makes you more credible.

- Disadvantages: Cost and more cost. Plus, it's hard to target, and since many people listen to the radio in their cars, they're not writing down your contact information.

Everything I've said about other forms of advertising applies to radio ads. Handle with care, and use them only as a way to accent your more targeted advertising. Don't build your Personal Branding around them. The only exception is if you have a radio program of your own.

CHANNEL 15: SEMINARS—PRIVATE

- Exclusive.

- Advantages: You get to make your pitch to a preselected group of prospects who mostly want to hear what you have to say. You can seriously target your best prospects with precision information.

- Disadvantages: Setup can be costly, and you have to be comfortable and polished in making a presentation to a large group of people. Turning such events into business also can require a lot of intensive follow-up.

Seminars take time, planning, and the ability to speak comfortably in front of groups of people. Consequently, they're not for everyone. Also, your profession may not lend itself to seminar-style presentations. However, 80 percent of the business owners I've talked with are in businesses where seminars would benefit them, so chances are that when you're ready, a seminar will help you grow.

In a private seminar, you make a presentation to an exclusive, invited audience, usually the personnel of a company or an organization such as a professional association, church, or civic group. The idea is to deliver your Personal Brand message in person to a large group, then get as many as possible of the members of that group to meet with you later individually to close them. Seminars are also a perfect venue for distributing materials and information. Sometimes you can even charge a speaking fee to come in and make your sales pitch, or at least get all your expenses covered.

There are several downsides to private seminars, however. For one thing, they take massive amounts of preparation and usually get expensive. You need, at a minimum, print handouts like a Personal Brochure and a presentation folder, perhaps a PowerPoint presentation, and possibly travel and lodging. The prep time can be equally daunting: writing your presentation, having your staff stuff attendee kits, polishing your speech, and so on. So you can't undertake private seminars lightly.

However, private seminars can be a great tool if you can

- Identify companies or organizations whose members are likely to need your services and fit into your ideal client profile.

- Speak comfortably in front of people.

- Make a presentation that's oriented toward the benefit to the audience.

- Distribute top-quality printed materials.

- Have a system in place for following up on individual leads and with the organization as a whole.

Some tips that I've learned through hard personal experience:

- Practice your presentation until you're reciting it in your sleep, and don't be afraid to change it.

- Keep it in the 60- to 90-minute range, no more. Most people don't want an all-day boot camp.

- At one seminar, promote your other seminars.

- Ask for the business! Make sure attendees know whom to talk to in order to schedule a private appointment with you.

- Make sure every person leaves with some printed material.

CHANNEL 16: SEMINARS—PUBLIC

- Inclusive.

- Advantages: You get to make your pitch to prospects who mostly want to hear what you have to say.

- Disadvantages: Setup can be costly, and you have to be comfortable and polished in making a presentation to a large group of people. Because these seminars are open to the public and are usually free, you'll attract all kinds of folks you don't want as clients.

The same advice I gave you about private seminars applies to public seminars, with a few changes. First of all, a public seminar is open to anyone who wants to attend, and you're the one reserving the space. You might be able to get a space for free, but you get what you pay for. If you want audiovisual capability and all the rest, you're going to have to pay for a hotel ballroom.

The other big difference with public seminars is that you can't screen who comes. If you're a retirement planner, you might advertise only in communities for people 55 and over, but you still don't know who's going to show up. You might spend thousands of dollars taking out a newspaper ad and sending out direct mailers, only to get 100 people of whom only 3 or 4 are ideal clients. That's the risk you take.

However, a public seminar is a great opportunity to educate the public about what you do and how you provide value. Even if the audience members don't suit your goals, they can still become referral sources. In any case, follow the same advice given for private seminars: give out classy materials, have a polished presentation, ask for the business, make your speech about audience benefits, and have a follow-up system in place.

In general, I recommend private seminars over public ones.

THINGS YOU CAN DO IN A MONTH

1. Complete your Personal Brochure and send five copies to your A clients, along with a letter explaining your new brand and asking them to pass four copies along to family or friends.

2. Get your telemarketing working—record an on-hold message, have staff start calling current clients to invite them to personal meetings, and so on.

3. Negotiate and sign your agreement with your new professional referral partners. Use an attorney if you feel it's necessary (unless you are one).

4. Talk to local schools, charity organizations, and churches about fund-raisers and other public community outreach events you could engage in.

5. Research customer relationship management (CRM) systems like Siebel and Salesforce.com. More on this later.

6. Finish the copy for your Web site.

CHANNEL 17: SPECIAL EVENTS

- Exclusive.

- Advantages: You make a personal connection with prospects in a casual, fun setting.

- Disadvantages: Can be expensive, and you might get dirty looks if you try to turn a social event into a sales opportunity, so be careful. Can take time to lead to new business.

Special events can be nearly anything where you bring clients and prospects together in a social setting for fun: parties, Client Appreciation Night, poker night, wine tastings, fund-raisers, sporting events, open houses, and so on. It's always the right time for a special event, and smart Personal Branders have turned their regular events into major draws on their community's social calendar.

The main thing to remember about special events is that they are selling-free zones. Period. No selling and no handing out brochures unless you are asked. You're putting on the event for one reason: to generate goodwill. You want people to think warmly of you and to enjoy your company.

Make sure you treat special events as you would a private dinner party: send invitations and collect RSVPs. Offer door prizes and games, and be creative. The object is to give everyone a wonderful time and make them associate those good feelings with you. This is a very effective channel, and I recommend it to most of my clients. They enjoy it as well.

CHANNEL 18: SPONSORSHIPS

- Inclusive.

- Advantages: Positive community attention and a more positive brand. You get to be associated with things that everyone likes or respects, like kids' sports or charity.

- Disadvantages: As with all advertising, cost and lack of targeting.

It's pretty simple: you buy an ad in the program for a high school musical, purchase an outfield wall sign for the local minor league baseball team, or put your name on the poster for a charity concert. Sponsorships do two things: create brand awareness and associate you with community involvement and generosity.

If you decide that sponsorships are right for you, be sure to check out all the opportunities in your area. Some organizations promote the daylights out of their sponsors, while others expect you to be grateful that you paid $2,000 to get your name on the bottom of a golf program. Make sure you're getting enough bang for your buck, and make sure you turn your sponsorship into a press release.

CHANNEL 19: TELEMARKETING

- Exclusive.

- Advantages: It offers multiple ways to target your customers.

- Disadvantages: We hate telemarketers!

I don't recommend cold calling, and it's largely illegal now anyway. What I'm talking about is "warm calling": using telecom technology to communicate with prospects and clients with whom you already have some kind of relationship. There are many kinds of telemarketing: outbound personal calls, on-hold narration, conference calls, teleseminars where you present to an audience that's strictly on the phone, and fax blasting to an audience that has agreed to let you fax to them.

Warm calling lets you create a relationship and ask for the meeting. On-hold recordings are a slam dunk for any professional, giving you an automatic pathway to communicating benefits, new services, special events, and more. Conference calls and seminars are easy now, thanks to services like GreatTeleseminars.com and InfiniteConferencing.com. I highly recommend on-hold messaging; the rest of telemarketing depends on your profession and your available time.

CHANNEL 20: TELEVISION ADVERTISING

- Inclusive.

- Advantages: Huge credibility builder.

- Disadvantages: Huge cost.

I discourage most of my clients from doing TV advertising simply because it doesn't deliver enough bang for the buck. When you add production costs to the cost of airtime, even on a local cable station, the expense can be substantial. And for many professions, TV advertising is simply not appropriate. What do we think when we see a lawyer advertising on TV? Ambulance chaser. What do we think when we see a doctor advertising on TV? Quack who probably pushes his own brand of vitamins on patients.

For most people, the downside of TV outweighs the upside. But if you want to pursue it, local cable TV advertising is your best option. It offers the best blend of manageable rates, targeted coverage, and usually production services. Talk to your local cable provider and see what kinds of packages are available.

One tip: *please* invest in good production values. Nothing hurts your brand more than a cheesy ad that looks like it came from the local used car lot.

CHANNEL 21: TRADE SHOWS

- Inclusive.

- Advantages: Fabulous networking opportunity and usually fun.

- Disadvantages: With travel, lodging, and the cost of exhibits and materials, a trade show can set you back more than any other channel except a self-published book.

You shouldn't even consider exhibiting at a trade show until you've been an active Personal Brander for at least a year. That's because your branding and marketing message will still be in the refining stages, not ready for the chaos and short attention spans of a big show. In addition, since you're going to have to pay for exhibit space, a booth, freight, airfare, accommodations, utilities, handout materials, giveaway items, and staff, the whole enterprise can cost a fortune. I recommend staying away from trade shows until you have the income to exhibit every year and can financially withstand a show that brings you zero new business.

Once you are ready, a trade show or conference can be a wonderful opportunity to set up an exhibit and get your story out face-to-face. People at trade shows are there as much to make contacts as to make buying decisions. Your collection of business cards following a big event will be worth its weight in platinum. A trade show is also a powerful way to step out of a regional niche and get wider exposure.

If you can worm your way onto a panel discussion team, you can further increase your visibility and reputation.

One of the best tactics I've heard of to make trade shows more fiscally manageable is to partner with some professional colleagues and share all costs. This might range from creating a completely informal partnership and agreeing to share leads all the way to forming an LLC just for show exhibition. But suppose you and three other insurance brokers split all the costs of a big show. Bringing your capital outlay down from $20,000 to $5,000 can make the impossible possible.

Some suggestions for making the most of trade shows:

- Try to use recycled exhibit booths and other show facilities. There are companies that specialize in this.

- Attend only those events that focus on your target market exclusively.

- Attend smaller events. The large shows may have the glitz, but you'll be lost in the crowd.

- Have a memorable giveaway item at your exhibit.

- Have a video or DVD demo of some product or service, if appropriate, to capture people's attention.

- Be certain to have a way to either get a business card or scan an attendee badge so that you can build a contact database from your show. It's the only way you'll get ROI.

- Turn your trade show attendance into a media event by sending press releases to local news outlets and sponsoring a big giveaway that the press can attend.

- Have laptops with wireless Internet connections at your exhibit so that people can immediately go to your Web site and give you their contact information.

THE RULE OF FIVE

Whew! That's a lot of ground to cover. But there's one other vitally important strategic point that I have to share with you before we move on, and that's this:

Have five ways to reach your target market.

To build and maintain a successful Personal Brand, you must have at least five channels by which you reach your target market with your branding message. Experienced brand builders use multiple channels, coordinated to work together. It's like attacking the same target from many directions; your chances of hitting it go up. So you might employ the three must-have channels—a Personal Brochure, a Web site, and professional referrals—and add outdoor advertising, special events, and teleseminars. That's six channels, and that's fantastic.

THINK SYNERGY

To get the most from the money you spend, get your channels feeding off of one another. You've got to generate *synergy*. That means that your channels have got to feed off of and support one another. That's how your branding machine really gets going.

Here's an example: You hold a public seminar to promote your legal services. At the seminar, you hand out copies of your Personal Brochure and explain the message. The brochure invites people to your Web site to download an information packet relevant to their legal situation, and in return for the download, you get their e-mail addresses for your e-mail newsletter. After the seminar, you send reminder e-mails to attendees and direct-mail pieces to people on your mailing list who didn't attend, giving them the highlight content. Finally, you tape the seminar, turn it into a packaged DVD that you can give out as a promotional piece or sell, and upload the video to your Web site, where people can watch it if they give you their e-mail address. You also send a DVD to all your local TV stations, inviting them to cover your next seminar.

Get creative and surprise me. Take the example of a branding client of mine, a financial planner who'd been using seminars to target widows over age 65. Because widows would generally rather find a financial advisor they like and trust instead of trying to understand a lot of Byzantine financial data, the seminars flopped. So our client switched to another tactic: sponsoring monthly bingo games at the local community center, even going so far as to call the bingo numbers personally. The bingo cards even featured his logo and phone number! His business has soared because of his creative use of a channel and his hard-earned knowledge of his market. Bingo.

BY NOW YOU SHOULD BE ...

- Deciding which branding channels you want to use

- Getting printing quotes for your branding materials

- Starting development of your Web site

- Holding meetings with potential professional networking partners

- Getting your press kit together

- Deciding on your new client-centric business model and fee structure

CHAPTER

CREATING CUSTOMER DELIGHT

For a long time, parents discouraged their children from worrying about what others think. They didn't realize how shortsighted and stupid that was. We need other people to think well of us.
—Mark Leary, social psychology professor, Duke University

In the cable TV industry, the connection from the outside main cable to the homeowner's TV is called the "last mile." Customer service is the "last mile" for your Personal Brand. The experience you provide your customers will either support or contradict the promises you make with your branding campaign. Performance turns your Personal Brand from hype to flesh; conversely, failure to perform alienates your prospects forever.

The third brain of a great Personal Brand is not customer service. It's creating customer *delight*. Remember that a brand is a relationship that carries an implied promise: that your clients will have a valuable experience that they can feel great about. Once your specialization has touched their emotions and your branding channels have gotten them in the door, the last step is to deliver on your promise and exceed it—again and again. When you perform as advertised repeatedly, you'll create the most valuable of all business currencies:

96

trust. You'll also create raving fans who will fall all over themselves to refer you new ideal clients. So how can you create customer delight and give people an experience that they'll talk about for days?

THINGS YOU CAN DO TODAY

1. E-mail your best clients to ask them for testimonial quotes.

2. Contact other clients to ask them about being on your client advisory board.

3. Pay one of your kids or a neighbor to regularly surf Weblogs and consumer forums such as Angie's List to see what's being said about you.

4. Close the deal on your mailing list.

5. Proofread everything.

6. Talk to the National Speakers Association about becoming a member.

WHAT TO DO

There are three secrets to creating customer delight:

1. Have a system.

2. Know what your clients want.

3. Underpromise and overdeliver.

Have a System

Smart business owners and professionals don't leave customer delight to chance. The best of them develop a proactive customer-experience program that operates on a preset schedule, without the boss's involvement, to continually reach out to customers and make them feel cared for, communicated with, and listened to at all times. It's a lot of work, but the benefits are tremendous:

- Happy clients who are easy to deal with during your relationship

- An unpaid sales force giving you spontaneous, gold-plated referrals

- Customer loyalty, leading to more consistent income

- Greater tolerance for change, such as price increases

- Less trouble when service problems arise

The best approach I've seen is to assign an individual to be your client experience director. I've also seen businesses create a "director of first impressions," which is a fantastic idea. In any case, this person's only job is to make sure that every client, from the moment he or she calls for the first meeting, feels taken care of, communicated with, and appreciated. The client experience director makes sure that thank-you and birthday cards are always sent on time, sends gift certificates to thank clients for referrals, researches and answers tough questions within 24 hours, and basically makes sure that everyone feels cared for and kept in the loop at all times—so you don't have to worry about it.

The other thing you must do in order to deliver customer delight is create a client service plan for your business that spells out every process in step-by-step detail:

- *Basic policies.* Create a manual that dictates everything related to your client communication: when mailings go out, at what stages in a relationship a client gets a phone call, each client's contact preferences, shipping options when you're sending gifts—everything. No detail is too small. Leave nothing to chance.

- *Gift providers.* Identify companies that offer affordable, high-quality cards, promotional items, wine, gift certificates, and such.

- *How to handle angry clients.* Determine what to say when a client complains: forms for taking a complete report, internal policies, and more.

- *Cues.* Identify things to look for when a customer is unhappy, which you can use to head off complaints before they occur.

- *Surveys.* Prepare survey forms that your employees can give out at the end of a visit or project to learn how you can improve.

- *Notes and preferences.* Make individual notes about each client, from how the client likes his or her eggs at breakfast meetings to key birthdays, anniversaries, and the like.

Most important, your service plan should spell out, step by step, what happens when a client makes the first phone call, at the first meeting, after the first meeting, at the one-year anniversary of being a client, after a productive referral, and so on. Every touch point should be scripted; every outreach should be planned. Spontaneity is great, but what you and your clients want is predictability. Remember, we live in a world where very few people deliver what they say they will deliver. As Shakespeare wrote, "Consistency, thou art a jewel."

Make sure everyone on your staff has a bound copy of the client service manual, and post it in a private section of your Web site. Also, sit down every six months with your staff to go over any and all customer complaints and/or praise. Look at the causes of complaints and examine ways in which your entire business can improve customer service. Constant improvement is the goal; in these feedback sessions, you should strive for the following over time:

- Fewer overall customer complaints per period

- More resolved customer complaints

- More referrals per period

- More positive survey results per period

THINGS YOU CAN DO IN A WEEK

1. Conduct demos and get free samples of customer relationship management software.

2. Write your first sample column for the local paper.

3. Train your staff on how to answer phones and transfer calls.

4. Write a stack of seasonal direct-mail messages for holidays, birthdays, anniversaries, and other such occasions.

5. Test-drive calendar software and handheld devices like the iPhone or BlackBerry that you and your key staff can use to keep in touch and stay organized.

(continued)

> 6. Begin fielding referrals from your old clients based on your letter telling them about your branding—and testing out your gold-plated referral service system.

Know What Your Customers Want

You probably know that the best referrals are unsolicited, and that when customers love your service enough to refer others to you without being asked, they're going to send tons of business your way. The question is: how do you provide that winning service and those incredible customer experiences?

You do it by learning what your customers want. You already know a great deal about them demographically (where they live, where they go to church, what their hobbies are) because getting that information was part of picking your target market. But what are their aspirations in life? What are their relationships with their kids or parents? What are their passions? Research—talking with clients and getting to know them—is the key to becoming a service provider who really enhances their lives.

With my clients, I recommend two ways to do this kind of research:

1. *Formal market research.* One way to learn more is to have your clients complete surveys. Create a survey that you can send them in paper form or put online and send to them via an e-mail (I recommend the Web because it's cheaper, it's easier for people who have enough paperwork lying around the house, and it doesn't kill trees), and once a year, ask them to complete the survey. Ask them questions like:

   • What keeps you coming back to do business with me?

   • What could I do to make it easier for you to work with me?

   • Where have I fallen short in the past?

- What services or conveniences would you like to see me offer?

This method can seem a little impersonal, but if your clients are willing to do it and give you honest feedback, it's a big time-saver for you. I recommend trying a survey just to see what the response is. If it doesn't work out, or if you'd like to do more, I highly recommend the following.

2. *Create a client advisory board.* If you have the time (and honestly, if you don't have the time to foster a relationship with your clients, why are you in business?), this is a fantastic option. It involves asking from 5 to 10 clients to serve on an informal advisory board to help you service all your clients or patients better. Most people are very flattered to be asked, so don't worry about imposing on them. They'll love that you asked them.

It's a pretty straightforward setup: you choose your location (your home, a restaurant), your time (breakfast, lunch, or dinner), your ideal advisory group (probably ideal clients, but you could also include professional referral sources), and how often you want to meet (I think every three months is an ideal interval). Then create an agenda of what you want to talk about at each meeting. It could be your business model, your overall service, the quality of your communication and marketing materials, or anything else that affects your business. Then your advisory board members show up and, based on the agenda, give you feedback. You can ask questions like the ones on your written survey or come up with new ones.

The goal, of course, is to create a regular feedback channel through which you will get valuable insights into how you can correct problems and improve service. When your meeting is done, log all the data you gather for analysis later. If you get consent, record the entire event. What you learn should tell you everything from how customers like your office wallpaper to their plans for retirement. This, in turn, can help you tailor your service to create the best possible experience. You'll also probably forge some great relationships that may last for many years.

BRAND SURGERY
THE PATIENT: BALANCING
PERSONAL AND PROFESSIONAL

- Don't share too much information. Some people think business should be all about business.

- Avoid controversial subjects, unless your target market thrives on them.

- Don't make up a lifestyle just to get into a lucrative market. Your lies will catch up with you and crush you.

- Be creative in building an environment that reflects your personality, but avoid clutter or tastelessness.

- Don't embarrass or anger your family or friends by telling personal stories.

- Don't take out ads that tell people how great you are. Show, don't tell.

- Make sure your eagerness to share personal information doesn't leave people scratching their head about what you do.

Underpromise and Overdeliver

Every client or prospect who comes to you will have a set of expectations; some of them will be reasonable, and others not. How you live up to those expectations will have a great deal to do with the customer's satisfaction. So you must *manage customer expectations*, and one of the best ways to do that is to tell the customer that something will take two weeks, and then do it in one. Or promise a certain amount of work for the price, and then do 50 percent more for the same money.

That's what I mean by underpromise and overdeliver. If you promise a reasonable level of service, that creates an expectation that you will live up to that promise. When you then deliver a much higher level of service, you'll surprise your client into a state of delight. But if you promise the moon—like some financial advisors

I've seen who promise 25 percent annual returns on their clients' portfolios—you're setting yourself up for disaster. The clients expect an extraordinary level of service, and when you deliver ordinary, they're angry and resentful. It's pure client psychological management. Promise a little less than you know you can deliver, then deliver more than you promised. It works every time. You'll know you were able to do the work faster or deliver more all along, but your customer won't.

Walt Disney theme parks are a wonderful example of underpromise and overdeliver. When you get in line for a ride, they have a sign that tells you that the wait will be 45 minutes. But when you board the ride and check your watch, it's always 30 minutes or so, and you're pleased. They've just made you happy to stand in line for half an hour.

BRAND CASE STUDY

The Brand: Daniel Will-Harris, Web designer, actor, author

Specialization: Jack-of-all-trades

Location: Marin County, California

Channels: The Web, his self-published book, his acting

Highlights: Having the store at the Museum of Modern Art in New York City sell the watches he designed

Online: www.danielwillharris.com, www.will-harris.com

The Story: Daniel Will-Harris is a funny guy. Just ask him. Any guy who would write and publish a book called *My Wife and Times* and produce a sarcastic bimonthly e-mail newsletter called the "SchmoozeLetter" can't be accused of being overly serious. That's been a big part of his successful Web design business, and now it's a part of another successful venture as an actor.

How It All Started: Will-Harris was an early adopter of the Web, posting one of the first 5,000 sites ever created on the Internet in 1995. He had already been doing his own publishing and design, and he thought the infant medium was perfect for promoting his design work.

(continued)

"Having the site got people to know I was there and see my work, and led to a job writing for CNet," Will-Harris says. "That led to working for NetObjects, which led to creating eFuse.com. You never know where things are going to end up." EFuse.com has become a very popular destination as a friendly place to learn the basics of building a Web site.

Will-Harris built his design business in a way that could only be called organic. "I moved to Point Reyes, but there wasn't any Web," he says. "I went around to local stores and restaurants and said, 'You know, your menu could look a lot better.' Restaurants have a very tight budget, so I would do work on spec for them, or I would work for food. The first year I lived here, I never had to pay to eat at that restaurant. There's something exciting about that."

Getting into acting was more of a stretch at first. "I turned 50 and I decided I was tired of spending all my time by myself at my computer," he says. "I wanted to work with people again. I didn't think it was a realistic thing to do. It's not a realistic career. But a friend encouraged me and said, 'Why don't you just give it a try and see what happens?' So I signed up for a class. Well, it used to be that you had to have an agent to find auditions. Now with the Web, I'm able to find my own auditions, and I'm getting cast in features.

What This Brand Stands For:

- *Web savvy.* There's no question that Will-Harris's Web site is the cornerstone of his success. It's arch, irreverent, and self-deprecating, with section titles like "EsperFonto" and "MyDailyYoga." It's the gateway to his highly popular SchmoozeLetter.com e-newsletter, a ramble about life, family flotsam, and occasionally the design biz.

  "I think the Web is fantastic because you can do it on your own, you can display your skills globally," he says. "I've had work on almost every continent, seen by people who would not have known I existed without the Web.

  "I think the reason my Web site stands out is because it's very personal. Businesses are afraid to do that; people think they need to be cold and corporate. I think the fact that you are an individual sitting in your home office is an advantage. When you are independent, you're selling your talents, skills, and personality. That stuff has to come across, and my site's always had a lot of humor and personality. Your Web site is your personality in pixels. It should really reflect how you are in person."

- *Mercurial interests.* Let's see, the man is a Web designer, a typeface developer, an author, an actor, and now a watch designer, with his watches being MOMA bestsellers. "That comes from my 'You never know' attitude," Will-Harris says.

- *Being personal.* Quite correctly, Will-Harris realizes that it's he himself, not his Web site or any other proxy, that connects with people. That's why his SchmoozeLetter, which has about 30,000 subscribers, is largely self-deprecating flotsam from his personal life.

X-Factor: A software accident that ended up making the Schmooze-Letter more popular than ever. "Once, the software sent out 12 copies of the newsletter to everyone, and people were mad. I wrote an apology, and when you connect to people on a personal level, the introductions start to get more personal. The more personal they got, the more people subscribed."

Branding Wisdom: "You never know what's going to lead to what," he says. "Doing what you love can lead to something totally unexpected. You can't have preconceived notions. I'm averse to people who say, 'In five years I'm going to be doing this.' Just do it and you may end up on a different path. Tuesday, I was modeling for an artist. You end up in places you don't expect. I'm just diversifying. I think when you're in your thirties and forties, you get really focused and you want to keep doing what you're doing, but eventually you burn out and you want to try other things."

CLIENT DELIGHT TENETS

Customer service is an attitude. Each time clients interact with you, they have a new experience. Creating memorable client experiences must become part of your business model. Will that experience enhance your Personal Brand or damage it? Here are the key tenets of client service and delight that every business should make fundamental to its business model:

1. *Love your clients.* You can't fake it. Everyone in your company must treat your clients with care and respect. If you don't love your clients, get another client base or another business.

2. *Develop a client-centered culture.* Your culture must naturally focus on meeting the clients' needs. Everything everyone does should be focused on this goal.

3. *Make client delight your mission.* The guideline is not, "You can't please all the people all the time," but, "We must make every client's experience as satisfying as possible, every time."

4. *Customer service is everybody's job.* Talk to everyone on your staff about what good service means for the business (strategy, referrals, and growth) and how it affects them (positive feedback, more pleasant work, better pay, and promotion). Make sure they understand how to answer the phone and transfer calls, how to greet a client, and how to handle the first stages of a client-service crisis. Most importantly, make sure everyone knows that even if their job title doesn't involve client service, client delight is still their first responsibility.

THINGS YOU CAN DO IN A MONTH

1. Print a year's supply of postcards with blank spaces for custom messages.

2. Launch your new Web site.

3. Have your Web development company engage in search engine optimization (SEO) to ensure that you show up on Google, Yahoo!, and MSN.

4. Nail down any sponsorships that you might want to do, especially if they are for events that close their deals months in advance, like county fairs or cultural festivals.

5. Find a quick printer who can overprint custom messages in black ink on your full-color postcards. The work should be affordable, be dependable, and have a 24-hour turnaround.

6. Send out an e-mail blast about your new Web site.

PEOPLE MAKE MISTAKES

It's not the mistake that kills; it's the cover-up. Nixon learned this the hard way; don't make the same error. Your customers don't expect you to be perfect, and you won't be. So when you do make an error, don't tap dance, deny, or "spin." That's the worst thing you can do. If your business is legitimately at fault, admit the mistake and go above and beyond the call of duty to fix it . . . at your expense. If the blame is shared, talk to the customer about the circumstances and about sharing the costs. In my experience, at least as many long-lasting business relationships have been created over the correction of a problem as over impeccable customer service. Why? Because when you pull out all the stops to make something right, you prove that you're as good as your Personal Brand. Here are my tips for recovering from a client-service crisis:

1. *Listen and acknowledge the complaint.* Show the client you care. Validate the client's displeasure with phrases such as "I understand how you feel" and "That's certainly not right, is it?" Let clients know that they are exercising their rights—and helping your business—when they complain.

2. *Take responsibility for the problem.* You're the captain of the ship, so even if it's a filing clerk who's been with you for three weeks who made the blunder, it's your fault. If the complaint is valid, own up. Admit that mistakes were made. Share your disappointment at what happened. Use phrases like, "You're handling this extremely well, considering the way you've been treated."

3. *Let them know you can do better.* Explain that what happened is very much the exception, and will not happen again.

107

4. *Ask what you can do.* Flat-out ask your client, "What can I do to make you happy?" or "What can I do to remedy the situation?" That's a scary question to ask, but it's mandatory. Losing valuable clients is scarier. Listen, give them feedback on the suggestion, then before you end the meeting, give the client a specific, itemized list of what you will do to make things right.

5. *Keep your client informed.* Let the client know that you're keeping your word. Call or e-mail to say something like, "I'm working personally on the situation, and by the end of the day tomorrow, everything will be as you requested."

6. *Thank your client.* The client alerted you to a problem that could have cost you business. You had a chance to correct it. Thank the client for the business and for giving you a chance to keep it.

IMPROVE AND NEVER STOP

The real challenge of customer service is that it never ends. You don't just institute a policy and leave it there. You must always be learning, listening, and adapting to continue giving customers experiences that they can brag about. If you can forge a love affair with your clients, you'll get rich and enjoy your work immensely.

BY NOW YOU SHOULD BE . . .

- Thinking about your next vacation

- Creating your client-service protocols

- Having photos taken

- Refining your new business model

- Surveying your best clients on what you do well and what could be improved

- Using your new logo everywhere and using your new business cards, stationery, note cards, envelopes, and mailing labels exclusively

PART III

ANATOMY OF A PERSONAL BRAND

In this section of the book, I am *not* trying to break down every possible Personal Branding tool and channel in granular detail. If I did, this book would be 100,000 pages long and filled with information that you'd never use. So I've focused just on the Personal Branding tools that, in my experience, busy professionals are most likely to use and that are most likely to give you a solid return on your investment of money and time.

If you're really dying to know more about running radio and TV ads, using telemarketing, doing seminars, or publishing your own book, you can find information about those and other secondary branding tools at www.thebrandcalledyou.com. I hope you'll use it as a resource. Now, let's look at the tools that any successful brander has in his or her arsenal.

BRAND IDENTITY

Microcelebrity is the phenomenon of being extremely well-known not to millions but to a small group—a thousand people, or maybe only a few dozen. As DIY media reach ever deeper into our lives, it's happening to more and more of us.
—Clive Thompson, *Wired,* December 2007

Now we begin the meat of Personal Branding: creating the tools that carry your brand message through your channels to your target market. We've found the three brains of our creation (none of them abnormal, for you Mel Brooks fans), and now it's time to start putting all the parts together. And we're going to start with the most basic tool of all, Brand Identity materials.

BRAND IDENTITY MATERIALS

You already have Brand Identity materials. They're called business cards. Even if you have no other printed materials that carry your brand, you have cards. Everyone does. These days, with companies like VistaPrint.com, it's so cheap to get beautiful cards that if you have cheapo ones printed on perforated sheets from Kinko's, you should be ashamed of yourself.

But the heart and soul of your Brand Identity materials isn't your business card; it's your logo. Your logo should be on everything that you do: cards, letterhead, envelopes, signage, ads, billboards, sponsor banners, your Web site, your e-mail signature—everything. If you don't have a logo yet, I'm going to walk you through the steps in creating one. Then your job is to find a good graphic designer, get some drafts, make changes, and pick a logo that dazzles you.

A logo has three parts:

1. Your company name

2. Your slogan

3. Your icon

Companies choose these elements with great care and often pay tens of thousands of dollars for slogans and icons because they know that these elements have the power to shape perceptions. A great example of the muscle a logo can wield is fashion designer Donna Karan. By developing the "DKNY" logo to symbolize Donna Karan New York, she did more than create a valuable branding graphic. She aligned her fashions with New York City, the place from which most American styles come.

Your logo is a single graphical image that represents your Personal Brand. An effective logo tells prospects almost everything they need to know about you: your name, what you do, your personal style, and how you create value. Done right, a logo benefits you in many ways:

- It becomes your surrogate, so that when people see your logo, they get an image of your face.

- It creates strong, widespread name recognition.

- It educates people on what you do.

- It appeals to the emotions and increases affinity.

So let's break down this vital piece of branding, shall we? We'll start with your company name.

THINGS YOU CAN DO TODAY

1. Research possible venues for public seminars.

2. Check to see if your phone service will support teleconferences.

3. Write down a list of personal contacts you have at companies that might sponsor a radio show.

4. Record yourself giving your elevator pitch and listen to how you sound. Are you talking too fast? Do you stammer?

5. Contact local movie theaters to find out their rates for onscreen, pretrailer advertising.

6. Have a staff member call your main competitors in your target market and request their marketing materials so that you know what you're up against.

COMPANY NAME

Fortunately, you already know what to name your company, don't you? We discussed it in the introduction; it was my first piece of branding advice. Repeat after me:

Name your company after yourself.

That's it. You are the business. Think of it this way: what are the most important goals of any company name? They are

1. To be remembered

2. To be referred

3. To be easily found

Notice that "to create credibility" isn't in there. That's because credibility doesn't come from a name. It comes from reputation and performance. If you're a financial planner, you can put "Executive Investment and Asset Management" on your business card until the cows come home and nobody's going to think you're Charles Schwab. No, your name must be easy for people to remember, easy to pass along to others, and easy to find in a phone book or online search.

Look at the names of businesses or practices similar to yours, and 90 percent of them will be very similar. In some cases, such as law firms, that's because the culture of that profession demands it. You don't call yourself "The Law Store" unless you want to be seen as an ambulance chaser. Your industry, and whether you're a sole proprietor or partner, will greatly influence the way you can name yourself. Some naming tips:

- If you can describe what you do in a one- or two-word phrase, go ahead and tack it onto your name. Examples: Creative Services, Chiropractic, Residential Renovation.

- If you're in a conservative business such as accounting or financial services, consider simply using your name with "Company" or "Inc." attached.

- If you use just your name with no descriptive add-on, make sure your slogan tells people what you do.

- Use the familiar version of your name. If your full name is William P. Jefferson III, but everyone calls you Bill Jefferson, use that version. In other words, exclude middle initials, suffixes, and designations from your company name.

- Don't add words like "& Company," "& Associates," or other professional descriptors. These words have been so overused that they no longer have any meaning.

NAMING MYTHS AND REALITIES

Myth: "If I name my company after myself, all my clients will demand to work with me. I want to create a system that doesn't depend on me."

Reality: Clients always want to work with the person in charge. Your name won't train them to want otherwise. The systems you put in place to service customers will.

Myth: "If I give my company a corporate name, it will create the illusion of something bigger than a one-person operation."

Reality: The quality of your branding and your service says infinitely more about your company than its name. NYSE-sounding names often mask one-man operations running out of garages. It won't take prospects long to figure out that you're small.

Myth: "If I change my company name, it will cause confusion."

Reality: Most of your clients don't even know the name of your company. They know *you*. Ninety-nine percent of them won't care one way or the other.

Myth: "I have a strange name that my clients won't remember."

Reality: We like strange names. Once you get them, you never forget them (Arnold Schwarzenegger, Monica Lewinsky). If you have a strange name, flaunt it and make people remember it.

Myth: "I'm trying to build equity in my company and eventually sell it. You can't sell a company based on a person."

Reality: Mary Kay, Schwab, Disney, Ford, Johnson & Johnson. Need I say more?

BRAND SURGERY
THE PATIENT: YOUR LOGO

- Reject all those weird typefaces created by design students. They're all over the Internet, but they often do not reproduce in the crisp, clean way that you need.

- Avoid clichés in your slogan as much as you do in your icon. Look at your competitors and see how many of them have variations on the same theme. Then go the other way.

(continued)

- Avoid thin white type on dark backgrounds, especially if it's your slogan. In printed form, the white will sometimes fill in, leaving your slogan unreadable.

- If you're in a creative business, be creative. Your logo should reflect how you want prospects to see you.

- If you're in a serious business, like anything related to mainstream health care or money, look serious and staid.

PARTNERSHIPS

What if you're in a business partnership with someone, like a medical or law practice? How do you handle naming? Some businesses get around the problem by coming up with a corporate-sounding name, but you know my reaction to that. Personal names are always best. Here is a quick-glance guide to handling partner naming:

Office Partners
You share office space but don't do any joint marketing. Solution: Your branding has nothing to do with one another. Use just your name.

Marketing Partners
You share space and perform some joint marketing that you both pay for. You do not share clients. Solution: Use your names individually, but give each other veto power over your branding, since it will affect the other person's spending and income.

Branding Partners
You are business partners, sharing all costs and servicing the same client pool. Solution: Use both your last names, exactly as if you were a law firm (which you might be).

In all these cases, it's perfectly kosher to add a brief descriptor after your name or names, like "Tax Accounting and Preparation" or "Adolescent and Family Counseling."

SLOGAN

Your slogan is the part of Personal Branding with which you're probably most familiar. After all, each of us can rattle off a few dozen of the most famous corporate slogans. Can you name the companies that use these slogans?

- The ultimate driving machine

- Think different

- Moving at the speed of business

- The best a man can get

- A diamond is forever

- Something special in the air

If you said BMW, Apple, UPS, Gillette, De Beers, and American Airlines, you're spending too much time parked in front of your plasma TV. But seriously, slogans have a lot of power. Your slogan has two purposes:

1. To tell people what you do

2. To tell them whom you do it for

That's it. Some marketers will tell you that your slogan should also tell people why your service is valuable, like a divorce lawyer's slogan I once saw that read, "Keeping divorce litigation simple." First of all, talk about overpromising. But more important, you have no idea what the people in your target market will value. What half of them value the other half might hate. That's too risky. Stick with the basics: three to nine words that transmit who you are, what you do, and whom it benefits. Craft your tagline specifically to address your target market:

- Strategic wealth planning for Dallas divorcees

- Gentle chiropractic for adolescent athletes

- Selling the homes of University of Wisconsin faculty

Your specialization statement should be the perfect guide to writing your slogan. Of course, you're really limiting your market when you make your slogan so precise, and I know that might make you nervous. But if you've picked a target market with more than enough potential to get you to (and beyond) your income goals, this isn't a problem. It's an asset. The more precise your branding, the more you'll come to "own" your market. Some tips for writing great slogans:

- Avoid the word *solutions*. It's so overused that it's lost its meaning.

- Be specific. Say what you do and for whom with precision.

- Check your grammar and usage. Mistakes like using "it's" when you mean "its" make you look foolish.

- Test your slogan repeatedly, and if the responses aren't to your liking, keep experimenting.

- Don't italicize your slogan or put it in quotes. Many companies do this because they think it adds drama to an otherwise bad slogan. It doesn't. It only succeeds in making you look like an amateur.

- Keep it to nine words.

THINGS YOU CAN DO IN A WEEK

1. Talk to people who might serve as branding mentors for you—retired colleagues, successful professionals, and other such people.

2. Test your crisis response procedures with a phony client complaint.

3. Review your sales materials—the materials you present to prospects when they come to your office for the initial appointment. Are they in line with your brand? Are they persuasive?

4. Call five clients to come to your office and give you their impression of the physical surroundings.

5. Take your Branding Timetable to a printer to get a wall-size copy run off.

GRAPHICAL ICON

Not all logos have icons; yours might just be your name in a nice typeface and your slogan, and that's fine. But the right icon can dramatically enhance the effectiveness and retention of a logo. An icon is a graphic element that enhances your logo by tying into the meaning of your Personal Brand. For example, if you're marketing to the sailing community, and you work a pencil drawing of a tall ship into your logo, it tells prospects without a single word that you're a person with a passion for the ocean and sailboats—and that's the type of personal connection that wins business. You don't have to use your slogan to tell people what you care about. Your icon can do it.

Your logo icon can be anything, from an elegant-looking graphic shape (often called a "dingbat" by designers) to an illustration that's suited to your target market, your profession, or your interests. But avoid the cliché icons that everyone in your profession uses. For example, how many real estate agents have you seen with a house icon on their business card? They probably all thought the idea originated with them. Here's a good rule of thumb: if a graphic image seems incredibly obvious for your profession—such as a chef's hat for a caterer or a quill pen for a writer—*don't use it*. Some other tips in choosing an icon:

- Don't use photos. They rarely reproduce well.

- Use something that can be drawn simply. Complex illustrations also don't reproduce well, especially in small sizes.

- Match your icon to the culture of your target market. For example, even if you're an avid surfer, putting a surfboard in your logo might not work well if you're trying to sell financial planning to seniors.

- Talk to a professional artist. This is the one area where do-it-yourself won't do. Unless you already know how to draw, it's worth a few hundred bucks to get something custom-done by a pro.

- Don't use your family crest. Such complex graphics rarely reproduce well in a logo format. Icons are usually small, and the finely lined detail of a family crest usually ends up a blurred mess.

BRAND CASE STUDY

The Brand: Marty Rodriguez, Realtor

Specialization: The top-selling Realtor in California, Century 21 superstar

Location: Glendora, California

Channels: Her sales, her staff, the Web, direct mail, cold calling

Highlights: Getting her own office

Online: www.martyrodriguez.com

The Story: Is Marty Rodriguez the world's greatest Realtor? By many yardsticks, yes. She's the number one agent for Century 21, which has recognized her as its top producer not only in America, but worldwide. Marty's name has become "top of mind" to home sellers in California's San Gabriel Valley. In a bad year, Rodriguez sells a home a day. In a hot market, she'll close 450 (or more) transactions annually. It's an astonishing pace, and you might think that Rodriguez's life must be all real estate. It is, and she loves it.

Century 21 certainly appreciates Rodriguez. In 1996, it created a franchise for her when she considered leaving the company. In recent years, she's been honored by *Hispanic Business* as one of America's 100 Most Influential Latino Businesspersons, has coauthored *The Complete Idiot's Guide to Online Buying and Selling a Home*, and has been profiled in *Fast Company*.

How It All Started: One of 11 children raised in a two-bedroom, one-bath home, Rodriguez discovered her zest for sales in Catholic school, selling more candy and Christmas cards than her classmates. When her husband, Ed, began building spec homes in the late 1970s, she got her real estate license so that she could sell them.

Her first six years in the business amounted to a learning curve. She and her husband were building a custom home, her children were young, and her business partner was carrying a sack of personal problems. As the crash of the early 1990s weeded out dilettantes and hobbyists from the profession, she asked herself, "What do I have to do to stay in business when everybody is going out of business?" Rodriguez quickly learned the answer: the successful Realtors were not always the best salespeople, but they were the best at building their personal brands.

What This Brand Stands For:

- *The team.* Marty's team, which includes her children, is an integral part of everything her office does. The team extends her brand much further than she could do on her own. "Clients know we are totally committed, here working late at night. If I'm not here, I'm at an appointment. They know we have systems, because it's all about communication. Even when a house isn't selling, we are communicating with sellers and letting them know what's going on, talking about price reductions. Communication is everything. Having that team means I can be in more places than most agents. That's why we do so much better as a team than as individuals. When you're number one, you can do things that others can't."

- *Ubiquity.* Rodriguez is everywhere in her marketplace—and if she's not, her team is. "My team is still cold calling or door knocking," she says. "You have to have the personal touch. In the bad housing market, the brand requires more of that personal kind of outreach. Before, everything was on autopilot," she adds.

  "I think it's just a matter of being everywhere," she says. And everywhere she is. Regular calls are important as a means of keeping in touch with past and present clients and protecting leads. Personal contact complements steady direct mail that drips regular "just listed/just sold" cards to clients and prospects. And in addition to a PR machine that lands Rodriguez regularly in newspaper and magazine stories, she sponsors the Marty Rodriguez Scholarship Fund for San Gabriel Valley students.

- *Total commitment.* For Marty, real estate is life. When she's not working, she's thinking about work. In the tough environment after the subprime mortgage meltdown, her sterling reputation remains critical. "My reputation is that Marty sells houses," she says. "People see me as tough, no-nonsense, someone who gets things done. They know that my office is open seven days a week. My

(continued)

121

agents are full time in an industry where most agents are barely part time."

X-Factor: Referrals and more referrals. With her unmatched track record selling area homes, Rodriguez gets them in abundance. "I get calls from people I don't even know," she says, citing a mortgage broker who brought her a ready buyer out of the blue. "She just sold my reputation," she notes. For that favor, the mortgage broker will get either a gift certificate or a check in appreciation.

Branding Wisdom: Rodriguez has built her franchise, Century 21 Marty Rodriguez Real Estate, around one concept: everybody does only what he or she does best. Each employee makes the most of a single focused attribute. Her buyers' agents don't prospect for listings, her marketing manager doesn't troubleshoot computers, and her listing coordinator doesn't perform inspections or run around removing lockboxes. Marty herself just sells properties. In simplicity is performance.

This business structure wasn't the product of any coaching session, but of Rodriguez's own vision. "There was nobody in this area that thought what I thought," she explains. After seeing her colleagues burn out from trying to do everything at once, she took a different tack. "I learned to delegate," she notes. "I don't cook; I don't do housework; I don't open the mail; I don't manage my own money. I focus on real estate."

PUTTING TOGETHER YOUR LOGO

OK, after weeks of naming, slogans, and choosing the right icon, you've got the pieces of your logo in place. Now you've got to put them together into a single unit. Your logo should appear to be one coherent graphic, with all three elements working together.

The most important step at this stage is simple: hire a professional graphic designer. Do not design your logo yourself. Designers bring to the table many more skill sets and knowledge than I can list here, including the many traps and tricks involved in getting your logo to reproduce well at the printer. Hire a designer and you won't be sorry.

Here are some logo-building tips.

Use Color Wisely

There are five main colors you can use in your logo: red, orange, yellow, green, and blue, and the variations on those colors, like aqua, gold, and violet. There are also three neutral colors: white, black, and gray. You'll probably end up using some combination of main and neutral colors in your logo, and we recommend that you limit colors to no more than two. Too many colors will cause your logo to look like a bed of Dutch tulips.

Colors on the red end of the spectrum are focused slightly behind the retina of the eye and appear to move toward the viewer (try it). Colors on the blue end of the spectrum are focused slightly in front of the retina and appear to move away. That's why red is the color of energy, excitement, and attention, while blue stands for peace, tranquility, and relaxation. In marketing, red means volatility and blue stability. Do you think Coca-Cola's color is red and IBM's is blue by accident? Think again.

As stated in *The 22 Immutable Laws of Branding* by Al and Laura Ries, colors tend to create moods or convey feelings:

- White = purity
- Black = luxury
- Yellow = caution
- Blue = leadership
- Purple = royalty
- Green = nature
- Red = attention

When selecting colors for your logo, consider the mood you want to convey. This will be your principal color, used for your name and probably your icon. We recommend using black as your other color. It stands out and is cheaper to print than the other neutrals.

Use Clean Typefaces

There are two kinds of typefaces: *serif*, the old-fashioned type that you probably see in your daily newspaper, and *sans serif*, the streamlined type without all the fancy curlicues and flourishes. You'll need to choose typefaces for your name and slogan; in making this decision, your most important factor is readability. Keep things simple; stick with proven basics like Times, Goudy, Arial, Optima, and Garamond.

Serif typefaces tend to be seen as more old-fashioned, so they are used more often for traditional, conservative businesses such as financial services. Sans serif type is seen as more modern and creative, so you'll often see it used by designers, architects, and the like.

The bottom line is, pick a typestyle that you like but one that's readable at small sizes. Ornate scripts are generally a bad idea. Most companies will go with one typeface for their business name and another for their slogan. As long as your typefaces are clean and readable, this isn't a problem. However, do avoid using all capital letters, especially in your name. It comes across like shouting.

Make Your Logo the Right Size

How big should your logo be? It depends on the medium. Once you size your logo for your business card, you'll see why I recommend keeping your icon simple. There's not a lot of space. Complex drawings turn to mush. But the basic guideline is, don't make your logo smaller than your prospects can read easily. In other words, if you're marketing to the over-65 crowd and your prospects have to squint to read your slogan, you're in trouble. Your logo should also be high-resolution enough that if it's blown up for an ad or banner, it remains sharp.

THINGS YOU CAN DO IN A MONTH

1. Read the main trade magazines in your industry to see if they contain any marketing ideas that you can borrow.

2. Create a six-month calendar of networking events you plan to attend.

3. Contact some of the companies listed in the appendix to get prices on client gifts.

4. Work with your copywriter to create a great cover letter to send with your Personal Brochure.

5. Contact any local celebrities you might know to discuss getting an endorsement.

6. Do a U.S. Trademark and Patent Office search (www.uspto.gov) to make sure that no one in your area and in your type of business is using your slogan.

YOUR IDENTITY SYSTEM

When your logo is done, you've got your first Personal Branding tool. The next step is to create your Brand Identity system: business cards, letterhead, envelopes, mailing labels, note cards, and any other materials you want to add. But those are the basics.

Creating the Brand Identity system is easy: have your graphic designer do it. There's a lot more to it than sticking your logo at the top of a piece of paper and calling it stationery. There are paper choices and textures, finishes, limitless layout options, color printing differences, and so on. Give your designer your logo, talk to him or her about your brand, and turn him or her loose. In the end, you should end up with a suite of coordinated materials that look and feel slick and polished and that all communicate the same qualities about your Personal Brand. Then you're on your way.

BY NOW YOU SHOULD BE . . .

- In the queue at your printer with your Personal Brochure and post-cards

- Meeting with professional referral partners

- Doing interviews with the local media

- Setting up seminars if you're going to do them

- Putting client feedback about your business and your brand into action

- Fully in sync with your staff about your brand and client service procedures

PERSONAL BROCHURE AND PERSONAL POSTCARD

There is much we can learn about personal branding from the legacy of Dr. Martin Luther King Jr. One of the reasons we find him unforgettable is his "I Have a Dream" speech. We remember him because everything about that speech makes sense to us. We align with who he was, what he stood for, and how he delivered his message. He spoke universal truth to an audience that was ready to hear it and get it.

—Gerry Foster, *Los Angeles Sentinel*

If there are two must-have printed pieces for any business, they are a Personal Brochure and a Personal Postcard. I'm going to tell you how to create both of these essential collateral pieces in one chapter. For both, the key word is *personal*. These are not sales tools. They are prospecting tools. They are built to carry a personal story or a personal message. Never forget that and you'll make the most of your investment.

PERSONAL BROCHURE

The business card isn't dead, but it's on life support, and a priest is being called. OK, that's an overstatement. I doubt that the business card will ever really go away. But when you're trying to make an impact in the market and really drive your Personal Brand home with a new contact or a prospect in your office, nothing works as well as a colorful, emotionally appealing, high-quality Personal Brochure. Many people give them out *instead* of their business cards. The Personal Brochure is the single most important branding tool you will ever have. It should be the cornerstone of your brand.

You probably have a mental image of a small-business brochure: three panels, fits in a No. 10 envelope, black ink, probably printed on a laser printer using some cheap Kinko's brochure template, filled with sales copy. Cut that picture from your brain. The Personal Brochure we're talking about is nothing like that. It's a professional-quality, full-color storytelling vehicle that's printed in an unusual size, uses beautiful color photography and gorgeous paper, and tells your personal story in a way that captures the reader's imagination.

Handing out a Personal Brochure will not get you business by itself. It's vital that you see that, or you'll waste your investment. A Personal Brochure is a tool for building rapport. It's a vehicle for your personal story and the qualities that will make you appealing to your target market. It tells readers who you are, where you come from, what's important to you, and so on. It's not a sale closer. It's a relationship builder.

A good Personal Brochure has two jobs. One is to let prospects *know you*. You should never fill a brochure with bragging points about your education, training, and certifications. That's sales information, and no brochure is going to close a sale for you. Your Personal Brochure's job is to help prospects feel a sense of connection to you, to break down their natural sales resistance by not trying to sell them. Great brochures talk about life lessons, memorable anecdotes from your younger years, exciting achievements—everything *but* the sale.

The Personal Brochure's second job is to help prospects *trust you*. That's less about the contents of the brochure and more about the look and feel. Think about how you've felt in the past when a service provider has handed you a cheap, flimsy brochure that looked like it came off a Xerox machine. You probably couldn't get to the door fast enough. Now think about how impressed you are when someone hands you a glossy, beautifully printed piece on expensive paper. Why do you think car brochures are so incredible? Because the makers are asking you to drop $40,000 on their product, and they know that if you feel better about and trust their product, you're more likely to do it.

THINGS YOU CAN DO TODAY

1. Record messages for your telephone on-hold system.

2. Get samples from digital and offset printers to compare quality and price.

3. Look at ways you can make your business more energy-efficient to save money that you can use for branding.

4. Drive around your community and look for creative places you can do outdoor advertising.

5. Get rid of outdated database and client management software.

6. Choose your branding channels.

Five Steps to a Great Personal Brochure
Step 1: Pick a Single Leading Attribute
You can't be all things to all people, and you don't want to try. Your objective in developing a Personal Brochure is to convey your Personal Brand in a way that's emotionally compelling and clear. You do that by choosing a *leading attribute*, one thing about you that will be the centerpiece of your brochure. Do this by asking:

1. What single benefit, feature, or value is most sought after by my target market?

2. What can I share about myself to express its value?

Your leading attribute can be anything that's compelling and reveals a lot about you. It might be your time in the military, your hobby restoring old cars, or your experience going to school at MIT. Choose what you think will make a great, revealing story.

Step 2: Make It Personal
Personality, not statistics, sells. The job of your Personal Brochure is to build rapport, and you don't do that with statistics, designations,

or degrees. The heart of your brochure is a biography that tells your story and makes the reader come away feeling as if he or she knows you. Great Personal Brochure text shares a person's history, appealing directly to the reader's emotions. People enjoy discovering how much they have in common with others.

Your personal story should occupy from 75 to 90 percent of your Personal Brochure. This is a soft sell in which the person is more important than the product. Consider talking about some of the following:

- How you grew up

- Family stories

- Your education

- Major life experiences that shaped you—travel, military service, and other such experiences

- First jobs

- Life lessons or mentors

You may think you're not interesting enough for people to care about reading your story. But who are you to judge? You're not objective; you've been you all your life. Trust me, people love reading other people's personal stories of obstacles and triumph. Think back on television coverage of the Olympics. Between events, the airwaves are bursting with personal stories, "Triumph over Tragedy" tales, and all sorts of inspirational tales about the athletes. Love them or hate them, we watch them because they're about overcoming obstacles to reach goals, something that touches almost every one of us.

Step 3: Write Your Story
Whether you or a professional writer does the job (and I highly recommend hiring a professional), follow these guidelines for more effective Personal Brochure copy:

- Use the third-person, objective point of view. Readers associate third-person writing with objectivity, and it makes your piece seem more journalistic.

- If you use the first person, talk only about your personal experience, not the results you have achieved. Otherwise, you'll appear to be bragging.

- Keep the text positive.

- Present your text in paragraphs, not bullet points. People like to read a good story, and research shows that narrative outperforms short, bulleted text every time. Use bullets sparingly.

- Be candid. Consumers have a strong internal lie detector, and they'll see right through equivocation or empty, overblown promises.

- Avoid clichés like the plague (rimshot).

- Use subheads to break up the text. Short headlines between major sections of copy make your brochure easier to read. Make the subheads powerful and interesting.

- Start the brochure with a strong headline that has emotional value.

- Finally, keep the text brief; 250 to 400 words on the interior of your brochure will be enough for most formats. You want to leave people wanting more, not tire them out.

Step 4: Create a Knockout Cover and an Appealing Layout

Your cover must scream, "Pick me up!" It should feature an image with "stopping power," that is, the power to catch someone's eye and make him or her pick up your brochure to see what's behind the intriguing image. Equally important, it needs a powerful headline that conveys a strong message about your Personal Brand.

Do not put anything on the cover that relates directly to your business, products, or services. If readers so much as smell a sales pitch, they'll toss your piece in the round file. Rather than sell, your cover should create unbearable curiosity, and the image should tie directly into the dreams or goals of your target market. Always put your company name and logo on the back of the brochure.

Once readers open your Personal Brochure, the interior layout should be clean and attractive, leading the reader into the text. Use plenty of "white space," empty space with no text and no graphics. Amateur designers think you must fill every inch of space, but pros know that dense copy and excessive graphics look ugly and unprofessional. Proper spacing and clean lines invite readers in to enjoy your story. This is one reason to rely on a designer to create your Personal Brochure.

When it comes to photos, go with a professional. Hire a pro to take two sets of candid, nonposed photos: one in a professional setting, and one in a relaxed, personal setting with friends or engaged in your hobby. Quality photos say a lot about you. To find a photographer, ask friends for a referral or visit www.photographers.com. Plan on investing between $1,000 and $2,500 for high-quality photographs.

And please, I beg you, avoid mug shots. They were fine for your high school yearbook, but they have no place in your Personal Branding.

THINGS YOU CAN DO IN A WEEK

1. Read magazines like *Communication Arts* to familiarize yourself with high-end graphic design and marketing.

2. Review your team's crisis response and make changes.

3. Develop your step-by-step new client intake process—forms, gifts, the interview, your waiting area, everything.

4. Start perusing blogs on branding and small-business marketing to find out the latest trends.

5. Revise your curriculum vitae; you'll need to include it in your press kit.

6. Test out the results from various Google AdWords.

Step 5: Choose an Unusual Brochure Size and Invest in Great Printing

Brochures in the usual 8½- by 11-inch format that fold into three panels are the death knell of good branding. They are a waste of your money, because it's easy to throw away a No. 10 envelope without ever opening it. The best shape for a Personal Brochure is usually a 6- by 6-inch, 7- by 7-inch, or 8- by 8-inch square, because square materials remind us of invitations and tend to be looked at more. If your budget allows, always go with an unusual size and format.

And if your budget allows, also make sure to invest in crisp, high-quality printing on rich, glossy paper. The quality, look, and feel of your branding materials say as much about you as the contents of your brochure. Always print your piece in full color unless your designer gives you a very good reason to print in sepia tone or black and white (and I have seen some stunning b/w brochures, so it's not out of the question).

Choose an experienced printer who can handle typesetting for you, and don't choose the printer who gives you the lowest price quote. You're not looking to save a few pennies here; you're looking for someone to produce your most valuable Personal Branding piece. Make sure that your printer uses a four-color press at a 175-line screen or greater, and make sure that you pay for proofs, also called "preflights" or "match prints." This is a necessary step, as this will be your last chance to proofread the brochure before it is actually printed. Print your brochure on heavy, high-quality paper, at least 100-pound gloss cover stock. As for quantities, we recommend that you print at least 2,500. If that seems like a lot, you'll use them. Your per-unit cost drops as quantities rise.

The emergence of digital printing has offered small companies new alternatives for producing brochures. Digital presses allow you to run smaller quantities at manageable costs and on shorter deadlines. The resolution isn't as high, and you can't do complex folds, but if you need a few brochures fast, digital is a great option.

Add it all up, and 5,000 brochures will typically cost you about $7,500, or about $1.50 each, when you factor in writing, design, photography, and printing.

BRAND CASE STUDY

The Brand: Dr. Todd Walkow, orthodontist

Specialization: Friendly orthodontia for adults

Location: Walkow Orthodontics, Newport Beach, California

Channels: The Web, referrals, promotions, branded giveaway items

Highlights: Community outreach and toy drives

Online: www.walkowortho.com

The Story: Walkow saw an opportunity in adult orthodontics, so he bought an existing practice from a Newport Beach orthodontist who had not been leveraging the full potential of his business. But rather than portray himself as having a large practice, Walkow made a very smart strategic branding decision: to build his business on his personal brand.

How It All Started: The doctor whom Walkow bought out had an office in a superb area of the affluent southern California city, a great clientele, and tremendous growth potential, but he was leveraging almost none of his advantages. Walkow saw the potential not only in the existing business, but in a unique orthodontic niche.

"There's a big, growing sector in adult orthodontics," he says. "People are looking into better aesthetics, so this is a huge, growing market. Most people predominantly thought of orthodontia as something for kids. But it's really for adults."

What This Brand Stands For:

- *Personal attention.* Walkow's business is built around making everyone feel special and engaged, and making the trip to the orthodontist's office something fun rather than something to dread.

- *Differentiation.* Walkow was one of the only orthodontic specialists in the region to focus on teeth straightening for adults, in an industry where the focus is usually on kids. By targeting an underserved audience that had money and a desire to stave off the effects of aging, he cornered the market in a lucrative business segment.

- *Fun.* Games, prizes, lunches, contests, recognition for proper dental hygiene—those are all part of Walkow's strategy for fostering patient and parent loyalty. It seems to be working.

X-Factor: A great Web site. Walkow's Web presence is breezy and fun, highlighting the orthodontist's identity as a young, hip father, and it also offers visitors games, "Beach Bucks" (which young patients can

(continued)

redeem for all kinds of special treats and gifts), and tons of valuable information for adults who are considering orthodontia.

Branding Wisdom: "When patients come here, we do internal and external marketing," Walkow says. "Internally, I try to make the experience the best I can, from having a really well-trained staff to patient care, making sure the patients are always getting the best care and attention possible. We have contests and special promotions; we always have things out for the kids, toys with my name on them. We have awards for people who take great care of their braces, Patient of the Day awards, the patient's name on a sign when he or she comes in. It's all about making patients feel like part of our dental family when they come in. We do all the little, special things we can to make it a better experience.

"Externally, we give patients things that have our name and the brand on them—T-shirts that kids wear to the beach and moms wear to the gym. We keep the community informed that we're here. We also do outreach to dentists in the area, bringing other dental practices to our office for 'lunch and learn' sessions. We want people to think of us when they think of orthodontics in Newport Beach."

Ten Ideal Uses for Your Personal Brochure

Once your beautiful brochure comes back from the printer, don't make the mistake that some proud Personal Brochure owners make: hoarding them because they are "too nice to give away." You're supposed to hand them out; they can't get you business unless they're in the hands of your prospects. Get them circulating and let them do their thing. You can always print more.

However, Personal Brochures are not cold direct-mail pieces. They're too expensive. Ideally, your brochures should be sent to people you already know or given to people by you personally. The first thing you should do is give a copy of your Personal Brochure to everyone who is remotely associated with your business: colleagues, media contacts, and friends. After that, choose any or all of these uses for your brochure:

1. Mail two copies to each of your current clients, one for the client to keep and one to pass along to someone who might need your services.

2. Mail a copy to each prospect in your database with whom you've had contact, along with a cover letter.

3. Give at least 24 copies to any professionals who are good referral sources and encourage them to pass the brochure along to their clients.

4. Use the brochure as part of your "12-Month Branding Campaign," as described later in the chapter.

5. Mail it to "cold" prospects as part of your "Six-Week Client Blitz" program, as detailed later in the chapter.

6. Use it as a substitute for your business card in networking situations. Hand the brochure out at public events and speaking engagements. If it's too big to carry, get contacts' business cards and mail them brochures as soon as you get back to the office.

7. Hand it out at seminars as part of your information package, prior to your presentation.

8. Include it in press kits and information packages that you send to the media.

9. Take plenty of copies to trade shows and special events. Every visitor to your exhibit booth should receive a copy.

10. Place it in appropriate locations, from chambers of commerce and hotel front desks to restaurants, golf courses, and theaters— anyplace that makes sense for your business.

BRAND SURGERY
THE PATIENT: YOUR PERSONAL BROCHURE

- Don't use a printer who uses a two-color press and runs your four-color job through twice. The color quality will suffer.

- Don't use photos of you at your desk or on the phone.

(continued)

- Make your type big enough to read easily.

- Consider designing your brochure to be a "self-mailer," with a mostly blank back where a label and bulk mail indicia can be placed. Without an envelope, your brochure is more likely to be read.

- Don't tell a personal story that will turn off the members of your target market. Know their values and their limits.

- Don't pose in your photos. Be natural and act realistically. Let your photographer capture you in your natural habitat.

- Pay for thick paper. You'll avoid color bleeding and get the truest colors possible.

- Quote out your print job to at least three printers. Do not necessarily take the lowest bid. You get what you pay for.

PERSONAL POSTCARDS: THE ULTIMATE DIRECT MAIL

A Personal Postcard is a full-color card anywhere from 6 by 9 inches all the way to 8½ by 11 inches in size. Your Personal Postcard is designed to match your Personal Brochure and give your branding consistency, but its real secret is that it's designed as a "shell." On the mailing side are your logo, your photo, and some brief Personal Branding copy, along with space for a mailing label and bulk mail indicia. On the message side is some thematic artwork, a little marketing copy that ties into your position—and a big blank space. That's where you're going to use a cheap, 24-hour printer to overprint all sorts of customized messages.

When you're ready to do a mailing, you just take your postcards to a local quick printer to have your message for that mailing printed on the "shell" of your Personal Postcard in black ink. This is cheap, maybe $50 per thousand. But you'll go through the cards fast, which is why I tell my clients to print at least 10,000.

Designing Your Personal Postcard

Direct mail has three goals: grow your Personal Brand, generate phone calls, and produce referrals. To accomplish this, your Personal Postcard must

- Build name recognition.

- Establish a positive emotional disposition toward working with you.

- Build your credibility.

Design your Personal Postcard using the same graphics, colors, and photos as your Personal Brochure; it should be the perfect complement to the brochure. Summarize the main copy from your Personal Brochure—your key experience, your main personal story, how you create value, and a call to action—in 50 to 60 words on the "message side," where the blank space is. Leave about two-thirds of the space on this side blank so that you can legibly overprint your custom messages.

On the mailing side, use your main Personal Brochure photo as large as you need it, with your personal photo, text, and contact information running over the picture. As always, I recommend hiring a professional designer to help you bring your Personal Postcard to life, and to make sure that you follow Post Office regulations for bulk mail.

Writing Your Personal Postcard

Because it's based on your Personal Brochure, designing your Personal Postcard is the easy part. It's the writing of your custom messages that will make or break you. You've got a fully customizable shell for your messages; now you need writing that works. These are the types of messages you can send:

1. Product and service marketing messages

2. Personal messages

3. Holiday greetings

4. Newsletters

5. Web site promotions

6. Event promotions (seminars, open houses, and so on)

7. Handwritten notes

Ideally, your strategy should include many or all of these types of messages scattered throughout the year. Here are my essential guidelines for producing postcard messages that get results:

- Always begin with a strong headline containing a benefit.

- Keep your text short—50 to 75 words.

- Use regular English, use colloquial language, and write with a relaxed, conversational style, like you're talking to a neighbor over the backyard fence.

- Get to the point.

- Give each message a benefit. It might be a discount offer, a bit of relevant news, or just Happy Thanksgiving. But always send something with a reason behind it.

- Connect with the emotions. Tell a story, offer advice, pass on a joke. Once you appeal to the emotions, you can suggest how you offer value and ask for a call or e-mail.

- Include a call to action. As long as you're not making a hard sell, it's fine to finish with an invitation to stop by your office for a cup of coffee and a chat, or something similar.

- Be original. Offer to take people to dinner, run a contest on your Web site giving away baseball tickets, offer a ride in a classic car, and the like.

To make this work, you've got to really know your target market. Know what its members like, what their goals are, whether or not they have kids and what age, what their values and faith are, and so on. Know them intimately, and you'll be able to write messages that really touch them.

Build In Response Channels

You also need to build "response channels" into your direct mail. This means offering the recipients multiple options for contacting you or requesting more information. The potential direct-mail response channels are

1. *Phone number.* Pro: You get high-quality responses. Con: People are uncomfortable calling for fear of sales pressure. Make sure you include a mobile number if you're out of the office a lot.

2. *E-mail address.* Pro: It's easy, and there's no fear of sales pressure. Con: It's impersonal, and people don't always check their e-mail regularly.

3. *Web site address.* Pro: There's no pressure; all your information is available without any effort from you. Con: It's hard to turn people from site browsers into prospects sending you e-mail.

4. *Fax number.* Pro: It's easy and accessible. Con: Almost no one communicates via fax anymore.

5. *Business reply card (BRC).* Pro: It's an easy way to let people contact you for more information. Con: Responses are usually low quality.

6. *Mailing address.* Nobody writes letters anymore. But you'll need to have it on your card to satisfy U.S. Postal Service regulations, so maybe you'll get lucky.

Printing Your Personal Postcard

Print your postcard on heavy, high-quality, glossy paper, just as you do your Personal Brochure. How your card feels in the hands will have as much effect on your prospects as the artwork or what it says. Maybe more. Spend what it takes to get thick paper, vivid inks, razor-sharp photos, and crisp print. It's worth it. As with your brochure, make sure that your printer is running the cards on a four-color press with at least a 175-line screen.

Save money by printing large quantities. If you feel your checkbook slamming shut at the suggestion, look at it this way: if you have a mailing list of 500 prospects, and you mail to them once a month for a year, that's 6,000 postcards. That's not even counting special mailings. But big quantities lower your per-card cost, so printing 5,000 cards may cost only $300 more than printing 2,500. That's why I recommend printing at least 10,000 pieces.

THINGS YOU CAN DO IN A MONTH

1. Develop a list of interview or story ideas that you can present to your local newspapers.

2. Review copies of local magazines that might be appropriate either for your advertising or for placement of articles.

3. Get an airtight contract for professional referrals completed by your attorney.

4. Send personal letters to the members of your local chamber of commerce explaining your branding project and asking about ways you can cross-promote the chamber.

5. Look into joining an organization like Toastmasters International to work on your speaking skills.

6. Research the viability of creating a package of premium services that you would offer to special clients at a higher cost.

A Few Other Tips

Buy a mailing list from a local newspaper or magazine that sells its subscriber lists. Assuming that your target market is limited to a certain geographic area, this is a great way to get only local names without wasting money on the names of people you'll never contact. Don't waste your money on lists from big list companies. Some have as many as 30 percent dead addresses.

For smaller mailings, such as 500 pieces, you can probably have your staff handle the mailing duties. Good label-production software is as close as your nearest office supply store. For larger mailings (more than 1,000 pieces), hire a mailing-fulfillment house. For a reasonable fee, such a house will print your labels, stick them on, bundle your cards, and get them in the mail stream while you handle other things.

Talk to your printer about "gang running" your postcards and your Personal Brochure. This means running both jobs on the same press at the same time. This can save you money.

Finally, make sure you get a bulk mail permit. Bulk mail lets you send batches of materials sorted by zip code for about half the cost of first-class postage.

Three Main Uses for Personal Postcards

You could just send your postcards off when the mood strikes you, but as I said before, direct-mail success comes from consistency and repetition. That means having a system. These are three systems I have seen used with great success:

1. *Twelve-Month Branding Campaign.* Each month, send a Personal Branding piece to your current clients, friends, professional referrals, and hot prospects. The object is to keep you on their minds for that time when they're ready to do business or refer someone to you. This "drip marketing" plan features a different type of mailer each month:

- *Month 1:* Personal Brochure with cover letter

- *Month 2:* Product/service marketing postcard

- *Month 3:* Personal Postcard

- *Month 4:* News postcard

- *Month 5:* Personal message

- *Month 6:* Personal Brochure with a letter asking for referrals

- *Month 7:* Web postcard

- *Month 8:* Product/service marketing postcard

- *Month 9:* Personal Postcard

- *Month 10:* News postcard

- *Month 11:* Web postcard

- *Month 12:* Handwritten holiday greeting

2. *Six-Week Marketing Blitz.* Send one Personal Branding piece per week to hot prospects for six weeks. This Six-Week Marketing Blitz campaign is designed to create instant brand awareness and get the phone ringing. Use the following mailing schedule:

- *Week 1:* Personal Brochure with cover letter
- *Week 2:* Product/service marketing postcard
- *Week 3:* Product/service marketing postcard
- *Week 4:* Product/service marketing postcard
- *Week 5:* Product/service marketing postcard
- *Week 6:* Product/service marketing postcard

This is your shot at turning "cold" prospects into hot ones. Repetition really does work, and this is the way to leverage its power.

3. *Timed campaign.* Identify each client's date-triggered purchasing needs and build a direct-mail campaign around that timing. For example, if you're a retirement planner, you could send a postcard with the headline, "20 Biggest Mistakes Retirees Make Prior to Retirement" and send a different message 20 times in the nine months before that client retires. Timed campaigns can also be linked to anything from childbirth to college graduation.

Making Mailings More Effective

So you know how to write and print your Personal Postcards. Great. But no matter how brilliant your postcard is, there are things you can do to improve your direct-mail response:

- *Make "warm calls."* With warm calling, the recipient has gotten one or more of your direct-mail pieces, so he or she knows your name. Once you've sent several mailings to your target market, start calling people to introduce yourself. Refer to your past mailers, but don't sell and don't ask open-ended questions like, "Is there anything I can do for you?" Ask people about themselves. I know one financial advisor who called her direct-mail recipients and invited them to kvetch about financial advisors. They *loved* it.

- *Follow up.* Have a follow-up plan for the people who respond to your direct mail. These folks should be your number one priority—they represent possible new business. Have a set procedure in place that goes something like this:

1. Receive a call or e-mail from a prospect.

2. If you speak directly, send a thank-you card within 24 hours.

3. If you do not speak directly, return the call within 8 hours.

4. Call within a week after your initial conversation to ask if there's anything you can do, any questions you can answer, and so on.

5. Ask for the meeting.

6. If the prospect invests time in meeting you, whether he or she becomes a customer or not, send a thank-you gift after the meeting, something like a book or a $20 restaurant gift certificate.

- *Have a system.* Work with your staff or a fulfillment house to set up a schedule that sends your direct-mail pieces out automatically. Assign essential tasks—printing labels, checking for deletion requests, sticking labels, bundling cards, going to the post office—then post a mailing schedule on your wall so that everyone knows when things go out. Always delete names from your database as soon as you're asked to do so.

- *Stick to it.* Most direct mail fails because people give up too quickly. Repetition and consistency are critical. Come up with a schedule and stick with it.

BY NOW YOU SHOULD BE . . .

- Getting your brochures and postcards back from the printer

- Prepariang to launch your new Web site to much fanfare

- Finishing the placement of any advertising you plan to do

- Contacting your B and C clients to start showing them the door

- Developing a year's worth of direct-mail messages

- Thinking about special events that you could throw for clients

---

CHAPTER

THE INTERNET

Personal branding associates an individual with the brand and therefore depends on the perceived trustworthiness of the individual as well as the product to fulfill consumers' needs and wants. Personal brands tend to get established more quickly since people are able to relate to the personality; however, they are also easy to tarnish because public perceptions of people are hard to manage.

—Doman & Amy Lum, *Business & Economic Review*

You've got to have a Personal Brochure. You've got to have a logo. And you've got to have a Web site. It's no longer optional. If you're in business, it's now assumed that you'll have at least a basic site up. If someone asks you your Web address and you say that you don't have one, that person is likely to take you less seriously. This is just a fact of the modern age of business and communication. This chapter is about the Internet, so I'm also going to talk about e-mail, Weblogs, and e-newsletters, but let's start with the Web.

Web sites are essential because the Web is an easy, sales-free way for someone to scope out a business without any sales pressure. With the average consumer being exposed to 3,000 or more marketing messages in a typical day, we all crave an information channel that we can use to research a service provider with no sales pitch and no spin.

That's the real appeal of the Web: it allows us to see if a business is worth spending our precious, limited time contacting. A great brochure on high-quality paper convinces a prospect that you're a player; a beautifully designed, technically superior Web site does the same. If you don't have one, get one. If you have one but haven't updated it in three years, talk to your developer about refreshing it. Just get online.

THE BIG THREE

There are three main reasons you need a good Web site:

1. *It builds credibility.* This is the main purpose of a Web site. It's a public relations tool, not a sales tool. It's probably not going to get you clients on its own. It's something that prospects see on the way to calling you, one more way to reassure them that you're a serious professional who knows how to run a business. A site also allows you to show prospects that you're a valuable resource by giving them useful facts, special reports, helpful links, and so on.

2. *It helps you maintain relationships.* Increasingly, small businesses are turning to the Web as a low-cost way of communicating with their clients and maintaining the relationship. Tools like blogs, e-newsletters, video clips, and forums help with this.

3. *It can generate leads.* It's not very common, but some accomplished independent service professionals with a lot of money to spend and time to invest have developed effective methods of using their sites to generate qualified leads. This takes careful strategy, since you want only leads who are your ideal clients, but if you have the time and money, you can turn the Web into an outstanding client generation center.

There are also two reasons not to be online: your target market isn't online, or you have no interest in growing your business. Even seniors, the least wired demographic in America, are going online at a 60 percent rate, so the first reason probably won't come into play. As for the second, if you're maxed out or nearing retirement and would like to scale back, save your money.

THINGS YOU CAN DO TODAY

1. E-mail the pastor of your church about a private seminar or presentation to the congregation.

2. Cancel orders for any cheap promotional items you might give out: pens, notepads, and the like.

3. E-mail colleagues who have excellent Web sites to get recommendations for a Web design and Internet marketing vendor.

4. Go to www.webaward.org to view award-winning small-business Web sites and be inspired.

5. Talk to your banker about possibly getting a business loan to pay for a truly aggressive Personal Branding campaign.

6. Start working out if you don't already. It will keep you healthy and alert during a potentially stressful period.

WHAT YOUR SITE SHOULD DO

There are a million and one options today for a Web site, and that can be as much a curse as a blessing. What do you spend your money on? First of all, back away from the fancy features and software like Flash animations and instant messaging. You're not going to want to waste bandwidth on that stuff. Your Web site must do four things:

1. Look clean, polished and professional, matching the look of the rest of your Personal Branding materials.

2. Be easy to navigate and use.

3. Read well, with brief copy that touches the emotions.

4. Give your clients and prospects paths to interact with you.

The last of these has become especially important. This is the age of Web 2.0, represented by sites like Digg, YouTube, and Netflix. Consumers now expect the Web to allow them to talk with companies, recommend those companies to their friends, and tap knowledge bases of other consumers. Today, small-business Web sites are communication centers that give clients a way to get updates on what a service provider is doing for them, prospects a way to take free online courses, and media the ability to download interview facts or a video clip. That means a lot more than giving somebody an e-mail link or posting a basic information site—what we used to call "brochureware."

Don't panic. You don't have to do all this. But you might need to do some of it, depending on your type of business and your budget. The best first step in creating your Web site is simple: hire a great Web developer, or even a small company that will give you planning, design, copy, programming, hosting, and even ongoing support. Pick a good company based on several recommendations, check out the company's work, and then listen to it.

And if you can do nothing else, at least put up a slick, beautiful site with easy navigation and great copy. That's much, much better than nothing.

THE BASICS

I'll get to the bells and whistles in a second, but first let's talk about the four pages that your Web site absolutely must have:

1. *Home.* This is the landing page that people will see first when they type "www.yourname.com" into their Web browser. It's got to make a knockout impression. It needs to be coordinated visually with all the rest of your Personal Branding, so it will probably use the same photos as your brochure and your postcards. In terms of copy, it needs to be powerful but to the point: who you are, what you do, and whom you do it for. It should be obvious to visitors upon arriving how to find what they want.

2. *Personnel.* This is the page that gives visitors your personal background and contact information, as well as that for all your key people. Feel free to pirate your Personal Brochure bio for this page and add some basic information about your education and qualifications.

3. *Products/services.* Here, you explain what you do and how you create value. If you're a lawyer, detail the legal services that you

provide. If you're a contractor, talk about the types of projects that you work on. Do not talk price; a Web site is the wrong place for that.

4. *Contact*. You must give your prospects multiple ways to contact you: your office phone number, your fax number, and your e-mail address. Give out your mobile number if you wish, but I don't recommend it. Wait until someone becomes a client before you give that person the means to reach you at dinner.

There are two other basics. First, go to a domain registry site like GoDaddy.com and grab "yourname.com" right now. Don't wait. It's about nine bucks a year. If your name has been taken (and it happens, especially if you have a common name), try these alternatives:

- Your name with a hyphen between first and last names—"joe-smith.com"

- Your name with your profession after it—"joesmithlaw.com"

- Your name with an action word before it—"calljoesmith.com"

- A more formal version of your name—"josephpsmith.com"

The other basic is that when you have your domain, all your e-mail accounts should come from that domain. You, your assistant, your First Impressions Director, everyone should have an e-mail address that's "name@joesmith.com." Do *not* use an e-mail address that ends in aol.com, yahoo.com, or gmail.com. It makes you look like an amateur.

THE BELLS AND WHISTLES

Maybe you don't want just a basic site. That's fine, as long as you have the time and money to invest. Here are some of the Web site extras that I think can work reasonably well to build relationships, enhance your marketing, and give prospects a little extra boost in calling you:

- A private, password protected area where clients can review medical records, financial portfolios, and other such information

- Original articles written by you

- A portfolio of your work if you're a designer, architect, or some other such professional

- Links to all kinds of useful resources

- A sign-up area that allows prospects to give you their e-mail address in return for something of value, such as a downloadable special report or a contest

- An online calendar of your speaking engagements, media appearances, and seminars

- A press center where people can see print articles about you or check out video or audio clips from radio or TV appearances, and where journalists can download your press kit

- A center for useful tools like financial calculators, a cholesterol level index, a link to the MLS, or other such goodies

- A page of testimonials from your happiest clients

- A distribution center where people can download helpful documents (original or not), such as tips for traveling with children from a pediatrician

- An appointment setter that lets users see your appointment calendar and request a vacant spot

- An online payment option that lets clients pay their bills electronically or even automatically

- Frequently Asked Questions, or FAQs

That's about as far as I would go. I had a client once ask me if I thought he should put a forum on his site, where his clients could post messages and interact. I thought about it for a second and said, "Sure, if you want your clients comparing what you charge them." His face dropped and he said, "Oh. Never mind." Each of these features offers added value to the Web surfer, which is why they make sense.

Beyond that, there are a lot of cool, advanced tools on the Net that you should steer clear of. If you surf around, you'll find them: instant messaging, photo sharing, recommendation engines, and more gewgaws than you'll find on the space shuttle. Just say no. You don't want to distract people. You want clients to love your site so much that they refer their friends to it, and prospects to think it's so great that they can't wait to call you. You don't want them playing around.

THINGS YOU CAN DO IN A WEEK

1. Get custom Rolodex cards printed and send them to editors.

2. Create a new "signature" containing your logo, slogan, and contact information for all your outgoing personal e-mails.

3. Cruise your target geographic area to make sure you have good cell phone reception from 90 percent of it. You don't want to be caught with no signal when you're trying to service a client or pitch a prospect.

4. Install and test an up-to-date wireless Internet system in your office.

5. Take sales appointments with your local newspapers to discuss purchasing their mailing lists.

6. Choose the settings for your high-end photo shoot: your office, your home, your boat, a client's home, or some other such location.

SOME WEB BASICS

By now, your head may be spinning. After all, when the Web was busy becoming indispensable, you were taking care of patients or in court, right? My bad. Let's backtrack and talk about basic Web terminology. Here's a quick glossary of terms you'll run into:

- *Bandwidth.* The capacity of your Internet connection to handle traffic. The more people you have coming to your site, the more bandwidth you need.

- *Broadband.* A high-speed Internet connection, usually DSL or cable.

- *Download.* What happens when someone grabs something from your site, like a PDF (see below) document, and transfers a copy of it to their computer.

- *Flash.* A very popular but rather frivolous and irritating type of software that designers can use to create incredible animations that won't help you in the least.

- *Hosting.* Your Web site exists on a server, a fast computer that holds the software and files that make up your site. Hosting is the service that you pay for each month that allows you part of a server's hard drive.

- *Hyperlink.* A line of type starting with "http://www" that, when clicked on with your cursor, takes you to another Web site.

- *ISP.* Internet service provider, the company that provides your link to the Internet. AOL and NetZero are ISPs.

- *PDF.* Portable Document Format, the standard for downloadable files on the Web. PDFs are quick to download and usually look great.

- *Server.* The computer that holds your Web site. (See "hosting.")

- *Shopping cart.* If people can pay bills or buy things on your Web site, a device that holds the items in their order until they are ready to pay.

- *Throughput.* The speed of your Internet connection in terms of both how fast you can access other computers and how fast things can reach your computer, like downloaded files or video signals.

- *Traffic.* The number of people who visit your site.

- *URL.* Uniform Resource Locator, a fancy name for your "www" Web address.

- *User interface.* The controls that people see on your site when they want to figure out how to find your portfolio or bio.

- *Wi-Fi.* Wireless fidelity, another name for a wireless Internet connection.

BRAND SURGERY
THE PATIENT: YOUR WEB SITE

- Don't be intimidated by the techno-jargon of Web development. As long as you hire the right team, you don't need to know the difference between XML and HTML.

- Don't walk away from your vendor without a "design document" that tells you costs, time frames, and deliverables.

- Don't promise anyone that your site will be up by a certain date. Like home renovation, these things tend to take longer than planned.

- Don't use your site as a substitute for face-to-face contact. Once your site is up, don't simply refer anyone who has a question to it. Personal interaction is always better, and will make your site more valuable.

- Know the latest technology, but don't fall into the trap of wanting to add the latest features every few months.

- Refresh your content as often as possible.

- Tell everyone about your site at every opportunity.

WEB DEVELOPMENT

Now you're ready to jump into the wonderful world of Web development. Who are we kidding, no, you're not! But you need a Web site, so you're going to do what people do when they come to you: hire an expert. Two "do nots":

- *Do not* hire a student to develop your Web site on the cheap. Web development is extremely complex, and doing it right takes years of experience and a lot of training. Find a small, responsive Internet development company that can give you a complete solution from one source.

- *Do not* use a ready-to-build Internet template from your ISP. The resulting sites look like bad off-the-rack suits and make you look like an amateur.

In development, you'll need four basic services:

1. *Strategic planning.* What pages should your site include? What software should you use? How fast a server will you need? How long will the project take? Your project manager will help you answer all these questions and create your "site tree," which shows every page and how the pages link. That's your project bible.

2. *Web design.* Your designer will work with your branding photos and logo to create the layout and look and feel of your site, including the user interface that visitors will use to get around. He or she will recommend colors, present you with several initial options, and work with the programmer to get your site looking and working great.

3. *Programming.* Programmers do everything from writing HTML code, the basic language of the Web, to choosing the custom software that manages video feeds, newsletter sign-ups, and other interactive features.

4. *Writing and content development.* Your writer will create copy for each page based on your existing branding copy. Other content can include articles, testimonials, downloadable brochures, and audio greetings.

When you get to the development stage, make sure you get three things: a firm price and how it's broken up; deliverable dates for design and copy drafts, a test version of your site, and a final version; and specific deliverables. Don't be surprised if the whole process takes three to six months.

BRAND CASE STUDY

The Brand: Kendra Todd

Specialization: Host of HGTV's *My House Is Worth What?* program; real estate and women's wealth expert

Location: Delray Beach, Florida

(continued)

Channels: Lots of television, her Web community, books, speaking, charitable work

Highlights: Winning the third season of *The Apprentice*

Online: www.kendratodd.com

The Story: Todd, a self-proclaimed beach girl from Virginia, came to national attention in 2005 when she became the first woman to win *The Apprentice*. She was hired by Donald Trump; published her first book, *Risk and Grow Rich*; and went on the national speaking circuit. But now, bolstered by the discovery of her personal faith, she's looking to move beyond being a real estate guru: she's transforming herself into a guide for women seeking financial independence.

How It All Started: Todd was an achiever out of college at the University of Florida. She launched a successful upscale magazine as her first business venture, but then fell in love with real estate, getting her license and going into the business not just of selling real estate, but of building a profitable portfolio of investment property herself. All this before age 27.

But when a friend convinced her to audition for *The Apprentice*, things changed. She made the show and quietly watched the histrionics of other people play out as she took mental notes. Finally, she stood up and took charge of one of The Donald's most challenging projects, the creation of a dazzling brochure for a new Pontiac automobile. Her leadership led to her being declared the winner of the third season, and much good fortune has come her way since. She's become the host of the *My House Is Worth What?* program, one of HGTV's highest-rated shows, is working with Montel Williams to build her brand as a money expert for women, and is building an enthusiastic online following. And in preparation for moving away from her real estate–centered personal brand, she's shut down her Florida real estate sales office to focus on Kendra Todd, financial guru.

"What I've tried to build and what I hope I stand for is an example of a young, successful female enterpreneur who overcame the obstacles that came at her, failed, picked herself back up, kept going, and found success. Hopefully, I'm perceived as someone who can guide people to making their best investments. I've tried to build a brand about caring about people and helping them make smart decisions for their lives."

What This Brand Stands For:

- *Authenticity and likability.* If you watched season three of *The Apprentice*, you noticed right away that Todd stood out among the histrionics and ego gratification of typical reality-show contestants. She's a very normal, nice, down-to-earth woman whose genuine caring and friendliness come through beautifully on the TV screen or in person. She comes across as someone you'd like to hang out with. In a world of phonies and hucksters, she's 100 percent real, and that's her greatest branding asset.

- *Achievement.* The other aspect of Todd that makes her a rising brand star is that she's walked the walk. She's not an empty suit telling other women how to get rich while she's never earned a dime. This is a woman who, before age 30, had launched a magazine and two successful real estate companies, accumulated a tidy portfolio of investment properties, landed a hosting gig on a red-hot TV show, published a book, and become one of the most popular go-to finance and real estate commentators for Fox News, CNN, MSNBC, and the other news channels. Todd's done what she claims to teach, and that makes her a shining example for young women who are trying desperately to figure the whole money thing out.

- *Channel smarts.* From appearances on every news and financial show under the sun to talk about the economy, real estate, and finance, to her growing Web presence and e-mail list, Todd has already built a thriving multichannel branding machine. She's published columns on Yahoo! alongside the likes of Suze Orman. She speaks all over the country with the likes of Trump and *Rich Dad, Poor Dad* author Robert Kiyosaki. She does dozens of live events. And she hasn't even launched her new book franchise yet.

- *Giving.* Todd's also become well known for supporting numerous charitable causes, including providing financial support for victims of Hurricane Katrina as they try to rebuild their lives.

(continued)

X-Factor: Obviously, the victory on *The Apprentice*. Winning the reality program was her entrée into many other opportunities that had little to do with the show, such as the HGTV hosting gig. For Todd, one opportunity has dominoed into another in an amazing rush of success, so much so that *The Apprentice* brand is almost forgotten. But it's not gone, she says.

"I'm not leaving it behind," she says. "It's just not the sole focus of who I am. This is what's important about my training: whatever opportunities are in front of you at the time, those will drive your brand. At the time I won, my brand was Kendra Todd, winner of *The Apprentice*. It's been a strong contributor to my success, because it brings with it the elements of success, business savvy, overcoming odds, and that a young female can be a success in business. But it's simply an element of a larger picture. Your brand evolves, whether you want it to or not. My brand stands for a lot more now, but *The Apprentice* was a great starting point; it helped establish me as an expert. Ten years from now, winning *The Apprentice* will still be an element of my brand.

"Part of creating a brand is picking and choosing the elements of different parts of your brand that you want to focus on. I have chosen to take the most important elements of the reality TV aspect of my brand—the young woman aspiring to success, the entrepreneur—and bring them to the forefront. I have left the parts of *The Apprentice* that may not be so advantageous behind. I've shaped my own brand awareness."

Branding Wisdom: "It's important to look at who you really are," she says. "The brand you try to create can be in conflict with the brand you're actually creating. How you see yourself and what you do can be at odds with how others see you. It's important that the brand you're creating be in line with you who are and what you value, or people will see right through it.

"There's no forcing a square object through a round hole. If your audience is at odds with the brand you're creating, you need to step back and listen to your audience. I started out building a brand that reached real estate investors, and that was very successful for several years, but because of the opportunities that had been placed in my path—the HGTV show, becoming a money expert on the *Living Well* with *Montel* series—my brand naturally shifted. I saw that I needed to change it to general wealth building, with real estate as a by-product of that. My audience became women and young people. When I talked about my next book series on Montel's show, more than 1,800 women signed up on my temporary Web site, and so many of them told me the same thing, 'You inspire me; now how do I figure all this out?'

"Build your brand and survey your audience. Your brand is always changing to serve your audience. You will evolve as a businessperson and an individual. Every experience you go through affects your brand. In the end, those who are down to earth and willing to share not only their triumphs but their defeats will make their audience realize that defeat is not the end of the road. People need to know that you're just like them, so that they know that anyone can do it."

GETTING PEOPLE TO YOUR WEB SITE

You can build it, but that doesn't mean they'll come. According to research company Netcraft, as of February 2007 there were somewhere around 29.7 *billion* individual Web pages on the Net, and more than 70 million Web sites. That's a lot of competition. Fortunately, you're not competing with the world. You're competing with other lawyers, accountants, designers, or caterers in your target market area. But you still need to drive traffic to your Web site. Here are some of the best ways to do it.

The simplest way is to put your URL on every single piece of brand marketing material you use: brochures, business cards, ads, signage, you name it. When you do a radio interview, mention your Web site at least three times. Remember, people are looking for a pressure-free way to find out more about you. They want to find your Web site.

That takes care of low-tech. There are four techier ways to drive traffic, but fortunately, none of them is too complicated:

1. *Search engine optimization (SEO for short).* This means writing your site copy and maximizing incoming links so that your site is easily indexed by Google and the other search engines. It's all about Google. Google does two-thirds of all searches, so if you're

going to drive traffic, you must appease the Google gods. SEO isn't for amateurs, so talk to your Web developer about it.

2. *Google AdWords.* Google really is the 800-pound gorilla on the block, so every traffic discussion starts there. Buying AdWords means that you agree to pay so much per search to have your business's name come up on one of those paid search results you see on the right side of the screen when you do a Google search. When someone in your town searches for "Corvallis Oregon chiropractor," you want your name to be the first one that person sees. AdWords is a great way to do that. Go to adwords.google.com to learn more.

3. *Banner ads.* Yes, banner ads are still alive and well. They are graphical ads that you place on Web sites that appeal to your target market. Your Web designer can create them, but you should decide which sites they go on. Look for sites that your ideal clients are likely to surf. If you're targeting fans of a local college basketball team, the college's basketball Web page and any fan sites would be ideal prospects for advertising. Contact them for ad rates.

4. *Google Maps.* Yes, it's Google again. You need to have your business on Google Maps so that people can find you. Local search is one of the truly booming areas on the Internet as people use it to find the things they need in their hometown. This is how to do it:

- Go to Google, click on Maps, and enter the name of your business.

- If your company appears in the listing, click on the More Info link next to the listing. Check your information: phone number, Web address, street address.

- If anything is incorrect or incomplete, scroll all the way down the page to "Edit this listing." You need to correct your company information. It's especially important that your company's Web site be listed. Google ranks Web sites by how many links from other sites they have coming into them, and in this case the incoming link is from Google, a *huge* source of links. You need your Web address in there.

- If you have a Google account, log into it. If you don't, don't worry; it's free. Follow the instructions and Google will send a PIN to your office phone number or street address to verify that you are authorized to make the changes.

- If you're not listed at all, access your Google account, go to Maps, and click on "Add/Edit Your Business." The site will walk you through all the steps.

TIPS FOR GETTING THE MOST FROM THE WEB

- *Post a privacy policy.* Web users are hypersensitive about online privacy, so if you ask people to fill out a form with personal information, have a link to a page where you promise not to share their information with any third party. Then stick to it.

- *Update your content regularly.* Nothing looks less professional than a Web site with outdated content. Set up a monthly updating and site maintenance plan with your Web company so that you'll have new content and updated features regularly.

- *Test your site before launch.* Before your site goes live, sit down and go through every page and every link to make sure that all links are active and all features are working. Have 10 of your friends do the same and send you "bug reports" with anything they find that doesn't work, including typographical errors.

- *Design for dial-up connections.* Millions of people still access the Web through dial-up modems. So unless you're marketing to a target audience in which a majority of the prospects have DSL or cable connections, make sure your developer designs your site to load quickly.

- *Check vendor Web sites.* Before you hire a Web company, scope out the sites it's built and talk to its clients. If any red flags appear, move on. This is too big an investment to trust to a second-rate firm.

THINGS YOU CAN DO IN A MONTH

1. Incorporate a customer relationship management program into your business model.

2. Write a telemarketing script and test it to see how consumers react.

3. Create a proposal for a regular column written by you and send it to the local print media.

4. Check into unique outdoor advertising opportunities in your area: blimps, skywriting, mobile billboards, and so on.

5. Hire a virtual assistant.

6. Hold your first Client Appreciation Night.

OTHER INTERNET TOOLS

The Internet is more than the Web, of course. There are many other aspects of it that you can use to build your brand—as always, if you have the time and money. To finish up the subject, here are three that are worth thinking about.

Blogs

You're probably familiar with Weblogs, or *blogs*. They're basically on-line journals that have become a very big deal. Political, gossip, or business blogs like Gawker, Daily Kos, and Club for Growth draw hundreds of thousands of readers per week. A blog is a chance for you to connect more personally with your clients and prospects about topics that matter to you, by writing regular entries in your blog.

Blogging is simple and free, thanks to free blogging Web sites like Blogger.com, TypePad.com, and WordPress.org. They make it very easy and intuitive to start, design, and run your blog.

Pros: Blogs offer a personal connection, you get to write about what's important to you, they're cheap, you can use comment boards to create a sense of community and get feedback, and you can really boost your feel of authenticity.

Cons: Blogging is time-consuming. You have to post several times a week to get people coming to your blog, and that's time that a lot of busy professionals just don't have.

Direct E-Mail

This is the tool that, for many small businesses, is replacing direct mail. Direct e-mail is dirt cheap and very easy to manage, as long as you have good lists. You can build your list by having a sign-up box on your Web site and attracting people with offers, contests, and so on. You can also buy lists, but that can become spam, or unsolicited e-mail that makes people mad. The best way to build your list is through "opt-in" lists, where people have chosen to be on your list.

The great thing about direct e-mail is that you can send it as often as you want for pennies, and it can replace or complement your direct mail. You can do a "drip" e-mail campaign, a Six-Week Blitz, or just about anything else. You can send richly designed HTML e-mails or pure text e-mails.

Pros: It's cheap, fast, and a great way to reach almost everyone in your target market.

Cons: It can take a long time to build a big opt-in list, and if you're not careful, spam filters can kill you.

Some tips on doing direct e-mail right:

- Make your subject line interesting. If your mail looks like spam, it will be deleted.

- Link to your Web site throughout the e-mail.

- Have a strong call to action that brings people to your Web site to enter a contest, download a report, or watch a video.

- When writing your messages, avoid words that will tend to get you picked up by a person's spam filters. Some of the most common ones:

  - Free!

  - 50 percent off!

  - Click here

- Call now!

- Subscribe

- Discount!

- You're a winner!

- Information you requested

- Million dollars

- Opportunity

- Compare

- Removes

- Collect

- Amazing

- Promise you

- Credit

- Loans

- Satisfaction guaranteed

Your Internet company should be able to walk you through the details of setting up a regular direct e-mail campaign that's 90 percent automated.

E-Newsletters

Print newsletters are time-consuming, and so are e-newsletters. E-newsletters have the advantage of being cheap. So if you have a loyal client base and a lot of information to share about finance, real estate, or other topics that are in the news a lot, an e-newsletter can be a useful tool.

If you want to create one, I have two words for you: Constant Contact. This company offers tools that let anyone create a free e-newsletter simply by picking a design, uploading copy, and providing your e-mail list. It even e-mails and calls you to talk about your online marketing and come up with strategies to make it more effective.

Pros: This is a cheap, fast way to deliver a regular flow of useful information to your clients and prospects. With Constant Contact, it's 100 percent turnkey and free.

Cons: It's time-consuming to write a bunch of news items and articles every month. You might have to pay a freelancer.

The main tip here is to make all your newsletter content practical, relevant, and useful. Don't talk about your family vacation except at the end; give your audience members tips, ideas, and news that they can apply in their lives immediately. As for creating an e-newsletter, there are software packages that will help you do it, and many Internet development firms will insist that these packages are the answer to your prayers, but I'd stick with Constant Contact. It's all the company does, and it does it well.

Now go surfing.

BY NOW YOU SHOULD BE . . .

- Sending your Personal Brochure to your best clients

- Beginning to see Web site traffic

- Showing up on Google searches

- Seeing your new ads running in the phone book and the newspaper

- Hearing unsolicited feedback from your clients about your office staff and your new business model

- Finalizing the details of your direct-mail and direct-e-mail lists

CHAPTER

10

PUBLIC RELATIONS AND COMMUNITY OUTREACH

If your brand is weak or inconsistent or contradictory, you won't get the deal; you won't get the promotion; you won't get the job. Why? Because other people will play safe, and rely on (and buy/promote/hire) the reputations they DO know. In the modern world, as in the Old West, you have to take control of your personal brand. You have to give people a reason to buy you.

—Rob Cuesta

In most communities, there's a Realtor or financial advisor or home improvement expert who writes a weekly column for the local newspaper. It may be short and not even that well written, but it's a big deal among the people who read the paper. That weekly piece brands that person as an expert—*the* expert—in his or her field. It puts one more piece of the puzzle in place for the consumer who's trying to figure out whom to call. One thing's for sure: that professional has mastered the public relations dance.

Public relations, or PR, is the art of getting the news media to write about, record, film, or interview you. It's a huge industry in this country; celebrities and corporations spend billions each year trying to get their names and their carefully spun stories into the right magazines and newspapers and on the right radio programs and TV shows. They do this for one reason: media exposure sways consumers. When someone appears on *Oprah* touting a new book, the sales of that book skyrocket. The right media can make the phone ring or, at the very least, give a fence-sitting prospect one more reason to choose you.

There's no reason why you can't do what Hollywood stars and the Fortune 500 do, albeit on a smaller scale: generate press coverage and use it to grow and strengthen your Personal Brand. Why would a reporter want to write about you? Why not? Where do you think newspaper and magazine editors get the material to fill up their pages, especially in small local papers where there may not be a lot of news? They cover local people—business owners, notable residents, and so on. You've got as much chance as anyone else of landing a prime spot in a local—or even a national—publication. You've just got to know how to do it. That means learning the PR dance.

HOW PR HELPS YOUR BUSINESS

Press coverage is the greatest, cheapest credibility builder on the planet. As you're developing your Personal Brand, at some point it becomes crucial to have corroboration, a neutral third party telling everyone that you're as good as you say you are. That's what press coverage does. People trust the news media. Rightly or wrongly, they assume that the media are objective—that a newspaper doesn't have an agenda when it writes a story about the award you received. So more than any ad, consumers trust the media to give them the straight story, spin-free. That's why PR builds credibility. Here are some other benefits of PR:

- *Name recognition.* Few things are better at making your name (or voice or face) familiar to your target market than PR. If you're a regular guest on a local public radio station's talk show on health issues, your name will become widely known quickly.

- *Prestige.* Having an article written about you or appearing on TV makes you more visible. Remember what I said about visibility? PR makes you a minor local celebrity; it has a sort of "halo effect" that makes you appear more important.

- *Perception of expertise.* If you're the subject of a newspaper feature story or are quoted by a trade publication for an investigative article, you must be among the elite in your profession. Right?

- *Marketing assets.* Newspaper clippings and video and audio files from TV or radio make great content for your Web site, CDs or DVDs you can give out to clients, or tools to garner even more coverage.

If you doubt the power of PR, I have two words for you: Tiger Woods. Name an athlete whose Personal Brand has benefited more from press coverage than the young golf champion. Woods isn't even particularly eloquent or charming; in fact, he's taken a beating in some circles because of his refusal to make statements about issues such as discrimination in sports. But the media can't get enough of him: he's young, ethnic, good-looking, and astonishingly talented on the golf course, a sport that makes for perfect photo ops. Woods's powerful Personal Brand owes everything to the media.

On the negative side, there's Al Gore. He's a Nobel Prize winner, a former senator and vice president, and probably the world's leading voice for taking action against climate change. But when I mention him, you know what I'm guaranteed to hear within the first five minutes? Someone saying, "After all, he invented the Internet." One small misperception, taken out of context, has haunted the man for eight years and counting, despite his accomplishments.

THINGS YOU CAN DO TODAY

1. Have your assistant go out and recover any cheap promotional brochures or other materials you might have left in the past at chambers of commerce, hotels, or other such places.

2. Subscribe to any online branding e-newsletters you find useful.

3. Research trade shows or professional conferences that would make ideal networking venues.

4. Place a classified ad for new staff, especially a client service manager.

5. Apply for a new business credit card that gives you rewards points for spending, helps you track your business expenses better, or both.

6. Brainstorm original article ideas that you could give to a free-lancer; these will end up as prime attractions on your Web site.

LORD OF THE DANCE

There are five basic steps in the PR dance, and whether you're targeting the editor of your hometown paper or of a national trade magazine, you've got to learn and follow them all:

1. Make things easy for editors, reporters, and program directors. Send information in the proper format, and be easy to contact.

2. Be respectful of journalists' time. They are busy, deadline-obsessed people. Send your press release, then follow up a week later with an e-mail. That's it. Don't hound them or make yourself a nuisance.

3. Know what editors and journalists need. Get to know the publications, radio stations, and TV stations in your area so that you'll know what kind of material they usually run. Then send them only those kinds of stories.

4. Be newsworthy. Create a new type of business, a new product, a new service—something worth covering.

5. Be different. Newspapers get dozens or hundreds of press releases and press kits every week. Most of them are conservative, boring, and unmemorable. Find some way to catch an editor's attention without being unprofessional.

In the end, all any editor or broadcast producer wants is a good story that can be gotten with minimal time or trouble. If you can provide such stories consistently, it doesn't matter who you are. You'll get coverage.

BRAND SURGERY
THE PATIENT: YOUR PUBLIC RELATIONS

- Don't pester editors for stories. Be patient.

- Promise a column or release and then deliver before the deadline, making sure you're within 25 words of the requested word count.

- Spell-check and manually proofread everything you send out.

- Don't send half a dozen press releases plus old articles in a press kit. No editor wants another stack of paper on his or her desk.

- If a reporter gets a fact wrong or quotes a competitor without getting a quote from you, insist on a correction or equal time.

- Make all your press materials—releases, past articles, video clips, and your bio—available on your Web site.

- Allow editors and reporters who visit your Web site to sign up for your press-release e-mail list, so you can send them your new releases automatically.

THREE TYPES OF PR

Most guides to public relations focus primarily on sending out press releases and getting articles or news items published. But I'm going to take you further by also talking about other effective avenues that can produce priceless coverage: getting your own writing published and establishing yourself as an expert resource.

1. Press Releases and Articles
This is PR bread and butter. Sending out regular press releases on your company letterhead is the easiest way to keep yourself in front of editors and generate occasional coverage. Doing this has several goals:

- To make editors familiar with you

- To keep your name in front of them

- To get your release used as a short "news brief" item

- To get a special event you're involved in listed in a calendar section

- To get the publication to write a feature-length article about you eventually

Editors need material to fill space. If they can't get it from you, they'll run house ads or filler articles from Associated Press. By providing material for short stories, you solve a problem for them. Then, as an editor gets to know you, you become a local or professional interest story. The more successful and prominent you become, the better story you are. It's a wonderful feedback loop.

So to whom do you send your releases? That depends on your target market. If you're primarily trying to develop your Personal Brand to attract local residents, you'll want to put local papers, magazines, radio stations, and TV stations on your mailing list. On the other hand, if you want to corral more professional referral sources or if you're targeting a group of people in a specific profession, such as engineers or teachers, the professional trade publications that cover your line of work are your best bet. I suggest starting with local media, then going after the trade books.

What can your press releases be about? Anything you like, as long as it's relevant to the publication. You'll find some PR gurus telling you to send a release every month, even if it's just to report that you hired a new secretary. Don't do that. Sending a release that wastes an editor's time is worse than sending nothing. Send a release when you have news that you think will interest the editor of a publication, even if that means sending three releases one week and not sending another for three months. Relevance is more important than frequency. Give journalists news they can use. Here are some possibilities:

- You win an award.

- You open a new location.

- You reach a milestone, like being in business for 25 years.

- You sponsor a sports team or charity event.

- You launch a new Web site.

- You publish a book.

- You start a new business.

- You hire the relative of a prominent local person.

- You launch an aggressive new business initiative.

- You join a community group.

- You run for office.

- You hold a seminar.

- One of your staff gets an award or a special honor.

BRAND CASE STUDY

The Brand: Melissa Rivers

Specialization: Queen of the red-carpet preshow fashion critique

Location: Los Angeles, California

Channels: The Web, books, television

Highlights: Annually capturing the attention of the world with her mother, Joan Rivers, while hosting their *Joan and Melissa Live* red-carpet events before the Oscars, Golden Globes, Grammys, and Emmys

Online: www.melissarivers.com

The Story: For 12 years, one of the guilty pleasures of Hollywood's awards season was tuning in to watch Joan and Melissa Rivers spend a couple of hours yanking the biggest stars in the world off the red carpet to ask them what they had been thinking when they dressed themselves. *Live with Joan and Melissa* became a ratings smash, and Melissa Rivers, derided at the outset by many people as riding her famous mother's coattails, distinguished herself as someone who knew how to handle herself on camera. Then came 2007, when the TV Guide Network cut Joan and Melissa loose from the franchise they had created.

Well, in a period of adversity, Melissa Rivers has proved herself in a way that she never did on the red carpet: she's become an entrepreneur, launching an AOL version of the red-carpet fashion-fest; starting her own Internet-based world à la Second Life; writing her first book, *Life Lessons from the Red Carpet;* and creating several new television shows. Witness the instant re-creation of a personal brand.

How It All Started: Rivers was a Penn grad working at *Entertainment Tonight* and becoming known as a producer when the folks at E!, the entertainment TV network, asked her in 1996 if she would join her mother on the live red-carpet preshow. "I was, to put it mildly, a nervous wreck," she writes in her book. "Why not? My mother and I were about to step onto the storied red carpet and directly into the sights of millions—no, let's be honest, billions—of TV viewers to create a new genre of live television for the E! Network: the real-time red-carpet interview broadcast and fashion extravaganza. No one had ever done such an audacious thing." The gamble paid off in a big way, making media darlings out of the Rivers women and giving the world a new awards-season pastime: trashing actresses' fashion judgment.

What This Brand Stands For:
- *Quality.* "I think the number one thing is always quality," Rivers says. "I don't want to put my name on something that's crappy. That doesn't mean there won't be things that aren't successful, but as long as I keep my eyes on quality and accessibility, then I'm OK. That applies to what I lend my name to as well. If I support a charity or cause, I don't just go to the event and smile. You know that I really believe in what they do."

- *Honesty.* "Mom and I have always been known for giving our honest opinions on things regardless of the fallout," Rivers says. "If I say I like something, people know I genuinely like it. That's why people loved the red-carpet shows. Honesty translates into quality."

- *Relentlessness.* Rivers may be one of the most underestimated individuals in Hollywood, regarded as someone who succeeded only because of her famous mother. But as she says, once she gets an

(continued)

idea, she doesn't let it go. That tenacity has led her to found a venture-funded Internet company that no one thought was possible, and to take the red-carpet magic to AOL, where she and Joan attracted more than 1.4 million unique visitors for their Oscar fashion postmortem.

Still, she knows she'll always be linked to her famous comedienne mother. "I'm definitely still identified as an appendage of my mother," she says. "I've made peace with it, but it hasn't been easy. Sometimes it's been very frustrating to just be 'Joan's daughter.' No matter what I do I will always be in her shadow . . . unless I become president, but I have way too many skeletons in the closet for that.

"However, that perception is changing slowly. Hard work and time are changing it. Stepping out on my own and doing things is making a difference."

X-Factor: Twelve years as the reigning co-monarch of the red carpet made Rivers a household name and allowed her to shed much of the baggage that comes with being the scion of a legend. Those fashion-filled evenings before the Oscars, Emmys, Grammys, and Golden Globes drew millions of viewers who either loved or hated the mother's and daughter's snarky asides about the attire of stars, giving Melissa the notoriety and influence to pursue multiple new paths in her post-red carpet era.

Branding Wisdom: "In business, I'm being perceived with a whole lot more respect, as someone who really believes in the changing face of media and who is actively participating in it," she says. "It has to do with the fact that I've been out there for over a year now beating the drum about the Internet and designing ways to integrate Internet, entertainment, and traditional media. I haven't gone to a meeting where I've pitched a show that didn't have an online component. I've been beating that drum for a long, long time, and people are finally paying attention.

"That's why I love what I do—it gives me the opportunity to knock on enough doors until someone listens."

How to Do It Right

When those newsworthy events come around, you'll want to send a news release or a press kit to your local media. Here are some tips for getting the best results:

- Know to whom you're mailing, whether it's a local community newspaper, an alternative weekly, an area magazine, a regional edition of a larger paper, trade periodicals, or all of the above. Read the publications and learn what they tend to publish. If they never publish your kind of story, don't assume that you're a special case. Don't send a release. Editors love news sources who know their needs and send them things that are relevant to their readers.

- Know the basic professional press-release style—contact information at the top, inverted pyramid format with the "who, what, when, where, why, and how" information in the first paragraph, and supporting information and a quote or quotes from you after that. Go to the press sections at any one of 100 corporate Web sites and you'll see professionally written releases to use as examples. Stick to this format until you become proficient at press-release writing. Then you can get a little creative.

- Avoid blatant editorializing in your press releases. Editors and reporters want facts in their releases, not opinion. When you master the press-release style, you can get away with humor or irony, but in the beginning, play it straight.

- To introduce yourself to editors, we recommend sending them a press kit with your first release. A press kit is a high-class folder containing your initial press release, your personal bio, your Personal Brochure, a business card, and a black-and-white photo of you. Send with it a cover letter explaining who you are and why you've chosen to send your information to this publication.

- Try to send a release at least once per quarter. You shouldn't send frivolous junk releases to editors, but you don't want them to forget you, either. Try to come up with something newsworthy at least every three months, and monthly if you can. Remember, what's not news to a national TV show may be news to your local 30,000-circulation paper.

- Start a relationship. When an editor or writer finally does call, take every opportunity to start a two-way relationship. Take the writer to lunch. Send the editor a thank-you gift if a story runs. Be easy and accommodating. Make yourself available as a source for future stories in your area of expertise. It pays off.

- Be responsive. Deadlines wait for no one, so when you get a request from a reporter, act fast. Get that reporter the information he or she needs within 24 hours. Reporters will love you for it.

- When your article runs, get copies. When your radio show airs, get a CD. When your TV interview airs, get a DVD. As long as you get permission, you can use this material to promote yourself.

- Don't forget about the online versions of print publications. They usually refresh their content much more often than their print counterparts, and many publications run Web-only stories. That means more space that you can fill.

Finally, if you have the budget and are prepared to make PR a major cog in your Personal Branding machine, hire a publicist. This can cost as much as $3,000 a month, so it's probably not even worth it unless you live in a large metropolitan area with at least 8 to 10 major print and broadcast media outlets. Publicists know how to do the PR dance like Fred Astaire, and they're skilled at creating relationships and keeping you on editors' and producers' minds. The best way to find great publicists? Ask the reporters and editors at your local newspaper. They know which PR flacks are real pros and which ones are pains in the neck.

THINGS YOU CAN DO IN A WEEK

1. Get a "hot-line" cell phone whose number you give out only to your best clients, key partners, and other such people.

2. If your laptop is important to your business, have it serviced by a professional and replace or update anything that needs it.

3. Write 10 direct-mail messages designed for very personal occasions: the death of a loved one, the birth of a baby, the breakup of a marriage.

4. Contact conferences or other events to find out about sitting on professional roundtables or symposia.

5. Sign contracts with all your key vendors (writers, designers, and so on), cementing important points like fees, confidentiality, and non-compete clauses.

6. Make sure your Web site is listed on any important online professional directories (like FindLaw.com for lawyers).

2. Publish Your Own Column

Getting your own column published, either in a local periodical or in a national trade paper, is a tremendous boon to your credibility. A disclaimer: many columnists who are not professional writers don't publish their own words, and you probably shouldn't either. Unless you have a background as a professional writer, hire a ghostwriter to write your column.

Why would a local newspaper or magazine want to publish your column? Because these publications are always looking for new material, and because you're an expert in your field. You're also (I presume) known and respected in your community. If you can deliver a well-written column about a subject that's of interest, you should be able to find a place to publish it, even if it takes a while to do so.

How to Do It Right

- Locate a good writer who can deliver a piece of a set length on deadline. Avoid the college journalism programs; you have no idea what kind of quality you'll be getting. A good way to find freelance writers these days is on Web sites like Guru.com and Elance.com. But perhaps the best way is to simply contact the writers who write for your local paper. Most reporters don't make a lot of money, and they would jump at the chance to make an extra $200 a month.

- Contact one publication at a time. Sending a proposal to more than one paper or magazine at a time is called a "simultaneous submission," and it's frowned upon. Compile a list of local and regional periodicals that have a need for what you can offer, then give each editor an exclusive shot before you move on.

- Choose your idea. Before you choose your publication, decide what you want your column to be about. It should be something that you're interested in, that you know a lot about, and that isn't already being covered in the publications you're targeting. For example, if you want to write about the ups and downs of the local real estate market, a regional lifestyle magazine might be best, but if your local daily newspaper doesn't already have a real estate column in its business section, that's a great prospect. Just as when picking a target market, look for an unmet need that you can fill.

- Get the editorial guidelines. Every publication has them, and they'll tell you how long a column should be, which subjects are kosher, what format to submit the column in, whom to send it to, and so on. Follow these to the letter.

- Pick your first publication and have your writer produce a sample column. Then send it with a cover letter to the editor. In the letter, explain who you are and why you think your column should be accepted, and offer three or four ideas for future columns. Then wait and see what happens.

3. Establish Yourself as an Expert Source

This is a great way to generate press coverage, because it involves very little work beyond the initial effort. You're establishing yourself with editors and producers, both local and national, as a knowledgeable, quotable source for news stories in your area of expertise. You become the guy reporters call for an opinion and a quote when they're doing a piece on emerging stocks, athletes in the media, class-action-suit case law, or whatever your field of knowledge is.

I've done this sort of thing myself. For a few years I was the Personal Branding expert *du jour* that CNN, CNBC, MSNBC, and other cable news outlets called when they wanted expert commentary on high-profile brands in crisis like Michael Jackson and Martha

Stewart. I'd do my three minutes of commentary and analysis and get some national publicity. I don't know how much it helped my business, but it was fun and good media training, and it certainly didn't hurt.

The wonderful thing about expert status is that once you're in their address book, editors and reporters will call you and put your name in the paper pretty regularly. They love having a knowledgeable professional that they can count on for easy access and a pithy quote. And beyond sending a thank-you card once in a while, you don't have to do a thing to get your name in the paper.

How to Do It Right

- Specialize. Even if you're a fantastic architect, don't position yourself to an editor as generic. That's too broad. Be the "architect with expertise in the county's design history and historic buildings." Package yourself as a specialist and you'll be treated as one.

- Have Rolodex cards printed to match your business cards, and send them to the editors at your chosen publications along with a cover letter offering yourself as an expert source.

- Be accessible. If you're going to be a source, you've got to be able to be reached. Provide editors with a mobile phone number and return calls as quickly as possible. Deadlines wait for no one.

- Be candid, then do research. When you are called to comment on a topic, if you don't know the answer, ask if you can call back after you've had a chance to crack the books. Then call back within an hour. Most reporters can wait a little while for an accurate answer. When you are quoted, tell a story. "Yes" and "no" are worthless answers.

- Every quarter, send your Rolodex card and a follow-up letter to editors until you receive communication from them. Some will tell you to buzz off. Some will thank you and promise to get back to you. A few will express real interest.

- Be opportunistic. When a news story breaks that's related to your area of expertise, contact editors *before* they need you. Tell them, "I'm sure you're planning a story about the drug recall, and I wanted to make myself available to provide medical information for your reporters."

THINGS YOU CAN DO IN A MONTH

1. Sit on a roundtable or panel discussion and use it as a networking opportunity.

2. Complete customization of a Constant Contact e-newsletter and begin sending it.

3. Decide on your incentive and thank-you gift choices for people who bring you referrals.

4. Save money by changing your office phone service to a VoIP service like Vonage.

5. Schedule a dinner with your 10 oldest/best clients and ask them to critique your branding strategies and materials.

6. Plan the agenda for your first seminar.

RADIO DAZE

I've focused mostly on print publications—newspapers and magazines—so far. There's a reason: they're easier to get into and less scary than radio. But you shouldn't ignore radio. The barriers to getting on the air are higher, but if you can do it, the rewards are potentially great.

Radio is great because, unlike with TV, you can't be seen. You just have to talk; you don't have to worry about being camera-shy or how your hair looks. Plus, many communities have either low-power FM radio stations, college stations, or public radio stations that are always eager for material that's relevant to the community. It could be tough to land a Saturday morning spot on the local Clear Channel affiliate, but smaller stations will be much more receptive.

There are two ways to make radio work for you: being interviewed and getting your own show. Obviously, being interviewed is much,

much easier. You can simply follow the same tactics you would use for print media: send regular, relevant press releases and make yourself available as an expert. Just make sure you're comfortable speaking into a microphone. Ask other people to rate your speaking voice. Is it too fast? Too hoarse? You may be able to get some voice coaching if you really want to be on radio.

Getting your own show is a much more involved project. First, you've got to have an idea and pitch it to program directors. More important, you'll almost certainly have to bring in your own advertisers or pay for the airtime yourself. I've found that few professionals have the time or connections to make this work, but if you're one of the lucky ones, having a regular radio show can turn you into a celebrity and really help your Personal Brand. Talk to a local station and ask what it takes to get your own show.

What about television? Well, the odds that a busy doctor, lawyer, or other professional will have the time, resources, and talent to make a TV show make business sense are long. Probably the best you can hope for is to establish yourself as an expert source for television news programs or interview shows. For that, you'll need a publicist to navigate the TV production company bureaucracy.

I did the national TV expert gig, and while it was fun, it didn't really make much of a difference in my business. Stick with local print and radio where your time is more likely to result in bottom-line benefits.

COMMUNITY OUTREACH

Community outreach and PR go hand in hand. Many times, what you do to create news that gets coverage will be creating a community outreach event. These are similar to the client events I talked about in the Chapter 5, but they are for either the general public or a large organization. Community outreach has two goals: creating news that gets you covered in the press, and generating widespread community goodwill.

Outreach can take many forms:

- Public-service seminars on subjects like identity theft or investment scams

- Charity auctions or sports tournaments

- School fund-raisers

- Tasting parties at local restaurants, wineries, or distilleries

- Entertainment for nursing home patients or children in local hospitals

- Groundbreaking for new buildings that you support financially

- Blood drives

- Guest speakers you bring in

- Roundtables with you and colleagues in your profession where you answer questions for the public

- Sponsored events like distance runs, where you earn money for charity with your athletic performance

With outreach, the key is that the event must offer a benefit to the community. Self-serving events will do you more harm than good. But if you do them right, community outreach shindigs can become highly anticipated annual events that become closely associated with your name.

As with so many branding ideas, this one also comes down to money and time. I suggest that if you want to engage in community outreach, you start small. Organize and sponsor a car wash for the local high school football team and see how you and your staff handle things and how manageable the expenses are. If it works out and you see a need, graduate to something bigger. Here are some ideas for making outreach pay off:

- Find partners or sponsors to share or cover some of the costs.

- At least 60 days before your event, start sending direct mail or direct e-mail to your lists, promoting the event and inviting them to participate.

- At least 30 days before, send press releases about the event and generate pre-event coverage.

- Invite the press. Don't just send a press release; send invitations to reporters and local TV and radio stations, and have your staff follow up with phone calls.

- Make sure there's a photographer present whose only job is to get shots of you with people in the community, special guests, and so on.

- Videotape the event, have the tape professionally edited, and send DVDs to your local TV stations.

- Post all photos and videos on your Web site.

- Send out a postevent press release talking about what happened, how much money was raised, and other such information.

There are many ways to become newsworthy, but the best way is to make yourself not just a valuable service provider, but a valuable member of the community. That's got rewards beyond getting your name in the paper.

BY NOW YOU SHOULD BE . . .

- Sending your press kit or press releases to editors regularly

- Making sure you're on the expert list for several reporters

- Starting your direct-mail campaigns

- Getting referrals from your professional contacts

- Using your "what you do and whom you do it for" line as your verbal elevator pitch with everyone you meet

- Getting useful feedback on your new client service and business systems

11

NETWORKING AND REFERRALS

Even ordinary Joes and Josephines crave a "personal brand"
that will earn them riches beyond the dreams of Croesus, or at
least an office with a window.

—Don Aucoin, *Boston Globe*

The common image of networking is the "schmooze": a bunch of guys in loud suits standing around chamber of commerce mixers with vodka tonics talking about their BMWs and their golf swings. But networking as done by smart Personal Branders is something else entirely. It's the art of creating relationships and seeding intrigue about yourself throughout a population.

Never is your Personal Brand more on display than in a networking situation. People probably don't have more than a couple of minutes to get to know you, so they *can't* really get to know you. They can get to know only your brand—who you are, what you do, and whom you do it for. In such situations, your Personal Brand is also thoroughly tested, because, as I said before, everything you do is part of your brand. Your clothes, your business card or Personal Brochure, your manner, maybe even subtle cues like your cologne or your watch—they all either confirm or contradict your brand. If you've got your act together, networking is a wonderful source of new business relationships.

Networking leads to referrals, and referrals are one of the engines of a successful Personal Brand. What's better than a referral client or patient who comes to you 90 percent sold on you? Nothing. Getting referrals from fellow professionals and from your satisfied clients should *definitely* be a cornerstone of your Personal Branding. I've had clients whose referral strategies were so successful that they stopped all their other brand marketing and made referrals their only source of new business. This channel is that powerful.

People often focus on networking contacts becoming clients, but that's too limited. There are many more ways someone you meet through networking can help you:

1. Refer clients to you.

2. Become a mentor.

3. Become a valuable advisor.

4. Provide you with needed services.

5. Offer expertise in areas like business plans or raising funds.

6. Provide media coverage.

7. Become a bridge to influential media members, corporate leaders, and politicians.

There are two kinds of networking, *formal* and *informal*, and in this chapter we're going to look at both. We'll look at networking and referrals, how they're related, and the ways to make both work wonders for you.

THINGS YOU CAN DO TODAY

1. Collect memorabilia from leisure activities to share with clients or use in photo shoots.

2. Cut costs by getting a quote from your printer for "gang running" your brochure, postcards, and other printed materials.

(continued)

3. Reserve any Web domain names that might be useful for future business ventures, including variations on your name.

4. Inquire about a toll-free number for your office.

5. Make a list of local charities you could get involved with as a PR strategy.

6. Write Frequently Asked Questions (and their answers) for your Web site.

FORMAL NETWORKING

Formal networking is where you attend an event that has been organized for the express or understood purpose of allowing people to network. That can be a networking organization like LeTip or BNI, a professional conference or association meeting, or even a high-ticket charity event. In all those cases, networking is either the raison d'etre or the main attraction. At formal events, you need to be prepared. Have your Personal Brand "elevator pitch" down pat: who you are, what you do, whom you do it for, and maybe a little touch of how you create value. Have Personal Brochures at the ready to hand out, and have goals in mind: in particular, to meet potential professional referral partners.

These are some of the best venues for formal networking:

- Chamber of commerce meetings

- Networking groups like LeTip

- Professional association meetings

- Trade shows

- Seminars

- Charity events

- Fine arts events like the opera and the ballet

- Boards of directors meetings

- Professional panels

- Organizational committees

- City council meetings

At formal networking events, you should be looking primarily for professionals in industries that are related to yours who could become professional referral sources. As we read back in Chapter 5, professional referral sources are colleagues with whom you create a formal quid pro quo referral agreement—you send them clients who need their particular services, and they do the same for you.

YOUR PROFESSIONAL REFERRAL NETWORK

Building a professional referral network, or PRN, is hands-down the best way to turn networking into a business growth engine. Truly successful Personal Branders will have a PRN of 7 to 10 referral sources in different industries, all sending them prequalified prospects. That's what you want to find in your networking: noncompeting, highly qualified, ethical people in *complementary* professions—people who are likely to have clients who also need the services you can provide. Spend 15 minutes and you can probably come up with 8 to 10 possible professions. For example:

If you're a family physician:

- Psychotherapists

- Physical therapists

- Chiropractors

- Alternative health-care practitioners such as acupuncturists

- Personal trainers

- Pharmacists

- Obstetricians

- Midwives

If you're a Realtor:

- Mortgage brokers

- Appraisers

- Home inspectors

- Title insurance sellers

- Contractors

- Homeowner's insurance brokers

- Builders

- Financial advisors

See, it's not that hard. But finding such professionals is only the first step. You need to find out if they are trustworthy, since you're going to send them business and rely on them to do the same for you. You also need to find people who are interested in being part of your PRN; some won't be. There's no magic formula for this stuff; you've just got to take the time and get to know these people. I recommend not bringing up a referral partnership at your first meeting. Just talk and build some level of trust. Then when you follow up a few days later, you can broach the subject: "Would you be interested in creating a formal agreement where we agree to refer each other business?"

The next step in creating a PRN is to get references from each professional—while offering the same to him or her, of course. Then you're going to make phone calls and ask candid questions about the way this professional takes care of his or her clients. You need to be certain that the people in your PRN are going to treat your clients like royalty; you can't afford even one bad experience, because the people to whom you refer your clients reflect on you.

Once you've done your due diligence and found a group of professionals whom you can trust, it's time to formally propose a reciprocal referral relationship with ground rules and benefits. Keep in mind that in some states, there may be laws against rewarding professionals for referrals, so do your homework. Talk to your certification or governing organization about whether or not incentives and rewards are kosher.

Keep in mind that you're not creating a circular network in which you and all your referral partners are sharing referrals with *one another*; that's just too complex to maintain. Some people get confused by this. No, you're creating a set of two-way referral channels, where let's say an appraiser, a mortgage broker, and a contractor send you business and you send business back to them, but they don't send clients to each other. It's likely that they'll never know about the others at all.

How formal you choose to make your PRN is up to you and your partner. Some are just handshake agreements, while others involve binding contracts prepared by attorneys. How you want to do it is, again, up to you, but I think it's wise to spell things out in writing. Here are the areas you should cover:

- *Right of first refusal.* You agree that when either of you has a client who might be perfect for the other person, you'll offer your referral partner the referral before offering it to anyone else.

- *Contact methods.* Spell out how you will contact your referrals, such as sending an introductory Personal Brochure and following up with a phone call, or having the referral partner send an e-mail icebreaker first.

- *Client service.* Spell out how you will handle client service, from how often clients will receive communication and updates to how fast complaints will be resolved.

- *Incentives and rewards.* If these are legal, specify what each of you will earn for sending a certain number of referrals who become paying clients. For instance, if you refer 10 new clients in a calendar year, you get a $100 gift certificate for a nice local restaurant, and so on.

- *Escape and renewal clauses.* If the partnership doesn't work out, you don't want to be stuck. Make sure that either of you can sever the relationship with 30 days' written notice, and make sure that at the end of each 12-month period, there's a mutual renewal option, so that you both have to agree to keep the partnership going.

- *Marketing support.* What marketing assistance will you provide? This could mean anything from just giving your partner 100 copies of your Personal Brochure all the way up to producing public seminars together. Spell it out.

THINGS YOU CAN DO IN A WEEK

1. Have one of your staff scrub your existing mailing list (the one you've put together yourself over the years) of dead or incorrect addresses.

2. If your office is in an unattractive area, explore other possible locations or talk to the city about beautification.

3. Follow up on press releases by e-mailing the editors or reporters to whom they were sent.

4. If you're going to do any door-to-door canvassing, create a detailed route map of your target market neighborhoods.

5. Attend three local networking events.

6. Call to follow up on any requests for information coming from your direct mailings.

Getting the Most from Your Professional Referrals

Professional referrals can be a gold mine for your business. But handled badly, they can permanently damage your credibility and reputation. Here are some suggestions for both avoiding disaster and leveraging your PRN for full benefit:

- Create a "referral response team." Assign one or two people on your staff the responsibility of making sure that referrals from your professional partners are treated better than incredibly. Create a PRN manual that spells out the timing and number of "touches," and train your team to spoil PRN referrals rotten.

- Deliver postservice reports to your partner. After you've done your initial work with the referred client (done his taxes, for example), report back to your referral partner on how things went and ask your new client to do the same via a phone call or e-mail.

- Don't list your professional referral partners on your Web site. It can be tempting to list them on a page called something like "Resources I Recommend," but then you're undermining your own partnership by allowing people to go around you directly to your partners.

- Do create a page on your site that says, "I know that often my clients/patients need service providers in related areas. I have put together a list of top professionals personally vetted by me, and I would be glad to speak with you any time about a referral." This encourages queries without poisoning your channel.

- Be wary about co-marketing initiatives. Anything where you're both putting in money, such as a direct mailer, can get sticky if the two of you don't agree on printing quality, copy, and other such matters. It's better to provide your own marketing tools to the other person but avoid mutual spending unless you're really in sync.

- Follow up with the clients you refer to your partners. It's important to make sure that the people you send to your partners are being cared for. Ask them. They'll tell you how they feel.

BRAND CASE STUDY

The Brand: Shiva Rea

Specialization: Yoga as conscious evolution

Location: Los Angeles, California

Channels: The Web, DVDs, classes, retreats

Highlights: Being the first major yoga teacher to give students digital tools that allow them to create their own home practice

Online: www.shivarea.com

The Story: Shiva Rea has become one of the biggest stars in the growing world of yoga. As more people seek spiritual content to their lives that does not involve organized religion, they have been drawn to her by her spiritual authenticity. Rea is a spiritual seeker and teacher first, and a businesswoman . . . well, somewhere far down the line. "It's funny . . . I still don't realize that there's a brand around what I do. I still don't have that processed completely," she says.

(continued)

How It All Started: What's in a name? Quite a lot for Rea. Contrary to what many people believe, she did not change her name in order to be more "exotic" for the yoga world. Her father bestowed it upon her, and when she began to explore its origins, she began to discover her path. "My father gave me the name when he was a 19-year-old surfer and art student. It's such an extraordinary part of my personal unfolding," she says. "Most people know Shiva as the dance of Shiva, half male, half female, the first teacher of yoga. In the mythology, all the yoga *asanas* (postures) come from the dance of Shiva.

"It's been a powerful name because one of the things I do, Yoga Trance Dance, I evolved out of my work in Africa and the Caribbean discovering indigenous dance. People are sometimes negative when they think I changed my name. Some people do change their name because it's important to them. But I can't stand exoticism in yoga; I like to feel that yoga is for everybody."

What This Brand Stands For:

- *Spirituality.* Above all, Rea walks the walk as a spiritual seeker. She says that her brand has grown completely organically, more because of the efforts of the business minds than of her own deliberate planning. She would rather be studying and embracing the traditions of the Krishnamacharya lineage, *tantra, ayurveda, bhakti, kalaripayattu,* world dance, yogic art, and somatic movement in order to develop her own unique style not just of yoga but of reaching personal enlightenment. Far from some more commercial, aerobic yoga brands, hers is first and foremost about the journey.

- *Global reach.* A cross-cultural flavor suffuses everything Rea does, with influences from Africa, India, the Caribbean, Latin America, and Asia. She is a global adventurer who has led more than 70 yoga retreats to many countries and sacred sites. This exotic feel and sense of worldwide unity can be found in her message, her speaking, and her teaching.

- *Eclecticism.* There's no must-buy regimen in Rea's yoga world; students and seekers can take what they wish and leave the rest. She has CDs, DVDs, books, classes and teacher training courses, and yoga clothing and accessories, but none of them are pushed on students with the aggressive marketing tactics of some of the more "Hollywood" yogis. Instead, each person is encouraged to find what works for him or her.

- *Respect.* The loving, positive, respectful, spirit-oriented language that can be found at every exposure to Rea's brand may make you think that it's all a big act. Nobody can be that compassionate and nurturing. But it's all for real, and it's part of her view that everyone has value, that the earth is a spiritual place, and that we are all on a journey of "creative evolution." Rea respects the people who buy her teachings and products, and that's hard to find these days.

X-Factor: Her *Shakti* DVDs. These home yoga courses were a revolution. "Previously, people with video couldn't even skip around to get to what they wanted to," she says. "So when I did *Yoga Shakti*, it let people create a custom practice, almost like a jukebox. I started to really get involved in media for yoga, and now I have 12 DVDs that are all unique, kind of a fitness brand, though not like Denise Austin. Ours is really about building a peaceful home practice in an inspiring, break-the-mold way."

Branding Wisdom: "I never choose any creative project based on money," she says. "What I find challenging is that people may think that's my intention, because if I go somewhere, I'll have a table that has 10 different kinds of DVDs. People assume commercialism.

"This is what I tell young teachers: focus on your garden," she says. "Make what you are growing and offering so incredible that people are naturally attracted to it. Don't put the cart before the horse. A lot of people get ambitious before they have something to offer. When you have something, people will start coming to you. I have a rule: never invite yourself anywhere. I think when you are invited, people are genuinely seeking what you're offering.

"The momentum of our lives comes from our own inner fire. Stoke that fire; look around like a point guard in basketball—I was a point guard in high school—be hyperaware of all the possibilities, then participate from your core. Once that momentum comes, so much creativity and vision are created. That's the brand."

INFORMAL NETWORKING

Informal networking happens when you attend a musical theater performance, go to a Little League game, or attend a private party. You have no idea whom you're going to meet. You probably don't have Personal Brochures with you, but you should have business cards to hand out. In these situations, you should be less goal-oriented and more yourself. No selling; just be you. Let people get to know you and ask questions. Odds are that you're going to meet either potential future clients or sources of personal referrals in these situations.

The downside to informal networking is that it's random. You don't know if you'll run into anyone of value, and you don't know if your new friends are going to create business for you. In fact, it can take a long time—two to three years, if you're new in community social circles—for informal networking to pay off in fresh bottom-line revenues. But that's OK. There are other reasons to do it: fun, meeting new people who might become friends, learning more about your community and interesting organizations, and polishing your own networking skills. But my advice to you is right out of the Nike handbook: just do it. Circulate and create relationships and prepare as much as you can. Put yourself in a position to benefit from informal social connections, but don't obsess over turning them into business. If you're authentic and clear about who you are, that should take care of itself.

One of the most important ways you can make informal networking pay is simply to put yourself in a position to meet influential people through your social life. What do I mean by influential people? Here's a partial list of the folks you can get to know in informal settings:

- Community leaders and politicians
- Business leaders
- Members of your local media
- Leaders of nonprofit groups
- Religious leaders
- Educators
- Activists
- Local artists and cultural figures

These individuals tend to be what marketers call "key influencers," people whose opinions affect the opinions of others. If a member of your city council comes to think you're a brilliant young attorney, she's likely to tell her friends (including those who don't need legal services), and her view is going to carry more weight with others than the view of the guy who delivers your newspaper. It's also quite possible to run into ideal prospects in informal situations, especially if you're in the environments that they frequent.

BRAND SURGERY
THE PATIENT: YOUR NETWORKING CONTACTS

- Don't ask for people's business five minutes after you meet them.

- Don't "just happen" to have Personal Branding materials with you. People aren't stupid. Tell them you brought copies of your Personal Brochure in case you met people of interest.

- Don't focus only on what people can do for you; instead, focus on what you can do for them.

- Don't monopolize people. No matter how valuable they could be as contacts, tag them and let them fly away free after a few minutes. This lets you both move on to someone else.

- Don't talk about how much money you make.

- Don't ask newly referred clients for referrals before you've even done anything for them. You've got to sow before you can harvest.

- Don't panic. You may well meet, wine, and dine valuable contacts and be referred to 50 potential new clients without a single bit of new business resulting for six months. It's normal. Things take time. Stay cool and don't start calling or you'll seem desperate. If you've treated people well, the networking and referrals will pay off in time—most likely in a sudden flood of new business.

BECOME A JOINER

That's the key. Informal networking works best when you go out of your way to put yourself where key influencers or ideal prospects are likely to be. That means joining arts organizations, subscribing to the opera or the symphony, joining civic clubs like the Elks, getting involved in local political causes or churches, or playing golf at the country clubs where the people in your target market usually play golf. Put yourself in situations where you're more likely to meet people. Sit next to others on a plane or in a movie theater. Dine in busy, energetic restaurants. Be the person who listens and meets others while other people protect their personal space.

Once you do this, follow a few basic informal networking guidelines that are really just common sense:

- Get involved. Don't just show up to hand out business cards. That will be obvious and will alienate people. Get your hands dirty in some way.

- Be real. Don't be the guy trying to build the legal or health-care empire. Just be yourself. Remember, a brand is a relationship.

- Have handouts that are appropriate to the occasion. Business cards only for highbrow events like the opera, Personal Brochures for more casual times.

- Keep showing up. The first time you're in a new environment, no one will know you, so you might not talk to many people. Become a regular and you will.

- Do some research on people who are likely to attend. For instance, if you're going to a charity fund-raiser, it's likely that the local head of the charity will be there. If you know something about him, you can make your conversation more relevant and more memorable.

SMART NETWORKING

Networking isn't about events. It's about seizing every opportunity to meet someone new, and laying the groundwork for a relationship with that person. Even more, it's about putting yourself in a position to meet someone new whenever you can. A fabulous example is Paul

Viti, director of sales and marketing for the New York office of Ernst & Young, a good friend and a networking monster. His secret is so simple it's brilliant: he catches a cab. His office is in Times Square near many upscale hotels, so when Paul walks out to grab a cab for a meeting, he's got a good chance of sharing that cab with a top executive from some corporation. When Paul gets in that cab with a CEO, CFO, or other top executive, he gets to know that person on a one-to-one basis. He told me once that he's laid the groundwork for more deals this way than through all other avenues combined.

With Paul in mind, here are some tips for making your networking more effective, whether it's professional or personal:

- Follow up fast. The day after you meet someone who is potentially worthwhile, follow up with an e-mail or a written note telling the person how much you enjoyed your conversation and hope to do it again. Calling can make you seem desperate, so generally stick to the Internet or the U.S. Postal Service.

- Keep people informed. Even if you haven't done business with a contact yet, keep him in the loop about your activities—awards, new hires, expansion, and so on. You might not want to put him on your monthly direct-mail list, but a letter or an e-mail every couple of months is ideal.

- Let them know about anything that builds your credibility. You want your contacts to form a mental picture of you as trustworthy, professional, and capable, so steer them to any information that completes that picture. That could mean telling them about a newspaper article in which you're quoted or giving them the names and numbers of a few happy clients to call.

- Build a community. Get your contacts together, whether it's via an online discussion board or a hosted lunch at a nice hotel. Get them talking, comparing notes, and creating synergy, and you never know what can happen.

- Be real. If you're new to your business, say so. If you have an irrepressible sense of humor, tell an appropriate joke. People who appreciate who you are will be drawn to you, and will respect you for not being artificial. Sure, you won't attract everyone, but who ever said you'd get everyone as your customer in the first place?

- Always be networking. This sales-inspired phrase should become your guiding principle. Always be in a mindset to meet someone new, to get to know him or her, and to let the person become familiar with your Personal Brand. You never know when you'll run into a new partner, client, or investor.

- Just get to know people. Don't try to extract any benefits from a person when you first meet. Remember, people want to be appreciated as people, not as clients.

- Listen twice as much as you talk in conversation, and ask people about themselves.

- Express interest in further conversation. Most people are just as interested in networking as you are. So when you meet someone who may benefit you, send signals that you're interested in getting to know this person better. Suggest lunch, hand over a business card, ask about a round of golf, and so on.

- Exude positive energy by smiling and being upbeat.

THINGS YOU CAN DO IN A MONTH

1. Run a complete test of all pages and features in your new Web site.

2. Have your copywriter write a list of 20 gold-plated testimonial quotes and send the list to your premium clients, asking each to sign off on the quote that he or she would like to attach his or her name to. This is a great way to get testimonials from very busy people.

3. Enter your Personal Brochure in any regional small-business marketing or advertising competitions.

4. Sign up for a free online clipping service like Clip&Copy, which will track coverage of you in the news media and send you alerts.

5. Produce a report for your best clients about how you are implementing their suggestions for improvement.

6. Track your direct-mail ROI—how many referrals and how many new clients.

PERSONAL REFERRALS: NOT JUST FROM NETWORKING

Networking often leads to referrals, but referrals don't come only from networking. Referrals, as you know, are hands-down your best source of new business. Personal referrals come not from colleagues but from your clients, when they tell a family member or friend, "You've got to call my mortgage broker. He'll take great care of you." There are three reasons why these referrals are so powerful:

1. Most people would rather find a new service provider through a referral than through any other method, because they trust the person providing the referral.

2. Referrals deliver presold prospects at a very low cost to you. Getting a new prospect in your door through direct mail, telemarketing, advertising, and the like can cost hundreds of dollars, but referrals are cheap.

3. If you can mobilize your current clients to bring you referrals, you can create a cadre of evangelists out there telling others how amazing you are.

With personal referrals, there's one commandment: *deliver incredible, mind-blowing service and quality to your current clients.* Make them fall in love with you. Thank them, do more than you promised, find innovative ways to save them money, remind them of anniversaries—whatever it takes to make them love you. No matter how small your budget, you can do this. Anyone can.

BE ACTIVE—ASK FOR THE REFERRAL!

So why don't more professionals cash in on referrals and get rich? Because they don't ask for the referral. Some businesspeople feel better about waiting for clients to refer new prospects on their own. This passive referral approach is never going to make you rich. Ask for the referral! If you've been treating your customers right, they'll be *thrilled* to help you out.

One of the best ways to do this is to work a referral request into your Personal Postcard direct mailings or direct e-mails twice a year.

When you mail to your clients, state candidly and politely that even if they don't have a need for your services right now, if they like what you've done for them, you would appreciate it if they would recommend you to their friends and family. People like to help others, so more often than not they'll be delighted. Other methods:

- Host a series of lunches or dinners for your best clients where you tell them that you'd rather not be in the marketing business, so you'd love to count on them to help you grow your company. This reverse psychology will turn your guests into your personal army of marketing crusaders.

- Host private, in-home miniseminars for your clients and invite them to invite their friends. This can be especially effective when you have people who have a common need, such as a large group of friends who are all approaching retirement.

- Place a function on your Web site that allows visitors to "Tell a Friend" about you by entering the e-mail addresses of people they know and sending them a prewritten message. As an incentive, you can enter site visitors in a contest for referring people.

Never be shy about asking for the referral. It's the only way you'll get it.

BUILD A REFERRAL SYSTEM

The most successful companies have well-oiled machines for leveraging this valuable business development channel. You've got to do the same. Here are our recommended components for a successful referral generation and management system:

- *Automate your direct mail.* As discussed, build at least two referral requests into your annual client direct-mail program. Do the same with any direct e-mail or e-newsletters you send: at least twice a year, expressly ask for referrals. I've even seen people give their clients a primer on what to say!

- *Mail copies of your Personal Brochure.* Nothing does a better job of communicating your brand than your key marketing piece. Once a year, mail half a dozen brochures to your clients with a personal letter asking them to hand them out when the opportunity presents itself.

- *Make sure your Personal Brand is clear.* You want clients to be able to communicate clearly who you are and what you do. If you're not sure that your brand is clear, ask your clients to describe you to yourself. If the description's fuzzy, take the time to make sure you clarify your brand.

- *Develop an incentive plan.* Offer your clients a program of incentives, such as restaurant gift certificates or movie tickets, for referring people who become paying customers to you. Make sure that clients know that the more high-quality prospects they send you, the more goodies they'll receive.

- *Go out of your way to thank referring clients.* Clients who refer their friends or family to you are doing you a favor. Thank them accordingly, even if the referrals haven't turned into business yet. When someone sends you a great prospect, send him a bottle of wine. When someone refers you 10 prospects in a year, send her and her husband to a bed and breakfast for the weekend.

- *Make sure your clients know how you're treating their friends.* People care about how you treat their friends or family because it reflects on them. E-mail them a quarterly progress report on how things are going with the person they referred.

- *Spoil your referrals.* Just as with professional referrals, develop a system to take fantastic care of personal referrals. Communicate with them, exceed their expectations, and give them added value. Remember, you'd like to turn these new clients into referral sources someday.

Finally (and it's surprising how many people forget this one), make sure your clients know the kind of referral you're looking for. Tell them explicitly what kind of person you want to attract to your business. Be careful talking about income, but if you're an investment advisor, I think it's perfectly fine to say, "Bill, I'm looking for fairly affluent, educated people who live in this area and are approaching the time for a 401(k) rollover. If you know some folks like that, those are the ones I would love to talk with." Meeting with and coddling nonideal prospects wastes your time and money; part of referral success is letting your client prequalify your prospects for you.

FIRST, MAKE FRIENDS

With networking and referrals, the bottom line is this: treat people with respect, dignity, empathy, and honesty. People may ultimately decide to do business with you because of your skill, but they will risk investing their time and effort only if they like and trust you. So forget about selling. Don't "make contacts." Start relationships. Make friends. The rest will take care of itself.

BY NOW YOU SHOULD BE . . .

- Sending referral requests to your best clients

- Seeing a trickle of new prospects brought in by your direct mail, advertising, and general brand presence

- Recovering from your first crisis with your new client management system

- Working on autopilot with your direct mailings and e-mails

- Enjoying your work more as you spend more time with clients you like working with

- Seeing a steady rise in your Web site traffic

CHAPTER

12

ADVERTISING

You already have a personal brand, whether you've consciously developed it or not.

—Lesley Everett, *Drop Dead Brilliant*

In doing a sort of *Gray's Anatomy* (the book, not the TV soap opera) of a Personal Brand, I've tried for reasons of space and practicality to talk about the tools that I think 90 percent of business owners and professionals will use. The last of those tools is advertising, and I talk about it somewhat reluctantly—not because it's not a useful tool in some cases, but because the expectations of what advertising can accomplish are so often unrealistic.

But you're going to do some advertising. We both know you are. It's the most visible form of marketing, so it's the first thing many business owners think about when they think about growing their business. It's also kind of a must-have for a local company or practice: you've just got to have a Yellow Pages ad. Everybody else does, so you feel you've got to have one, even though it's not always a great investment. It's a matter of keeping up with your competition and being at least as visible as they are. So since we can't ignore advertising, let's burst some of the bubbles surrounding it.

The major misconception about advertising is that it's great at making the phone ring. In general, this is not true. Sure, if your ad is

201

someone's fourth or fifth "touch" of your Personal Brand—if this person has already been exposed to your Personal Brochure, a direct mailer, and your Web site, for instance—then an ad in your local newspaper might be the last exposure that drives him or her to make the call. But by itself, advertising very rarely generates leads or new business.

This is in part because of the nature of Personal Branding. You're trying to get your personality across and portray yourself as an elite, top-flight professional who's different from your competitors. But a black-and-white newspaper ad lumps you in with a bunch of other advertisers and usually makes you look a little cheap and cheesy (it's rare to find a designer who can make a quarter-page newspaper ad look truly elegant and creative), so it's not a great match for Personal Branding. Of course, the really elegant advertising vehicles, such as full-page ads in glossy real estate or lifestyle magazines, are way beyond the budget of all but the most successful professionals, who don't need them anyway. So advertising can be a Catch-22: you advertise to stand out, but advertising makes you seem more like everyone else.

THINGS YOU CAN DO TODAY

1. Talk to local organizations about speaking opportunities.

2. Write a "Referral Promise" that you'll print in a classy form and give to all your clients, specifying how you'll treat anyone they refer to you.

3. Make sure that all e-mail addresses in your organization are changed to name@yourname.com.

4. Have your Internet marketing company shop around for the best deal on Web hosting—the best blend of price, service, speed, and reliability.

5. If you're targeting a specific company or organization (like a school), inquire about opportunities to publish in its internal newsletters or magazines.

6. If you have marketing or business partners, take a strategic lunch to make sure you're on the same page with branding and spending.

THE STUFF YOU'LL ACTUALLY DO

The other big myth about advertising is that it can convey something about your Personal Brand, like your values or your sense of humor. That's probably not true. When it comes to thinking about advertising, most people labor under what I call the "Budweiser fallacy," which is that advertising is all about huge budgets and the slow process of building a penetrating brand. That's fine if you're a huge corporation with $200 million to blow each year on TV spots and $8 million to spend on Super Bowl airtime. But if you're a small-town veterinarian or an interior designer, you can't afford that luxury. You need your ads to get results or you won't be able to afford to run them.

Most small-business advertising is about accomplishing two things: making your name and face more familiar, and making people aware of practical offers and discounts that will hopefully make the phone ring. Some ads do both. But most of the time, a small-business ad, whether it's in the newspaper or on a billboard, is your photo, your logo, your contact information, one sentence about what you do and whom you do it for, and maybe a quick "starburst" about a special offer for people who mention the ad when they call. There's not much room for personality or humor.

I don't want you to waste your money on bad advertising. I wrote this book to help you invest in your business the right way and give you an edge over the guys who are sinking all their cash into marketing that doesn't work. So in this chapter, I'm going to spend 95 percent of the time talking about the five types of advertising that make sense for your business:

1. Phone directory

2. Newspaper and magazine

3. Outdoor

4. Online local business directories

5. Sponsorships

THE OTHER 5 PERCENT

The other 5 percent is about television and radio advertising. You're probably never going to do either one. Either it's too expensive, it's totally inappropriate for your profession (medicine, law, and mental health come to mind), or you don't have viable broadcast outlets in your community. Don't lose sleep over it. For most professionals, being on TV or radio is about one thing: ego. They want to say, "Did you see my ad on Channel 8?"

That's not to say that television and radio ads can't be great for building your Personal Brand; they can be. But the risk-reward ratio is completely out of whack. Producing a radio or TV spot that doesn't sound or look like something done in your basement is tough and expensive; you've usually got to hire professional voice-over people, actors, producers, sound people, and so on. The rates, even for local radio and cable TV, can be outrageous. And if you decide to appear in your own ads, there's the very real possibility that you'll make a fool of yourself. On the reward side, you might get the phone to ring . . . maybe.

I advise my clients to steer clear of radio and TV ads until they've been branding for at least five years, or until their father buys the local station. It's good advice. There's plenty of opportunity to reach people with the other five types of advertising.

THINGS YOU CAN DO IN A WEEK

1. Talk to your IT pro about an automatic data backup system that backs up all your client files and vital data every day.

2. Use e-mail to promote your first teleseminar for your clients.

3. If you're thinking about writing a book, check out CreateSpace.com, an Amazon.com company that lets you sell books that are printed only when a customer orders them.

4. Ask three friends to critique your professional wardrobe and make changes if needed.

5. Plan a dinner to reward your staff members for their hard work in handling the branding transition and all the accompanying changes.

6. Negotiate a rights agreement with your photographer to allow you to use your main branding photos in a wider range of settings.

PHONE DIRECTORY ADS

Yellow Pages ads are just something you have to have; everyone does. I used to try to talk people out of running them until I realized that it was a completely futile gesture. Nobody wants to take the risk of being the only divorce lawyer in town without an ad in the section under "Attorneys." And really, this isn't a bad investment of your marketing dollars, because the phone directory is the one print advertising vehicle that people go to when they are ready to make a decision about a service provider. Most of the rest of the time, when someone encounters your ad, it's by accident.

So you're almost certainly going to run a Yellow Pages ad. Fine. Here are some tips on doing it right:

- Spend the extra money for accent color. The red or other colors in those ads definitely attract the eye.

- If you can, buy a full-page ad. Most ads are smaller, so you'll stand out.

- Always negotiate your ad rates.

- Buy a full year if the directory gives you a good discount. You can save a lot of money.

- Keep your ad simple: your photo, your logo, and a powerful headline that "declares the pain," as marketers like to say. In other words, use a few words to call out the reader's need. If you're a divorce lawyer, maybe your headline is "Specializing in Scream-Free Divorces." Then include a few bullet points that highlight your main services and include your phone number and Web address. That's it.

BRAND CASE STUDY

The Brand: David Riley, David Riley Associates Advertising Design

Specialization: High-end brand design and development, especially for Christian clients

Location: Costa Mesa, California

Channels: The Web, portfolios, direct mail, referrals

Highlights: Creating and writing a book on branding and image development

Online: www.rileydra.com

The Story: David Riley Associates doesn't do anything on the cheap. It's become known as one of the more expensive boutique branding and design shops in Orange County, California, but you can see the money in the results: gorgeous packaging, collateral, ads, coffee-table books, and more for major real estate developers, churches, and companies like Aqua Lung. All the way, David Riley's personal brand has guided the agency and brought his personal design aesthetic to the forefront.

How It All Started: "I left Disney 22 years ago," Riley says. "I had worked for Disneyland as creative director and art director. I planned to leave and start my own business, and they became my first client." Riley found offices in the beautiful coastal enclave of Corona Del Mar and started his agency with 3 people. Now it's up to more than 20 people and a client roster that includes Paramount Parks, bestselling author Joel Osteen, New Horizons Learning Centers, and Coldwell Banker Real Estate, to name just a few.

What This Brand Stands For:

- *Faith*. Riley is a devout Christian, and many of his clients are churches, Christian universities, or high-profile ministers such as Billy Graham. Not only does this open up a huge and growing market of companies and organizations for David Riley Associates, but it also creates a humane and positive attitude throughout the agency. Even with the constant deadline pressure, you've never seen a more laid-back ad shop than David Riley Associates.

- *High cost that's worth it.* "I consider us expensive," says Riley, "but that shows in the unique, memorable work we've been in a position to deliver. Being expensive works in our favor because it positions us as elite. People tell us, 'I hear you're expensive.' Now I go along with it. We're right there with the big firms. The high cost pays for the quality of the work that we do.

  "Price also helps us prequalify our clients. I don't mind being more expensive. The beauty of our business is that clients are buying art, so they're willing to pay more for creativity."

- *Beauty.* Riley's shop is becoming well known in the industry for producing marketing and branding tools that look gorgeous and even feel great to the touch. That's a vital part of his brand in a business where everything is about appealing to the audience's emotions.

X-Factor: Old-fashioned portfolios. Yes, this is the age of the Internet, and all ad agencies have their portfolios online because it's cheaper and easier than constantly reprinting expensive books. But Riley says that sometimes there's just no substitute for something you can hold in your hand.

"I still send out a quarterly publication that highlights some of our recent clients and projects," he says. "Now I'm producing a coffee-table book on the firm showing our work and our clients. A beautiful piece carries a huge amount of weight. I deal with presidents and CEOs, and they don't look at the Web. They would rather touch and feel something; they like looking at print pieces. We find that a lot of companies will research us on the Web, then when we go in for the presentation, the top people haven't seen us on the Web, so it's a nice leave-behind for me."

Branding Wisdom: "Listen to the client," Riley says. "Find out who they are, what their attitude is, how they run their business. Are they conservative or progressive? Are they serious in the way they do business, or light-hearted? I think a lot of creatives think they have the answers before they talk to the client.

"It's not just your logo. What is the voice and attitude of your organization? We get hired to create the logo, but I want to translate the

(continued)

attitude into the logo and the print material. Do you have a sense of humor in your business? Do you have a vision? People comment on my business card. They'll flip it over and see the irreverent comments on our people and they laugh, and I tell them, 'You've just gotten the flavor of my business.'"

NEWSPAPER AND MAGAZINE ADVERTISING

Newspaper advertising is definitely more common; not all communities have local magazines, and color advertising in some periodicals can be very costly. But after Yellow Pages advertising, this is the most common type of advertising. Newspaper advertising is familiar and reaches a cross section of a community, two reasons why business owners are comfortable with it. The greatest benefit of newspaper advertising comes from the nature of the newspaper itself: it's a regularly published medium. If you advertise in a daily paper every day, your name and face are reaching people constantly, reinforcing their awareness of you and making them more likely to remember you when they need the services you can provide.

With newspaper ads, there are several keys to success. The first is to know which section of the paper is best for your business. Does your paper have special weekly sections on things like health care and real estate? Those might be the best spots for your ad, depending on your profession. If you're in a financial field, the business section might serve you best. Talk to the paper's advertising manager about opportunities and rates in different sections. The ad department may have statistics on which sections have received the most response from readers.

Another key is, what do you want to achieve with your newspaper advertising? If you want to make the phone ring, you need to fill your ad with incentives and offers. On the other hand, if your goal is just to build brand awareness, running a nicely designed ad that tells people who you are and what you do, together with your contact information, is enough. Your goal will affect your ad design—an offer-filled ad will be plain and utilitarian by necessity, while a brand image ad needs to be clean, attractive, and professional. For branding ads, the look is everything; modern typefaces, a great photo of you, and a simple, powerful headline are about all you need.

The last key to newspaper advertising is negotiating rates and perks. For example, if you run a quarter-page ad daily, can you get a full-page "advertorial" once a week in the Sunday paper? Advertorials are faux articles that are actually ads for your business, and I've seen some fantastic ones. One of the best is a piece that runs every week in the *Santa Barbara Independent*, a weekly newsmagazine. It's by an attorney who specializes in drunk driving cases, and it tells the reader step by step what will happen when he or she is pulled over and how to handle each step in the process. It's an informative, gripping read. I've actually read the advertorial at least four times, which is unheard of. When you're negotiating ad rates, make sure to ask about special benefits, discounts for running a larger ad, and so on.

Magazines Are Different

Magazine advertising is a little more complicated, if only because magazine ads tend to be in color and therefore more costly to produce. Magazines are also specialty publications rather than general interest, so you'll reach only a targeted audience with them, and they have smaller circulation than a typical daily newspaper. So if you're considering spending your money on magazine advertising, I recommend doing it only if you can find a publication that hits your target market right in the bull's-eye.

A perfect example is *Homes and Land*, the regional real estate listing periodical. Most metro areas have multiple publications about homes for sale, and these are great ad locations not only for a Realtor, but also for a mortgage broker, appraiser, or inspector. On the other hand, if there's no magazine aimed at your profession, you can try one about lifestyle. If most of your ideal prospects are golfers, and there's a magazine in your area about golf, that's where your ads should go. A chiropractor or massage therapist might advertise in a local wellness magazine, but a general practitioner might not. If you can't find a magazine whose readership is ideal for your business, stick to the newspaper.

The exception would be if you have a big marketing budget and you're targeting the very affluent. Then, those glossy affluent lifestyle magazines that pop up in so many localities are a good brand-building tool. You see ads for Realtors, financial advisors, CPAs, lawyers, and other professionals all the time in these rich, beautiful periodicals. Advertising in them points up the great difference between magazines and newspapers: the design standards are much higher for magazines. You need better photos and a much more sophisticated look to make magazine ads work for you, because you have only one goal: brand building. No magazine comes out often enough to be a lead generator. The only thing you can do is communicate your brand's core points: your elite status, your quality, and your class.

BRAND SURGERY
THE PATIENT: YOUR ADVERTISING

- Be wary of "group" advertising deals, where a bunch of similar businesses pool their money to buy ad space. All this will do is tell readers that you're just like the others.

- Don't rely on figures that tell you the total number of visitors to a Web site when considering Web advertising or sponsorship. You need to know how many *unique* visitors the site gets each month.

- Don't confuse cleverness or creativity in ads with effectiveness. You're not interested in helping your designer or copywriter win an award; you want to bring prospects in the door.

- Do your homework before you sponsor an event you're unfamiliar with. You don't want to be associated with something your target market might find unsavory.

- Use Google Maps' "Street View" to scope out the perspectives on outdoor ad locations from many viewpoints. It's not available for every intersection, but it's a great tool.

Newspaper and Magazine Advertising Tips

- Always get a media kit. Verbal citations of ad rates or circulation mean nothing.

- Find out how each publication wants its ads delivered. Many are all-digital now, meaning that your designer can just e-mail high-resolution files. But some in smaller communities still work off of physical ad printouts. Find out what they need.

- Make sure your ads work with other channels. Include your Web address and include a call to action: "Call for a beautiful free brochure!" or an announcement of an upcoming seminar.

- Try to get a guarantee that your newspaper ad will run in the same *location* on the same page every time. Readers become accustomed to seeing a certain ad on a specific piece of page real estate, and this helps them remember you.

- Remember, all publications now have online counterparts. See if you can get a package deal of print and online advertising for a single price.

- Make sure all your ads maintain the common look of your Personal Branding: the typefaces, colors, and so on.

- Ask about special editions that might suit your business—a special section or issue on health care, for example, is a perfect opportunity for a doctor, dentist, or chiropractor.

OUTDOOR ADVERTISING

Billboards, bus-stop shelters, the sides of buses—these are some of the common places you'll find outdoor advertising. Outdoor ads can be very useful in making your presence known and establishing your Personal Brand over the long term. Outdoor ads are frequently something that you buy and leave alone, so after six months you "own" the billboard at the corner of First and Main. But remember that outdoor advertising can take a lot more forms these days:

- Building murals

- Temporary graffiti

- Posters

- Electronic signage

- Skywriting

- Banners towed by aircraft

- Ads on parking space dividers

In big cities, you can even find ads that automatically detect a person's wireless phone signal and send a customized ad about a coffeehouse or restaurant to that person's phone as he or she walks by. As with all forms of advertising, this may not be available in your area and may not be appropriate for your business. But when you're trying to get noticed and rise above the "noise," creativity helps. What helps even more, however, is where your outdoor ads appear. The central rule of outdoor is the same as in real estate: location, location, location. You want your ads to be visible to as many people as possible, and especially to your target market. So if you're a retirement planner, you probably don't want a billboard across from the high school, but you'd love the one across from the Hometown Buffet.

The keys to success with outdoor ads are not much different from those for print: negotiate smart deals, create packages if you can (buying ads on bus stops, billboards, and bus sides, for instance), and keep the design simple and clear. The design issue is especially important because most people are mobile when they see your outdoor ad. A driver might view your billboard for three seconds. If you try to do too much with it, you'll either confuse him or cause a fender bender. So keep outdoor advertising dummy-proof: a big image, a big headline, a big phone number or Web address, and that's it. Make the design more startling and creative (as compared to print advertising) so that it grabs the eye, just as with your Personal Brochure.

Most of all, don't overlook the most important piece of outdoor advertising you'll ever have: your signage. I see this all the time, and it's such a missed opportunity. Whether you have a curbside sign or a sign on your building, great signage should be your first investment in outdoor advertising. Make sure you check with your municipality to find out what kind of signage is allowable, but regardless of what you can do, follow the three rules of business signage:

1. Visibility

2. Visibility

3. Visibility

The main purpose of your signage is to make it easy for people to find you and for clients to refer you to others ("Just look for the big yellow sign on Main right after Chestnut"). If it helps burnish your brand, that's great, too. Make sure that your signage continues the look and feel of your main brand and that it's classy. Having a temporary banner on your building because your sign is still at the factory is worse than having no sign at all.

In trying to make outdoor ads work for you, you've really got to do your homework. Figure out through observation (outdoor ad companies sometimes have statistics on this as well) what age or income groups are most likely to frequent the areas where you might place ads. Ideally, you want to locate your ads in spots that receive a regular flow of foot or vehicle traffic and give you regular exposure to your target demographic. Think creatively: if you're going after women under 50, then maybe taking out an ad on that bus stop across from the Curves franchise is a good idea. On the other hand, if you're a landscape designer, the billboard facing Home Depot might be a winner.

THINGS YOU CAN DO IN A MONTH

1. Inquire about running ads in quality e-newsletters that reach your target market.

2. Look into creative outdoor advertising possibilities, such as paying for the naming rights of a nature trail.

3. Talk with a video production company about creating a DVD-based video presentation of your business that could run at trade shows.

4. Get cost and time quotes for designing and building a trade show exhibit booth for your company.

5. Talk to colleagues in your same line of work about co-exhibiting at a trade show.

6. Contact the alumni association of your university or graduate school and inquire about speaking at an alumni gathering. You might also ask about being written up in an alumni publication.

ONLINE LOCAL BUSINESS DIRECTORIES

We've already talked about Google Maps. But local search is one of the fastest-growing areas of Internet advertising as consumers use the Web to find service providers in their area and entrepreneurs try to accommodate them. Yahoo! has its own local business search service, as does Ask.com. Companies like Citysearch have built their businesses around providing complete local information, and directories like YellowPages.com capitalize on their existing print directory brand names to capture users.

Thanks to smart devices like the iPhone, local business search is also going mobile. Most companies like YellowPages.com have mobile services that allow you to search via your cell phone, and with smart devices, it's child's play to pull up Google Maps to find a local Indian restaurant or dry cleaner. How is all this relevant to your business?

I'd suggest focusing on searches done at home for the most part. Mobile searches tend to be impulse searches, and few people select a lawyer or an accountant on impulse. So you have two goals: to register with any free services like Google Maps' business finder, and to check out paid advertising packages with the paid directories. With the free services, the best you can do is make sure that they have your business in their database so that people can find out about you. With the paid services, you want to appear at or near the top of search rankings for your community.

There is a place for mobile search in your strategy: making sure people can find you. When prospects are en route, it's vital that they be able to use their smart device to locate your address and maybe even get a map to your location. The best advice is to see if you can bundle computer-based local search advertising with a mobile plan, so that you have the home and the car covered.

SPONSORSHIPS

Sponsorships are not right for every business. If you're strapped for cash, you're better off spending your money on direct mail and generating referrals. Also, if you're in a profession like criminal-defense law, advertising on the outfield wall of your local Little League may not be the way to go. But if you're tapped out on other tactics and are looking to become more widely known in your community, sponsorships are outstanding.

Basically, you pay to help support an event, sports team, or nonprofit institution, getting some free advertising in return. Some of the best things to sponsor are

- Local baseball and soccer teams

- Museums, symphonies, and other arts organizations

- Charity events like golf tournaments and 10K runs

- Concerts

- High school organizations

- County fairs and festivals

Sponsorship gets your name in front of a wide range of people, attached to something positive. It also paints you as someone who cares about your community and/or important causes. For a few thousand dollars (often much less), a sponsorship can buy you a great deal of goodwill. Some tips:

- Attend the event that you sponsor and carry business cards. Let people know that you're a sponsor, and make sure they know what you do.

- Leverage the sponsorship as a PR opportunity. If the event doesn't issue a press release about your sponsorship, issue your own.

- Provide your own program ad or signage. Don't let the organization create an ad for you by scanning your business card. You need something classier than that.

- Approach other sponsors of the same event about cross-promotion.

- Local radio and TV stations and publications are often sponsors of local events, so use your own sponsorship as an opportunity to create relationships with local media figures.

That's enough of the major brand marketing channels and tools that you're likely to use. As I said before, if you need information and tips on more tools, please visit www.thebrandcalledyou.com. Now let's get down to the real business at hand: creating a strategic plan for your Personal Brand and putting it into action.

BY NOW YOU SHOULD BE . . .

- Starting to analyze your return on ads, direct mail, and other tools and beginning to make adjustments

- Building a steady e-mail list from your Web site traffic

- Planning your first community outreach event

- Distributing your Personal Brochure to all the appropriate point-of-purchase locations in your city

- In the address book or Rolodex of most of the editors and program directors in your area, and maybe even have done a few interviews

PART IV

IT'S ALIVE! BRINGING YOUR BRAND TO LIFE IN 12 MONTHS

13

CREATE YOUR BRANDING STRATEGY

This democratization of personal branding is not likely to slow anytime soon. In fact, more and more "regular" people are joining the content-creation party.

—Beth Snyder Bulik, *Advertising Age*

If you've been reading the "By Now You Should Be . . ." sidebars at the end of each chapter, you might think that by now you should already be well on your way to using your Personal Brand to make a million dollars. Not so. True, with the information I've given you, it's possible to jump headfirst into brand marketing and be successful, but for the great majority of professionals, having a detailed plan increases the chances of success by an order of magnitude. You're a very busy person, and there aren't enough hours in the week for you to personally oversee every detail of your branding, marketing, and client service. That's what a One-Year Branding Plan is for.

The One-Year Branding Plan (OYBP) helps you do something that every businessperson needs to do: turn your investment of time and capital into new clients and new income as quickly as possible. Your OYBP maps out everything you'll be doing and spending and creates *systems* to make sure everything happens when it needs to happen and is handled by the right person. Believe me, systems are your friends. The busier you get as your Personal Brand fuels the growth of your company, the more you need automated systems to handle the important but routine work that you can't handle. Systems like the OYBP help you become successful without that success wrecking your health, your company, and your life.

BRAND CASE STUDY

The Brand: Tony Little

Specialization: America's personal trainer

Location: St. Petersburg, Florida

Channels: Infomercials, infomercials, infomercials. Also the Web, retail, books, and a presence in our cultural psyche

Highlights: Becoming the number one direct seller of all time

Online: www.tonylittle.com

The Story: Tony Little is so big that he's parodied. That's big. But he is an easy target: a buff dude with a ponytail and way too much adrenaline chewing on the sets of dozens of infomercials for his Gazelle line of cardio workout machines, screaming lines like, "You can do it!" In reality, Little is a calm, very nice man who just happens to be the most successful direct salesman in the history of television—more than $3 billion in products sold in 81 countries so far. Now he's a one-man industry, with books, food products, shoes, apparel, and, of course, his line of Gazelle aerobic gliders, which you can see almost any night if you're up late enough to watch the infomercial ecosystem come to life.

How It All Started: Little really was a riches-to-rags-to-riches story. He was an acclaimed junior bodybuilding champion who was bound for glory when he was struck by a school bus while driving. He sustained serious injuries but somehow managed to compete in a major bodybuilding event. However, the aftermath was a downward spiral of depression and painkiller addiction, with Little winding up 60 pounds overweight.

One day in 1985, he had had enough. He decided to get back in shape and change his life. In the process, he realized that what Americans were being told about fitness was misleading. He became determined to share his message of aerobic fitness combined with strength training and mental fortitude—the attitude that you can do anything if you stick with it and never give up. As a certified personal trainer and bodybuilder, he had the knowledge. What he lacked was the opportunity. But Little soon changed that.

"Too many people quit before they get there," he says. "When you come up with an idea, you have to act on it. I'm not afraid to ask questions. When I met Bud Paxson (creator of Home Shopping Network and PAX TV), it was because HSN had turned down my product. But I didn't say that was the end of my career. I found out that Bud's son owned a gym, so I went to the gym and made a deal with his son that I would promote the gym in return for a meeting with Bud. I drove behind Bud's son to the house, the gates opened, and when I met with Bud, he said, 'You've got five minutes.' I made my pitch and got the deal." And the rest is infomercial history.

What This Brand Stands For:

- *Passion*. Little isn't the same hyperkinetic guy you see on the infomercials, but he cares intensely about personal fitness and about quality. "The ability to train mom, dad, and the kids via TV or video or multimedia is what I'm all about," he says. "I developed my brand with the concept that I was a high-integrity, high-motivation personal trainer with a lot of experience, and that I could help them change their lives. But the whole thing has expanded into health and nutritional products. Now one of my biggest areas is my sleep category. I've sold 3 million of my pillows already. That was funny, because everyone thought, 'This guy's so hyper and energetic, he never sleeps.' But when you have a passion for something and you really believe it's going to benefit people, you can sell it."

- *Wellness*. Early on, Little was really indignant about how the American public was being sold a bill of goods about fitness. The prescription was cardio and eat lots of grains. Nothing about
  (continued)

221

strength training, nothing about flexibility training, nothing about sleep or attitude or self-belief. So he has set out to address all those concerns and give people what he believes is a complete solution to keeping mind and body healthy.

- *Tenacity.* I think the story about coming back from a devastating car accident in six weeks to compete in a bodybuilding event, then getting himself back in shape after drug addiction, *then* creating a million-dollar sales career out of nothing says it all. Little doesn't know the meaning of the word *quit.*

X-Factor: Parodies and TV. Everybody who's anybody has taken a crack at Little's ponytailed, too-much-caffeine muscleman persona. I mean, the guy did one of those wacky Geico insurance commercials like Joan Rivers. Little loves it all. "I have quite an imprint," he says. "I was mentioned in the movie *Juno.* I've done all the talk shows, and footage of me doing my infomercials has been licensed and used on TV and movies about 80 times. I just licensed footage of me doing an infomercial for the Rock 'n' Roll Stepper on HSN for a Jim Carrey movie called *Yes Men.*

"I was written into a Bruce Springsteen song, '57 Channels and Nothing On.' I figure he got home from a gig and wanted to watch some TV and couldn't get away from me. The line was something like 'Tony Little, will you please kill yourself.' That cracks me up. I love the parody stuff. I love comedy and laughter. There was an Alec Baldwin parody where he dressed up as me, I think on *Saturday Night Live. Beavis and Butt-head, South Park,* all of them have done me.

"I've done two *MADtvs* and I've done a sketch with (wrestler) Steve Austin. I did a sketch for VH1 that was a parody on Matthew McConaughey where he was selling the 'McConaughsizer,' a picnic table made into an exercise machine. I love all of it."

Branding Wisdom: "You find a way to get it done and think outside the box. Traditional doesn't work. You have to find creative ways to get it done. I back things all the way. There's no overnight success."

BUDGETING

How much does this Personal Branding stuff cost? The answer is, it depends. It's not cheap. If you're used to doing everything for your business in the lowest-cost manner possible, you're going to have to change your ways. Remember, Personal Branding is about marketing you, but it's also about attracting superior clients who make you more money. That means enhancing your image, positioning you as an elite, top 1 percent player in your profession—one of the best of the best. You can't do that with cheesy brochures and a template Web site. You need quality in every aspect of your business, and quality translates to money.

Successful professionals usually spend between 15 and 25 percent of their gross income on marketing their Personal Brand. OK, if you just spit your coffee all over this book, please wipe it up and go get another cup. Yes, you read right. That's a lot of money, but you can't create a brilliant, winning brand on the cheap. There are always ways to save, of course, but in the end you're going to have to hire other specialists to give you the services you require to make your brand come alive: printers, designers, Web developers, copywriters, signage makers, interior decorators, photographers. They're going to want to get paid what they're worth. If you go to a cheap alternative, you're going to get what you pay for.

Think about what you tell your clients when you're doing their taxes, guiding them through the legal system, or selling their house: *when something is this important, the cost of using the best is much lower than the cost of not using the best.* I think we can agree that it's much cheaper to pay $750 for a top CPA to do your taxes than to be audited by the IRS. Heck, think about what you're going to tell your ideal clients when you've cut loose your B and C clients and raised your fees by 25 percent! You're probably going to say, "I'm working to take my skill set and service level to the top 1 percent of my profession, and I need to charge accordingly," or something to that effect. The point is that quality always costs, but you really do have to spend money to make money. The key is spending it right.

Remember when I said that good Personal Branding was worth a 100 percent increase in gross revenues for a typical business in the first 12 months? Let's say you gross $100,000 today and you normally spend about $5,000 a year on marketing. You decide you're going to spend $20,000 on a complete Personal Branding campaign. It's going to be a challenge, and you're going to have to tighten your belt, but you know it's the only way you're going to get off the treadmill. So you launch your brand, and over the 12 months, you actually need to increase your spending to $25,000 for the year, but your gross income doubles in that time, to $200,000. Yes, you've spent $25,000, but you've also increased your income after marketing expenses from $95,000 to $175,000—a jump of 84 percent in a single year! It's not what you spend, but what you make that counts.

THINGS YOU CAN DO TODAY

1. Collect minor facts about your business and keep them in a file to use in future marketing.

2. Talk to your more socially adept staff members about going to networking events in your place, so that you can be in two places at once.

3. Talk to someone at your local post office about the best ways to use direct mail.

4. Talk to a local radio station about bartering on-air advertising time for your professional services.

5. Offer to give free speeches to groups like the Elks or Kiwanis.

6. Join a networking group like LeTip.

STEP 1: DO THE NUMBERS

If we're going to move on, you're going to have to trust me. So forget about the scary numbers and let's look at creating our budget. But before you can start, you need to set your revenue goals:

Your previous 12-month gross revenue: _____

Your goal for the next 12 months: _____

Now you need two budgets:

1. *Brand launch budget.* This is going to be the amount you'll need to spend at the expensive Personal Brand creation stage, where you're having things designed and written and programmed. It's the start-up costs of your renewed business. There's a pretty basic formula for this that I like to give my clients:

   Additional income desired ÷ _____
   = brand launch budget

   The number in the space depends on your situation:

   • If you have a lot of money but little time, divide by 3.

   • If you have a lot of time but little money, divide by 5.

   • If you have little of either, divide by 4.

   So if you decide that you're looking for $80,000 in new business in the next year and you have plenty of time but little capital, your brand launch budget would be $80,000 divided by 5, or $16,000. If you have plenty of cash but no time, it would be about $27,000. Why the difference? Because if you have time, you can do things yourself that you would otherwise have to pay someone to do, like label postcards.

2. *Client retention budget.* This is your annual budget for ongoing brand marketing, from overprinting Personal Postcards and postage to gifts for professional referral sources and travel to networking events. I've got a cool formula for this one as well:

   Previous 12-Month Revenue × 10% = _____

   So if you made $80,000 last year, you should plan on spending $8,000, or about $667 per month, to maintain your client relationships and branding. That covers expenses like buying ad space, traveling to networking events, and paying the postage for Personal Postcards, in addition to your regular costs like paying your staff.

   Add the two and you get what you should expect to spend during your first year as a Personal Brander. In the case of our hypothetical example (assuming that the person is time-rich and cash-poor), the total branding budget would be $16,000 plus $8,000, or $24,000. That's a lot of money to spend when you're grossing $80,000 a year. But if you can be grossing $160,000 at the end of 12 months, isn't it worth it?

You're going to want to find out what branding services really cost, and that gets tricky. Some prices are going to be different in different markets. In the following table, I've given you my best experienced estimates on the costs of some services while suggesting the best ways to find out others:

Expense	Guesstimate/Resource to Contact
Printing	Shop the same job to 3 printers
Photography	Get quotes from 3 photographers
Graphic design	$50–$100 per hour
Copywriting	$50–$100 per hour
Postage	If bulk rate, depends on the number of pieces mailed; see your post office for detailed information
Photocopying	3 to 6¢ per copy
Mailing fulfillment house fees	Usually by the job, depending on volume; call for proposals
Direct mail lists	Can vary widely; contact list companies for specific numbers
Web hosting	Shouldn't be more than $50 a month for full-featured package, $25 for basic
Advertising space	Ask for or download media kits
Sponsorships	Contact the organization behind the event
Gifts	Varies; see the Appendix for a list of gift websites

At this stage, it's also time to ask some important questions about what you want to achieve—not just for your business, but for yourself. Remember, the purpose of building a brand isn't just to make more money but to create a lifestyle. How much do you want to make, and what kind of life do you want that money to buy?

- What is your broad goal (e.g., to be in the top 1 percent of insurance brokers in the state)?

- This year my pretax income was _____.
- My pretax income goal for next year is _____.
- My pretax income goal for three years from now is _____.
- My pretax income goal for five years from now is _____.
- To reach next year's income goals, I need _____ ideal clients.
- I also want to reach this milestone:

  _____

- I'd like to reach this milestone, too:

  _____

- Remember, I'm doing all this so I can:

  _____

That last one is critical. The reason you're doing everything is to create the lifestyle you want. Never lose sight of that. Personal Branding is expensive and unnerving, and it can take a while to show results. During the first three months, you might have moments of panic when you feel like you've thrown your money down a black hole. During those times, it can help to remember that every smart decision you make brings you one step closer to your vacation home and every Friday off to spend with your kids.

THINGS YOU CAN DO IN A WEEK

1. Create a "work-free zone" at home, a span of time that's just about family and relaxation, not about branding.

2. Begin an "advocate list." These are people who can be counted on to rave about you and your services. Stay in touch with them at least every 30 days.

(continued)

3. Set up an evening of coaching and Q&A for 20 ideal prospects.

4. Rent time at a recording studio and have a friend interview you *60 Minutes* style about your business. This gives you a ready interview for radio stations.

5. Contact charities about donating your services, such as legal services.

6. Research marketing or success speakers and seminars that sound promising. Sign up for the ones that fit your budget and that you think you'll like.

STEP 2: HOW DO PEOPLE SEE YOU?

You already have a Personal Brand. Your customers and prospects already have an image of you, perceive your abilities in a certain way, and have a few words that come to mind when your name comes up. So you're not working in a vacuum, which can be a mixed blessing. On the one hand, clients may have a strong, positive perception that's in line with what you would like your Personal Brand to be. On the other hand, your target market may hold some damaging misperceptions of you. Before you set out to create your Personal Brand, you need to know what kind of "brand baggage" you're carrying around.

You can't know where to go unless you know where you're starting from. The solution to this is to talk to people. Put on your journalist hat and start by interviewing your clients. You could e-mail them a written questionnaire, but the response rate for these is abysmal. I suggest inviting 20 clients to lunch and asking them the following questions in person, tape recording the answers so that you miss nothing:

1. What do you like most about working with me?

2. What do you like least?

3. What three words do you think describe me best?

4. How do I provide value for you?

5. What do you think I stand for in the community?

Don't stop there. Interview colleagues, business leaders, and others who aren't your clients. Ask them:

1. What do you think my strengths are?

2. What do you think I do?

3. What do you think other people say about me?

When you break down all your interviews, you should be looking for certain patterns and sets of data: words or phrases that come up repeatedly, words you've never heard used about you, and opinions that either confirm what you think about yourself or contradict your own self-image. The sum total of this information will tell you how you are perceived in the community today. That is your Personal Brand right now.

The key question is this: how does the way you are perceived today differ from the way you want to be perceived as part of your new Personal Brand? A good way to track this is to write two columns on a sheet of paper:

How I'm Perceived   How I Need to Be Perceived

Complete the second column first. Write down the qualities you want to be associated with the Personal Brand that's going to make you rich: expertise, family man, and so on. Then be brutally honest with yourself, go through the comments from your interviews, and write down how people perceive you. How similar are the two lists? If they're fairly close, then most of the work your brand needs to do is to reinforce the perception that people already hold. If they're far apart—if your Personal Brand needs to position you as "conservative," but people perceive you as "a flaming liberal"—you've got some work to do to change people's minds.

Most likely, you'll be somewhere in the middle. About 90 percent of business owners and professionals fall into that category, and if you're one of them, you don't need to do anything extraordinary. Just create your Personal Brand with care and market it with originality and persistence. Time will take care of the rest.

BRAND SURGERY
THE PATIENT: YOUR BRAND STRATEGY

- Don't promote your "individuality" to the exclusion of all else. Prospects don't care about your quirks. They want value.

- Don't create a brand that promises public behavior that you can't continue in private. If you brand yourself as a paragon of virtue but can be found drinking in dive bars at 2 a.m., you'll alienate clients.

- Don't overpromise. If you're inexperienced, focus on something else. Once you get more experience, you can rebrand, but if you promise too much and can't deliver, those bridges are just waiting for a match to go up in flames.

- Don't be shy. If you're hesitant about telling people how good you are at your specialty, get over it. Personal Branding isn't for the timid.

- Do be aggressive in setting yourself apart from your competition. More than one branding campaign has been over before it began because the business owner lost his nerve and became "just another insert-profession-here."

- Don't interview friends about how you're perceived. They won't be honest with you. Talk to clients who know you well, ask them to be honest, and if they hurt your feelings, take it. Like medicine, it's good for you.

STEP 3: BUILD YOUR PERSONAL BRAND

Now it's time to decide what your Personal Brand really is. Two factors drive this decision:

1. Your values, your personality, and the things you care about

2. How you need people to perceive you if you are to reach your income and growth goals

You must be authentic above all else. However, you also need to know what qualities you should emphasize or what aspects of your service need to be brought out in order to earn the money you want to earn. You should never adopt personality traits solely to attract more clients, but if your target market values convenience and time savings highly, there's nothing wrong with emphasizing those areas of value in your brand and adjusting your business model to match.

This process has three steps of its own.

A. Choose Your Target Market

You can't finish your Personal Brand until you know your target market. Take a close look at the types of customers you've been working with over the past year or two and answer these questions:

- Which clients produce the highest hourly earnings?

- Which clients generate the most referrals?

- Which prospects seem most receptive to my work style?

- Which prospects have the potential to make me the most money?

- Which prospects have the most growth potential?

- Which people do I enjoy working with most?

- Which prospects do I have the most in common with, in terms of lifestyle and personality?

The result should be one group of clients that stands head and shoulders above the rest. Once you have this, answer these questions about the group:

- What do the members of this group have in common?

- Can I reach my income goals with this group?

- Is there an unmet need that I can meet?

- What is that need?

- Based on their culture, values, and background, will the members of this group perceive the value in my Personal Brand?

- Can I afford to market to this group?

- Are there marketing channels that will reach these people?

- Is the market free of any dominant competitors?

If the people in this group have some things in common, such as geographic location, interests, religion, or life stage, and the other answers are in the affirmative, you've got your target market. If not, set that group aside for later and choose another that passes the test. Now describe your target market in the most specific terms possible. Examples:

- Affluent couples living near the Breezewood Country Club

- Boeing engineers less than three years from retirement

- Divorced women in their forties

- Cycling enthusiasts

- People of Pacific Islander descent

- People interested in organic, "green" lifestyles

Estimate how many households there are in this target market. How many of those do you need to capture to reach your income goals? How many of them are your clients now? If you need to capture more than 20 percent of a target market to make the money you want, then that market is too small. Make sure your market is sufficiently large to allow you to grow realistically.

B. Write Your Specialization Statement

You know to whom you're marketing your brand. Now you need to determine what that brand is. Specialization is the most important branding decision you can make, because it decides whether people will perceive you as unique or as just another service provider. Keeping in mind how people perceive you now and how you want to be perceived, go through the parts of the Specialization Statement.

1. Who You Are

Keep it simple. Just tell the market what you do. You're a physician, a physical therapist, a real estate agent. Be clear and quick.

2. *What You Do and Whom You Do It For*

Here's where you can start to slip in some more precise branding and suggest how you create value for the people you're targeting. Let's say "who you are" is a physical therapist. Describing what you do as "helping people rehabilitate from injuries" is generic and boring. It does nothing to enhance your brand. But once you focus on your ideal client and target market, you can be more precise. So your statement becomes, "Helping pro athletes get back on the field."

This statement not only tells people whom you specialize in working with, but suggests that you understand the professional athlete culture and know about sports injuries.

This imaginary professional's Specialization Statement would be: "A physical therapist helping pro athletes get back on the field." That might lead to a slogan like, "Helping pro athletes get back in the game."

C. Choose Your Leading Attribute

We can't finish without adding some personal elements that make you You. This bit of "personality" is your *Leading Attribute*, a quality that makes you different from everyone else in your market. It won't be part of your Specialization Statement; instead, you'll use it to direct the look, feel, and style of your brand marketing. Your Leading Attribute can come from your lifestyle, education, family background, religion, hobbies—whatever genuinely reflects the distinct person you are. It should also be likely to appeal to your target market. Examples:

- Surfer

- Harvard graduate

- Classic-car collector

- Former Air Force pilot

- Native of Germany

- Born-again Christian

Whatever Leading Attribute you choose to build your Personal Brand around, it will become central to the *expression* of your brand. Let's say our physical therapist is a woman who runs triathlons in her spare time. That's an attribute that's sure to appeal to ultracompetitive professional athletes. So her Personal Brochure might feature a cover photo of her running in the desert, while her logo might feature a runner as an icon . . . and so on. Your brand's Leading Attribute will influence how you express your brand in photos, graphics, copy, colors, office design choices, gifts, and even where you locate your office.

THINGS YOU CAN DO IN A MONTH

1. Get three to five friends in any profession together to create a "mastermind group" that gets together monthly to share ideas, life goals, and support.

2. Check into getting a marketing coach, an experienced marketing professional who can help keep you motivated and on track. Find him or her by searching online under "marketing coach."

3. Turn some of your most dramatic client/patient stories into case studies that you can use for marketing. Keep in mind that you'll need to change the names to protect confidentiality.

4. Brainstorm ways in which you could create a simpler, more streamlined, lower-cost version of your current service offering.

5. Brainstorm ways you can save your clients' time, then use time savings as a major branding message.

6. Select a Client of the Year and plan something special to honor that person.

STEP 4: CHOOSE YOUR WEAPONS

Finally, what Personal Branding channels are you going to use? The 21 branding channels are these:

1. Buzz marketing

2. Canvassing

3. Client referrals

 4. Direct mail

 5. Indoor advertising

 6. The Internet

 7. Networking

 8. Outdoor advertising

 9. Point-of-purchase display

10. Print advertising

11. Professional referrals

12. Public relations

13. Publishing

14. Radio advertising

15. Seminars—Private

16. Seminars—Public

17. Special events

18. Sponsorships

19. Telemarketing

20. Television advertising

21. Trade shows

I recommend that no matter what business you're in, you use the following channels because they are very cost- and time-effective:

- Direct mail (Personal Brochures and Personal Postcards)
- The Internet (a Web site)
- Professional referrals
- Special events

In terms of branding tools, you've got to have a Personal Brochure and Brand Identity—logo, business cards, letterhead, and so on.

Those are the essentials. But because of the Rule of Five, you'll need at least five ways to reach your target market. So think of other channels you might use with the tools you're going to create. You might use your Personal Brochure as a networking tool and attend a ton of professional networking events, or turn your logo into spectacular exterior signage, a form of outdoor advertising.

Review the channels and see which ones best fit (1) your time, (2) your budget, (3) your personality, and (4) your target market. Then choose your weapons and list them here:

The Channel I'm Using	The Tool I'm Using for It
Point of purchase	Personal Brochure
1. _____	_____
2. _____	_____
3. _____	_____
4. _____	_____
5. _____	_____

Congratulations on making it this far! You've climbed a huge hill: deciding what your Personal Brand will be and how you'll communicate it to the world. Now it's time to move to the next step: getting organized and launching your brand.

BY NOW YOU SHOULD BE . . .

- Determining if you need to increase your budget

- Starting to see some professional referrals

- Seeing a change in how people treat you after receiving your Personal Brochure

- Meeting more people who know who you are and what you do

- Charging more!

14

LAUNCH YOUR ONE-YEAR BRANDING PLAN

I would like to see the Pope wearing my T-shirt.

—Madonna

All the pieces should be in place by now: your Specialization Statement, your Leading Attribute, your target market, your goals, and your choice of channels and tools. You have at least some idea of what you want your Personal Brand to be and whom you want to capture as your perfect wealth-producing clients or patients. The only thing left is to, as Alan Shepard said in *The Right Stuff*, "light this candle." Welcome to the end of the beginning—launching your One-Year Branding Plan.

At this time, there are a few questions I find it helpful to ask:

- Do my attire, my jewelry, and even my car support my brand's image?

- Do the trappings of my lifestyle support it?

- Has everything been proofread and all print jobs inspected for quality?

- Are there any pieces missing, such as signage?

- Do I know what I'm going to say when someone asks me, "Why the change?"

- Have I planned a surprise event to thank my staff for helping me launch my brand?

It's easy to get nervous as you get ready to spend all this money and put your professional future on the line, and simple, grounded questions like these not only help you clear your head, but also help you address small issues before they become big ones. Now, let's get your Branding Timetable together and launch this thing.

THINGS YOU CAN DO TODAY

1. Create a real or online suggestion box for your staff.

2. If your business is seasonal, such as tax preparation, check into special seasonal advertising rates.

3. Think about any non-English languages in which your marketing materials might need to be produced.

4. Does your signage need to be visible at night? Take a look.

5. Designate one day a month as "Q&A Day." On this day, you won't see any clients. You'll just take calls and answer questions, no obligation.

6. Do sample searches on the major Internet search engines and see where your business comes up when you use different search terms.

YOUR BRANDING TIMETABLE

A good first step is to recap all the pieces you have in place. Write down

1. Your goals

2. Your target market

3. Your Specialization Statement

4. Your Leading Attribute

5. Your Branding Channels and tools

Great. There's really only one thing you need in order to get going, and that's a master plan to determine what happens when for the next 12 months. Amazingly enough, that's what I'm going to help you create in this chapter: a Branding Timetable.

Your Branding Timetable is a week-to-week, month-to-month matrix that lists all your Personal Branding channels and lays out when everything involved in making each of those channels work needs to happen, and who is responsible for making sure that it happens. It's the master calendar of your branding efforts, and when you finish it, I suggest that you print it about eight feet long and post it on the wall of your office so no one can miss it. Your Branding Timetable should list

1. Your Branding Channels.

2. The activities and deadlines related to each channel; e.g., under Direct Mail, you might put "Copy," "Printing," "Six-Week Blitz," "12-Month Drip," and "Personal Brochure."

3. Who is responsible for ensuring that each of these activities gets done.

4. Columns for each month of the year, broken into weeks.

Your Branding Timetable should look something like this:

Branding Timetable											
Month	July				August				September		
Week	7	14	21	28	5	12	19	26	1	8	15	22
Activity												
Prof. Referrals												
Lead generation	X				X				X			
Resp: Patti												
Meetings		X				X				X		
Resp: Patti												
Relationship			X				X					X
Resp: Patti												

(continued)

Branding Timetable (*continued*)											
Month	July				August				September			
Week	7	14	21	28	5	12	19	26	1	8	15	22
Activity												
Client Events												
Venue booking		x										
Resp.: Geoff												
Invitations						x						
Resp: Geoff												
Entertainment								x				
Resp: Geoff												
Direct Mail												
Printing		x										
Resp: Mary												
12-Month Drip	x				x				x			
Resp: Mary												
Personal Bro.										x		
Resp: Tom												
6-Week Blitz				x	x	x	x	x	x			
Resp: Mary												

You end up with a full year's schedule spelling out every branding activity and logistical action that needs to take place, when it needs to happen, and who's responsible for making sure that it happens. You can also add a column at the end of each activity to enter how much it cost, and a field at the end of each month totaling how much you spent that month on your branding activities. Some people even add a field below that to enter how many new clients they added each month. These are great ways to track your return on investment in real time.

I would also suggest reproducing your Brand Timetable in electronic form using free calendar software like Yahoo Calendar or Google Calendar. These calendars are marvelous tools because they can be accessed anywhere with a computer and an Internet connection and

---

BRAND SURGERY
THE PATIENT: YOUR BRAND LAUNCH

- Don't launch your brand piecemeal by sending your brochure one week, direct e-mail the next, and so on. Instead, it's wiser to use a "flip the switch" strategy, where you get everything in place—ad placement, direct mail, Web site, press releases—and roll it all out within two or three days. This creates greater impact and awareness.

- Celebrate your brand launching with a special event like a Grand Re-Opening party at your newly decorated office, and invite the press.

- Inspect all your printed materials thoroughly before approving them. With your first round of mailings, perfect quality is especially crucial.

- Focus on the "new" in your brand messaging for the first 30 days after your launch. This will remind people that you're doing something special.

- Drop the "new" messaging after 30 days. You want everyone new to assume that you've always been this polished, suave marketing machine.

---

because you can program them to send e-mail alerts or wireless phone text messages when certain tasks are due. Make sure that everyone in the office knows how to use and update your online calendar.

Once it's done, your Branding Timetable becomes your brand marketing bible. It's the master schedule for every activity; it should be the first thing you and your staff look at when you come into the office in the morning. It's going to be the prime mover of all marketing activity for your business, and the great thing about it is that even when you're away, the tasks can still get done. This frees you to sell less and network, speak, or vacation more. Make yourself the responsible person for as few Personal Branding activities as possible. This frees you to travel, take a vacation, or focus your time on what you do best: providing the valuable service that keeps clients returning.

THINGS YOU CAN DO IN A WEEK

1. Have one of your staff come up with a list of books that would be helpful and of interest to your clients, and create a waiting room library.

2. Establish a finder's fee for anyone who refers you a new prospect who becomes a client.

3. If you send invoices to your clients, use them as an opportunity to send branding materials or information about special offers.

4. Plan your first lengthy vacation (no working!) six months after you begin your branding campaign, no matter what the results.

5. Spend some time commenting on blogs run by others in your profession in order to build up your reputation and draw people to your Web site.

6. Consider and price car signage.

YOUR BRANDING HANDBOOK

The second tool you'll need for your brand launching is your Branding Handbook. This is a tabbed three-ring binder or a Web page (preferably both) that details all the minutiae involved in managing your brand. Some of the information that should be in your handbook is

- Names and contact information for vendors (printers, mailing houses, designers, and so on)

- Prices for each service you're receiving, from graphic design to Web hosting

- Names and contact information for your professional referral partners

You may want to combine your handbook with your client-service procedures so that everything is in one place. I also suggest building "triggers" into your Branding Handbook—preset conditions that, when they occur, set certain events in motion. For example, when you gain a new client by referral, a notation in the "referral clients" section of your handbook reminds a staff member to send a thank-you gift to the person who gave you the referral.

Use automation whenever you can to extend your and your team's capabilities. With direct e-mail companies, e-mails can sometimes be scheduled and locked in months in advance, while things like client updates can be provided online and clients notified by e-mail. Automatic systems can send reminders of their appointments to clients' mobile phones. Make technology your time-saving ally.

BRAND CASE STUDY

The Brand: Kathy Kaehler

Specialization: Celebrity trainer and spokesperson

Location: Los Angeles, California

Channels: *Today Show*, Exercise TV, Lifetime Network, books, newspaper articles, the Web, personal training

Highlights: Thirteen years on the *Today* show

Online: www.kathykaehlerfitness.com

The Story: Kaehler always intended to have a career in fitness, earning a B.A. in Exercise Science and Dance Education and interning at the Coors Wellness Center. But she never set out to be a celebrity personal trainer. She began working for Jane Fonda at her exclusive Laurel Springs Retreat in Santa Barbara, California. Eventually, she was the official fitness expert for the *Today* show, the author of seven books, and known around Southern California as the "personal trainer to the stars." Yes, she regularly helps major celebrities like Julia Roberts and Kim Basinger stay in shape, but that's only one small part of who she is and what she aspires to.

How It All Started: "I just fell into being at the right place at the right time, meeting Jane Fonda," she says. "She was looking for someone to

(continued)

be her program director and trainer for a very private, small spa that she was going to have on her property in Santa Barbara. Her customers were from the entertainment business. So that's when I started training celebrities.

"After two years of driving from Santa Barbara to L.A. every day, I started picking up more clients. I would start with the first at 6 a.m. and take my last at 7 p.m. But I ended up with a list of A-list clients, and that led to me getting on the *Today* show a year after Katie Couric started. I wrote a letter to Katie saying I'd like to be on the show, and within 24 hours I got a call back from Katie herself. I said, 'The *Today* show has been on all my life, but you guys don't do anything for fitness, you should have me on.' I met with her, they took me upstairs, I signed a contract, and I was on for 13 years."

What This Brand Stands For:

- *Fitness*. Kaehler has planned her brand every step of the way and has a manager, a publicist, and an agent who assist her in making the most of opportunities. As a result, she is very well-known in the fitness world. However, she is still first and foremost a working personal trainer who conducts training sessions every week with a very exclusive clientele. "I still teach five days a week, when I'm in town," she says. "I teach a semiprivate circuit class in my home. It's very fulfilling to me because that's my whole job, stemming from what I've learned by training people, and I still love it. That's my brand: I am a trainer. I can get someone who's unfit fit."

- *Professionalism*. Kaehler isn't starry-eyed about her role as a personal trainer for the bold and the beautiful. Like any professional, she's dedicated to doing her job, but she's aware that training the famous has helped her career. "I don't mind the 'personal trainer to the stars' title because my first clients were celebrities, and I continue to work with celebrities. It's been a very interesting chapter in my life, and a way to generate my message and get it out there."

- *Communication*. She's written seven books on health and well-being for women, teens, and people who have busy lives. She's great at breaking down an intimidating topic like fitness into bite-size pieces, such as her five-minute workouts—small, rigorous sessions that can slip into any busy day. Her next product is a piece of fitness equipment that she has designed and developed herself: Gym in a Box.

X-Factor: She's become the go-to trainer for the hit reality show *Keeping Up with the Kardashians,* and is also working on Exercise TV. It seems like Kaehler is popping up everywhere: *Time* magazine, the new Nissan Master Trainer, and in a series of workouts for *TV Guide.* She's proof that you don't need a horde of paparazzi following you around to be famous.

Branding Wisdom: "I'm known for my simple approach to fitness. My training techniques are easy to do, but challenging. Yes, I am a celebrity fitness trainer, but I can train someone in a state-of-the-art facility, a celebrity home gym, or someone's garage. My goal is to educate and motivate people to live active, healthy lives. I stay with those core beliefs and message so people always know what they're getting."

THE FIRST 30 DAYS

There's so much to do in launching a Personal Brand that it can seem overwhelming. Once you finish your brand strategy, the clock starts ticking, and this list is enough to get you started.

1. Get your logo designed and print your new business cards.

2. Print new stationery, mailing labels, note cards, and envelopes with your new logo and slogan.

3. Order new signage or anything else that will feature your logo.

4. Complete your Branding Timetable.

5. Get top-quality photos taken.

6. Design, write, and print your Personal Brochure and Personal Postcards.

7. Design and launch a basic version of your Web site: home page, bio page, services page, portfolio or case studies page, and contact information. You can always add other pages and features later.

8. Send out your initial press kit.

9. Take out a phone directory ad, if that's appropriate to your business.

10. Send a personal letter to your current base of clients, colleagues, and professional contacts explaining your Personal Brand launch, your reasons behind it, and what you hope to do for them in the future.

11. Send Dear John letters to your B and C clients, wishing them well and referring them to other providers.

12. Redo your office as appropriate to work with your brand and your new client-service philosophy.

13. Create your Branding Handbook and client-service guide in hard copy and online.

14. Buy or compile your initial direct-mail list and/or direct-e-mail list.

As you implement each step in the brand launching, check it off on your Branding Timetable. Right after this 30-day period, you'll want to start sending your direct-mail pieces and starting your professional referral outreach. You'll have your Personal Brochure, Personal Postcards, and Web site, so you're in a great position to network, ask for referrals, send people to the Web to learn more about you, and make a fantastic impression.

THINGS YOU CAN DO IN A MONTH

1. Have your graphic designer create a "style manual" that details every element of your visual branding, from typefaces and sizes to colors and the position of elements.

2. Consider (and check into the legality of) a satisfaction guarantee, if this makes sense for your profession.

3. Become a regular contributor to the Answers section of LinkedIn .com.

---

4. Think of a contest or competition and run it by your client advisory board.

5. If this is appropriate for your practice, consider saving money by sharing office space with another professional.

6. Speak to 10 high-profile local celebrities about the possibility of endorsing you.

WHAT TO SAY TO PEOPLE YOU WORK WITH NOW

It's important that you let your current clients and prospects know why you're launching a new Personal Brand and what it means to them. Direct mail is OK; personal contact by phone or face-to-face is better. Either way, explain that you're launching this new identity to help you grow your business and to focus on the areas where you provide the greatest value to your clients, and that this will in no way change your availability for them.

It's reassurance, it's courtesy, and it's good business sense. Who knows? If your clients or colleagues understand marketing, they might help you spread the word.

THE PEOPLE ON YOUR TEAM

Throughout this book, I've talked about your staff or your team. But that's not a one-size-fits-all issue. You may have a staff of six people working under you, or you may have no staff at all. So it's not as simple as saying, "Have your staff do it." As you get ready to launch your Personal Brand, the issue of who's going to help you launch and maintain it becomes vitally important.

My basic advice is this: *don't launch your brand alone*. It's nearly impossible for one person working solo to launch and maintain a complex Personal Brand while also providing sterling-quality work and client service. If you try to do it all, you'll more than likely wind up angering clients, wasting money, and pushing your goals years farther into the future. My advice would be that if you're working alone today, find the money to hire at least a personal assistant. Better yet, hire a person and designate her Brand Manager. She becomes responsible for implementing all the steps on your Brand Timetable and making sure your client-service processes get followed. Then I would suggest going out and contracting with a virtual assistant (Virtual Assistant Networking Association, www.vanetworking.com, is a great place to look), someone who will handle your basic needs, like phone calls, faxing, record keeping, and so on. Virtual assistants will charge you a flat monthly rate to handle the clerical basics, freeing your Brand Manager for the important task of keeping your branding socks pulled up and your shoes tied.

If you have a bigger office or a bigger budget, or if you already have a staff, consider either hiring a new person or reassigning and retraining your people to be brand-focused. In a perfect world, this is the office staff I would love to see you have:

- *Brand Manager.* This person is responsible for all the daily demands of your Personal Branding campaign, from negotiating advertising rates to booking interviews to getting quotes from the printer.

- *Office Manager.* This person runs your office, handling everything from payroll and human resources to security and maintenance.

- *Client-Service Manager.* This person oversees all aspects of client care, from first impressions to account updates and billing to gifts and crisis resolution.

- *Personal Assistant.* This person is your right hand, dealing with phone calls and e-mails, maintaining your calendar, and doing whatever needs to be done to ensure that you have time to be your best.

You can outsource all the other services you need to contractors. You'll get IT support from your Web hosting and Internet marketing company. You'll get design work from a freelance graphic designer, and copy from a freelance writer. If you can manage it, build this core staff in-house, on your payroll, so that these people are working only for you. Then supplement them with contractors to keep your costs under control.

One last thing about your people: *take great care of them*. If they help you reach that 100 percent income growth figure, treat them like gold. Reward them with gifts and recognition, because good people who can help you be your best do not grow on trees. Care for them, acknowledge their hard work, and compensate them well (I've seen companies that gave employees bonuses based not on revenue, but on how delighted clients were), and they will take care of you.

BY NOW YOU SHOULD BE . . .

- Seeing the first responses to your direct mail

- Writing your e-newsletter or blog if you have time

- Finishing your Brand Timetable

- Making the guest list for your first client event

- Starting to see a difference in your monthly income

- Realizing that you're less stressed because you're not working with unpleasant clients

15

MAINTAINING AND DEFENDING YOUR BRAND

Personal branding is today's buzzword. There is no one-strategy-fits-all. If you feel your personal best in a suit, wear a suit. If you want to be more relaxed, you can be. Just show respect for yourself.

—Mary Lou Andre, president, Organization by Design

Well, that wasn't so bad, was it? All right, it was stressful and expensive and a little terrifying. But you got through it. You got your new Personal Brand launched. You sent out your postcards and Personal Brochures, launched your Web site, contacted the clients you no longer wanted and gave them a polite brush-off, and held your Grand Re-Opening gala (two local reporters even showed up!). So now it's time to put your feet up, relax, and watch the money roll in, right?

You know the answer to that transparent trick question. The work is just beginning, and you've got two big tasks ahead of you: maintaining your new Personal Brand and living up to the promises it's making to all those people who are coming into contact with it. Hopefully, you won't ever have to deal with the third task: defending your brand when it's in crisis, such as when someone accuses you of cheating him by taking money for services you didn't provide, or sues you for malpractice. I hope you'll never be in that position, but as I like to remind all my clients:

Hope is not a success strategy.

Unfortunate things happen no matter how diligently we plan, so I'll address crisis branding in this closing chapter as well.

THINGS YOU CAN DO TODAY

1. Compare your monthly income before you raised your fees with your income now.

2. Create a promotion with an expiration date and see how that affects your response.

3. Review your business model to see if it is friendly to the disabled or visually/hearing impaired.

4. Ensure that if you deal with the elderly (such as in retirement planning), your materials are easy for someone with reduced vision to read.

5. See to it that your office is child-friendly if you deal with parents of small children.

6. Order business cards for all your employees. Yes, they all need them.

BRAND MAINTENANCE

There are two kinds of brand maintenance. The first involves staying on top of all the services and timed events that need to keep happening to keep your Personal Brand out there in the marketplace. This means making sure that printing gets done on schedule, mailings happen when they're supposed to, business cards get ordered, Web site updates occur on time, gift baskets are sent, RSVPs for client events are received, and a million other details that take a thousand phone calls or e-mails a day are seen to.

Honestly, this is why you have to have a Brand Manager. Just making sure that the basic infrastructure of your Personal Brand doesn't come crashing down like a rotted wooden bridge is a full-time job. There's no way you can possibly do it and practice medicine, law, or financial planning. It's essential that you have a person whose only job is staying on top of the printers, the mailing houses, the photographers, the designers, and the caterers. Someone who makes sure that you're paying the rate you agreed to for your newspaper advertisement, not some higher rate that a sales rep tried to slip by unnoticed.

The second aspect of brand maintenance involves communication with your clients. You need to be communicating with them regularly via mail, e-mail, or phone, keeping them updated and making them feel cared for. One of the reasons this is so important is that human beings hate feeling that they are being kept in the dark. When you call a company's customer-service number and you can't get an answer to why your PC isn't working, what really makes you angrier than anything else (other than being on hold for 45 minutes)? It's not being able to get a straight answer. If some smart IT professional gets on the line and tells you that you probably need a new computer, fine, you can deal with that. It's uncertainty that we humans don't handle very well.

So when your clients don't receive regular communication from you, they feel left in the dark. This can make them resentful, and that resentment only builds if the first time they hear from you in six months is to ask them for a referral. That's the "he only calls when he wants something" mindset. It's bad enough if you're an ungrateful son, but to be an ungrateful CPA? You'll be seen as uncaring, calculating, and opportunistic, and you'll lose business.

Remember, Personal Branding is a relationship built on an implied promise, and healthy relationships take constant communication. That means having systems that allow you to stay in touch with your current clients at least once per month: an e-newsletter, e-mail alerts, a print newsletter, a personal letter from you, a phone call, even a seasonal greeting card. It's not about need, financial statements, or referrals. It's about "touch." There's a reason that marketing professionals call it that. We're social animals. We like to be around others, like to know that the people we trust and respect value us as well. Regular communication tells your clients that you value and respect them. That kind of goodwill building will get you more referrals and cut down on complaints.

BRAND SURGERY
THE PATIENT: BRAND MAINTENANCE

- Don't leave anything to chance. Plan everything.

- Don't assume that people know who's responsible for what task. Assign everything.

- If you want to drink or behave like a college freshman, go on vacation.

- If you're small, use free automated tools like Yahoo Calendar as a sort of CRM lite.

- Make personal contact with every one of your clients at least once a year.

- If you can't beat a competitor in your target market, try partnering.

Customer Relationship Management

The newest tool in handling customer communication is powerful software called customer relationship management software, or CRM. Sold under brand names like Salesforce.com, CRM tools used to be known as sales force automation because they were designed to enable sales executives to keep track of their prospect and client database and manage their appointment calendars.

These days, CRM tools are much more widely available, and I recommend them to many of my clients who maintain larger offices or who are working with one or more professional partners in a large practice. Some CRM systems are strictly Web-based, with no software to buy, while others, such as that sold by Siebel, actually reside on your computer network. Either way, CRM products give you a suite of extremely powerful features for managing and optimizing client relationships:

- Operating your own call center for telemarketing and client-service questions, with instant access to the client's complete history.

- An online client portal that clients can use to get answers to their questions from an online knowledge base, and that you can customize to deliver personalized information to different client groups.

- Having incoming client e-mails automatically routed to the right person.

- Controlling and automating your direct e-mail campaigns.

- Managing your e-mail and direct-mail lists.

- Analyzing your return on investment data.

- Storing all your relevant documents for easy electronic delivery to a printer or prospect.

- Providing automated lead capture from your Web site, including sending a personalized greeting e-mail to the site visitor.

If you're a small organization, CRM is probably not necessary, nor is it likely to be within your budget. But if, for example, you're running a growing legal practice with 6 attorneys, 50 clients, and more of both coming all the time, you probably need a tool to make sure that the lines of communication remain open, vital documents don't disappear, and confidential matters remain confidential. CRM gives you complete control over the inflow and outflow of information by e-mail, phone, and print. If you're big and getting bigger, I highly recommend checking into it *before* you launch your Personal Brand.

THINGS YOU CAN DO IN A WEEK

1. Attend a trade show or conference and network like a fiend.

2. Establish a day and time when you always stop working to enter any new contacts into your database.

3. Start a "swipe file," a file of clippings, brochures, and other good ideas that you can "borrow" from later on.

4. If your community warrants it and you're comfortable with it, find ways you can make your business more friendly to the lucrative gay and lesbian market.

5. Create a client complaint form on your Web site and ask clients to tell you about anything, no matter how minor, that they didn't like about their experience.

6. Record your first podcast and make it available on your Web site.

Adjusting on the Fly

Let's talk about Steve Jobs, cofounder of Apple Inc. There's no question that he's a brilliant brand technician and visionary; the Jobs "reality distortion field" alone is said to be responsible for the runaway success of marketing monsters like the iPhone. But think back to 1996, when Jobs came back to Apple, the company he had created with Steve Wozniak. Things were not good: the company was losing ground to Microsoft's inferior but entrenched Windows operating system, and its product line was confusing. Most experts figured that Apple was little more than a takeover target.

What Jobs did was stunning: he ignored all that had gone before, threw many long-standing projects over the side of the ship, and completely revamped the company. Boring was out; design was in. The results—the iMac, iPod, iTunes, iPhone, and so on—have turned a moribund corporation into a culture-changing dynamo. The lesson: inertia kills. You have to be willing to change things on the fly when they're not working. That's true for CEOs of major computer companies, and it's true for Personal Branders. It's absolutely essential that you be willing and able to adjust your strategy as time goes by.

Remember, way back when, that I suggested taking your client advisory board to breakfast every three to six months to talk about how you could improve? You should be doing the same kind of self-assessment with every aspect of your Personal Branding: your spending, your flow of new clients, your marketing effectiveness, your penetration into your new market. This is why it's so important to track everything you do, from the dollars you spend on newspaper advertising to the number of calls you get after each round of direct mailings.

Train your staff to ask new prospects where they heard about you and log the information. I would even recommend creating a Client Intake Form that you can use to quiz clients on which of your branding channels they've come into contact with.

Then every six months at least, sit down with the data and ask these questions:

- Am I sticking to my budget?

- Am I seeing the number of high-quality prospects I need?

- Am I getting enough new ideal clients signed and sealed?

- Am I bringing in enough new income? If not, what do I need to do?

- Are all my branding channels delivering a healthy response? If not, which ones do I need to consider changing?

- Am I getting enough traction in my target market?

- Am I working the number of hours I want to, or do I need to scale back my branding?

- Am I enjoying this?

For instance, if you've been running ads in the local lifestyle magazine for the last six months, but not one new client has mentioned seeing the ad, it might be time for you to consider pulling it and spending your money elsewhere. Or what if when you were researching your target market, you overlooked a powerful competitor? When you launch your marketing, you suddenly find that you're fighting an uphill battle against someone who "owns" 40 percent of the clients you're chasing. That's the time to consider retrenching and going after a similar but less challenging group of prospects. And if you have the pleasant problem of your Personal Branding working too well, you need to decide how best to handle the flood of business. Do you slow down your marketing, turn away new clients, or expand and find partners to handle the demand?

Regrouping and assessing two or three times a year can help you rein in spending that's become unsustainable, dump ineffective channels or tools and replace them with effective alternatives, and make sure that your Personal Branding is doing what it's supposed to do: giving you a career and a lifestyle that you can really enjoy.

THINGS YOU CAN DO IN A MONTH

1. Advertise in a publication for a few months, and then meet with the advertising manager to discuss special pricing or benefits such as advertorials.

2. Invite a reporter to spend a typical workday with you as a human interest story. Even better, if you have a dramatic client or case, invite a reporter to "ride along."

3. Record a "weekly update" on your phone system, allowing prospects to call in to get new information every week.

4. Conduct a mail survey of your prospects to find out how fast their Internet connections are. You might also be able to get useful information from the local phone or cable company.

5. Protect all your content with a copyright symbol, and speak to your lawyer about trademarking any processes or unique products that you've come up with.

6. If you don't take credit cards, inquire about a merchant account so that you can accept them as payment.

A BRAND IN CRISIS

You're no Michael Jackson, and you're no Martha Stewart. I was asked by the cable news networks to comment on the state of their powerful Personal Brands when they were on trial for child molestation and fraud, respectively. Be grateful; your transgressions aren't likely to be tracked by a national audience and debated on CNN. But that doesn't mean that your Personal Brand can't land in a lot of hot water. If it does, you've got to know how to prevent it from being cooked.

A brand crisis is really a simple matter of trust and doubt. Something happens that makes the people in your target market or your wider community doubt that the identity you've put forth via your Personal Brand is really who you are. People start wondering if you're a hypocrite or a phony. And since negative gossip spreads far faster than good word of mouth, the bad stuff can race ahead of your business much faster than you can imagine.

A crisis doesn't have to mean that you "had sex with that woman" or something else salacious. In fact, it's usually brought on by a simple misunderstanding that gets out of control. Some examples:

- Someone accuses you of copying a competitor's advertising.

- You're sued for breach of contract.

- You say something that inadvertently offends the wife of a government official.

- You foolishly claim that you went to an Ivy League college when you didn't, and someone calls you on it.

- Someone accuses you of sending e-mail spam to all your clients.

None of these is a major issue that should affect your Personal Brand or your business, but each one of them can do so if you let it spiral out of control. That's why it's especially important to monitor your image in the marketplace and to respond fast if any potential scandals or misunderstandings occur. Some crucial damage-control steps:

- First, determine whether the problem has gone public or not. If it's still private, meet with the party involved to sort things out. Explain any misunderstandings and offer compensation if appropriate.

- If it's gone public, talk to your attorney about what you should say without increasing your potential liability. If you have a publicist, talk to him or her about whether you should demand a retraction from a paper, issue a press release, or hold a press conference.

- If you've made a mistake, take full responsibility and act to correct it immediately.

- Do not go into hiding. Denial only makes things worse.

- Apologize as quickly as you can if you can do so without putting yourself in a bad legal position.

The other factor that makes branding crises so challenging is that thanks to the Internet and wireless technology, we live in a news-in-a-minute culture. A video of you dancing at a company party in a makeshift toga with a bottle of Jack Daniels in your hand can be seen by 100,000 people on YouTube the next morning. Bloggers can spread rumors about you that are read (and believed) by thousands. Old MySpace, Facebook, or LinkedIn profiles can come back to haunt you.

Your basic stance should be: *beware*. Be cautions and circumspect. Assume that whenever you're in public, you must live up to your brand's promise. Even well-meant ribald behavior, taken out of context, can do damage. And send someone tech-savvy around the Web to erase any incriminating things from your past—college fraternity pictures, bad poems, political rants, movie clips. Don't give any competitors or evil-minded members of the community the chance to try to take you down. Remember, you're a Personal Brand now. You're public. You have a responsibility to live up to the promises you've made.

BRAND CASE STUDY

The Brand: Rev. Carlton Pearson

Specialization: Pentecostal heretic and preacher of the Gospel of Inclusion

Location: Tulsa, Oklahoma

Channels: His New Dimensions Church, books, television

Highlights: Appearing on *Dateline NBC* after losing his ministry

Online: www.gospelofinclusion.com, www.newdimensions.us

The Story: Few people have climbed as high as Carlton D. Pearson, or fallen so far so fast by their own doing. Once one of the fastest-rising

(continued)

stars in the Pentecostal branch of the Christian church, labeled by some as the black heir to Oral Roberts himself, he had it all: a huge church with a huge following, a pulpit from which to shout his message to millions, status, money, and influence. But he threw it all away because he decided one night that he didn't believe in Hell. The uproar destroyed his church and his career. Now he is reinventing himself as the custodian of a revolutionary message: the Gospel of Inclusion, which says that all men are saved, not just believing Christians. It's as controversial as, well, Hell, and it's the subject of his first book, *The Gospel of Inclusion*.

How It All Started: "The men in my family were either preachers or convicts," Pearson says. A dapper, charismatic man, he grew up in a mixed-race, mixed-faith part of San Diego County, part of a long, long line of African American Pentecostals. It seemed foreordained that he would become a preacher himself. And did he ever follow that path: attending Oral Roberts University, starting the revival-like Azusa Festivals that drew tens of thousands of the faithful, captivating audiences with his mesmerizing preaching. His star seemed impossible to stop.

Then came the night when he was watching the news about starving women and children making their way back into Rwanda on his big-screen TV while eating dinner. "I said, 'Lord, I can't believe you would let these people suffer like this only to suck them into Hell,'" he says. "And I heard a voice say to me, 'Is that what you think we're doing? Can't you see they're already there?'" That was the beginning of a revelation for Pearson that would shatter his faith, his preaching, and his career and cost him his livelihood and nearly his marriage: Hell is a place on earth. There is no eternal pit of fire. Everyone is redeemed by Christ, and religion is the problem, not the solution.

You can imagine what happened in the conservative Pentecostal community when Pearson started preaching this message: "I was labeled a heretic. I used to have 4,000 people at my services, and within a few months I had only 300." Bottom line, he lost everything. Even Oral Roberts, his white father, condemned him. Ironically, one segment of the community that embraced him, among a few others, was the group that his conservative faith had always railed against: gays, lesbians, people with AIDS, and transsexuals. They gave him hope and helped him resurrect his career as a religious revolutionary.

What This Brand Stands For:

- *Courage.* How many people who had the soul-shaking experience that Pearson had would have given up their lucrative career and potentially ruined their lives to follow their convictions? Few, I'll wager. Pearson did it, and he's earned the respect of nearly as many people as think he's an agent of Satan. The drama of his story has landed him media coverage on *This American Life, Dateline,* ABC's *20/20,* and other media. HBO has bought the rights to his story. "I couldn't have done things any other way," he says. "God spoke to me for a reason; I couldn't deny that."

- *Vision.* Pearson's Gospel of Inclusion envisions a world in which all humanity sheds the anxiety and fear that come with believing in a hateful God who damns most of His creation to Hell, where religions act as uniting forces instead of bearers of controlling dogma, and people pursue peace. "The religions of the world are not about building bridges to God or others but about controlling people through fear," he says. "Once people live in Christ Consciousness, with the knowledge that all are and have always been not only saved but safe, that will change everything."

- *Revolution.* He knows he's got an uphill battle, having been condemned by practically every mainstream Pentecostal and Evangelical leader in the country. He actually takes that as a positive sign. "First they ignore you, then they laugh at you, then they fight you, and then you win," he says, quoting Arun Gandhi, the Mahatma's grandson. "I believe that. I want to be a part of what I see as a significant movement in history. Everything starts with an often unassuming man, and then becomes a movement. Eventually, we build a monument to commemorate how things have changed. We're at the movement stage now."

X-Factor: Books. His first book, *The Gospel of Inclusion,* came out in April of 2008. His next, provocatively titled *God Is Not a Christian,* promises to ruffle even more feathers. But books are tangential to his real mission: changing hearts and minds. "I'm in the second half of my

(continued)

life, and I know what I'm here to do," he says. "If I have a brand to create and manage, then it's in the service of this message, and I can't imagine anything more important."

Branding Wisdom: "Know that you might pay a price for a brand that's more about your passion than about traditional wisdom," he says. "I chose to listen to the voice that spoke to me and to follow it to a reevaluation of everything I was and everything I did. That cost me dearly, but I have no regrets. There's a reason that we talk about the fires of passion: passion burns. The journey of Christ to the Cross is called 'The Passion' because passion can be about pain, and usually is. But if your passion is worth it, you will endure. I have a greater life now than I ever could have had if my eyes had remained closed, because now I see the truth. The awakening is my happy and holy liberation."

BRAND CONSISTENCY

Consistency in the timing of your branding and in the message is critical to the healthy growth of your Personal Brand. Prospects must see the same visuals, the same value points, and the same emotional message over and over before they make an impression. If you change your message on a whim, deliver direct-mail cards whenever you feel like it, or show up at networking mixers whenever the mood strikes you, you'll appear unprofessional.

Here are some tips for keeping your brand marketing consistent:

- Always check your latest message against your Specialization Statement.

- Follow your Brand Timetable to the letter.

- Update your Web site content at least monthly.

- Use your logo everywhere.

- Train your staff to support the values in your Personal Brand.

- Ignore trends.

- Ignore what competitors are doing.

- Give your marketing 12 months to generate results before you consider changes in the writing or the design.

- Assemble a team of skilled contractors—writers, Web developers, printers, and other such professionals—and use them for everything.

BE YOUR BRAND

Finally, it's not enough to market your Personal Brand. You've got to live it. This is why it's so important to choose a brand that reflects who you really are and what you really care about. If your Personal Brand reflects your true passions, lifestyle, and personality, it's going to be easy and fun for you to build, and you'll do a better job as a result.

If your Personal Brand says that you run marathons, run marathons. If it tells people that you're a serious jazz fan, know your Stan Kenton from your Dave Brubeck. *Be* your brand. Make this process foolproof by building your brand around what you do well, what you love, and how you live, including your flaws and foibles. That way, you don't have to change a thing. Now go and get rich.

BY NOW YOU SHOULD BE . . .

- Networking like a fiend

- Running a network of at least four referring professionals

- Seeing your income increase

- Seeing your company show up more often on Web searches

- Drawing praise for your client-service methods

- Recovering from your first successful special event

RESOURCES

Caveat emptor (buyer be-ware). We've assembled this library of personal branding resources based on our own experience and the recommendations of clients, but we haven't done due diligence on them, nor is this an endorsement. As with all things, use them with your eyes open.

Advice

- AllExperts.com
- Business.gov
- BusinessAdviceDaily.com
- BusinessNetworking Advice.com
- BusinessTown.com
- Businessweek.com
- Entrepreneur.com/ marketing
- Inc.com
- Online Business Advisor— Onlinebusinessadv.com

Business Needs and Services

- AllBusiness.com
- Cbiz.com
- Expectsolutions.com (office design consulting)
- Finewaters.com (bottled water with your company name on it)
- Greatland.com
- Officedepot.com
- Officemax.com
- Officescapesdirect.com
- OfficeWorld.com
- Quill.com
- Score.org
- Small Business Service Bureau—sbsb.com
- Staples.com

CRM Solutions

- Clpsuite.com

- Legrandcrm.com
- Microsoft Dynamics CRM
- Salesforce.com
- Shoestringcrm.com

Freelance Vendors (Designers, Copywriters)

- BizReef.com
- Craigslist.org
- Elance.com
- Getafreelancer.com
- Guru.com
- ifreelance.com
- Odesk.com
- Project4hire.com

Gifts

- 1800flowers.com
- BirthdayChocolates.com
- Cardstore.com
- CookiesByDesign.com
- Giftcards.com
- Giftcertificates.com
- GiftTree.com
- Harryanddavid.com
- Hersheysgift.com

- Omahasteaks.com
- Proflowers.com
- Shop.mms.com
- Starbucks.com

Mailing Services

- Direct Marketing Association —the-dma.org
- Directmail.com
- DirectMailQuotes.com
- FedEx.com
- PostcardMania.com
- SonicPrint.com
- TFC Marketing Support Services—tfcinc.com
- Usps.com/directmail

Photographers

- Asmp.org/findaphotographer
- Photographers.com
- PhotographyPros.com
- Respond.com

Printing

- Areaprinting.com
- GotPrint.com
- iPrint.com

- OvernightPrints.com
- PrintDirect.com
- PSPrint.com
- Uprinting.com
- VistaPrint.com

Research

- Business.com
- DemographicsNow.com
- HighBeam.com
- Hoovers.com
- MarketResearch.com
- NicheBOT.com
- Nichemarketresearch.com
- QuestionPro.com
- ResearchInfo.com
- SurveyMethods.com
- Wikipedia.org

Signage

- AccentSignage.com
- BuildASign.com
- FastSigns.com
- Signsnow—standout inacrowdedworld.com

Virtual Assistants

- CallRuby.com
- IntelligentOffice.com
- IVAA.org
- PersonalFriday.com

Web Developers/Internet Marketing

- ConstantContact.com
- DesignFirms.org
- Dice.com
- EmailLabs.com
- FindMyHost.com
- FindMyHosting.com
- GoDaddy.com
- ImnInc.com
- MailerMailer.com
- Mailworkz.com
- NetworkSolutions.com
- PRWeb.com
- Topica.com
- Web-development.com
- WebDesignFinders.net
- WebHero.com
- Xemion.com

INDEX

A-list, ideal clients, 35–36, 41–42
Ability *vs.* visibility, 29–30
Advertising, 201–216
  brand surgery, 210
  case study: David Riley, 206–208
  goals, 203
  indoor advertising channels, 72, 235
  newspaper and magazine, 203, 208–211
  online local business directories, 203, 214
  outdoor, 76, 203, 211–213, 235
  phone directory, 203, 205
  radio, 86, 178–179, 204, 235
  sponsorships, 90–91, 203, 214–216
  television, 204
  things you can do in a month, 213
  things you can do in a week, 204–205
  things you can do today, 202
Advice resources, 264
Affinity as brand response, 20–21
Agreements, referrals, 80–81
Apple, 255
Articles and press releases, 168–174
Authenticity, 29
Awareness as brand response, 20

B-list clients, 35, 41
Bach, David, case study, 9–12
Bandwidth, 150
Banner ads, 158
Bateson, Gregory, 6
Be your brand, 263
Blogs, 160–161
Bly, Robert, 65
Bottom line benefits, 43–45
Brand, personal (*See* Personal Brand)

Brand crisis, 257–259
Brand identity, 111–125
  brand surgery: logo, 115–116
  business card, 111–112, 125
  case study: Marty Rodriguez, 120–122
  company name, 12, 113–115
  graphical icon, 112, 119
  logo, 112, 115–116, 122–124
  partnerships, 116
  slogan, 112, 117–118
  system of materials, 125
  things you can do in a month, 124–125
  things you can do in a week, 118
  things you can do today, 113
Brand launch budget, 225
Brand manager, 248
Brand response, 20–21
Brand surgery
  advertising, 210
  balancing personal and professional, 102
  brochures, 135–136
  budget, 28
  business relationships and specialization, 61
  logo, 115–116
  maintaining your brand, 253
  networking, 193
  OYBP, 230, 241
  public relations (PR), 168
  selling and marketing, 34–35
  Web site, 152
Branding channels and tools, 67–95
  buzz marketing, 68, 234
  canvassing, 68–69, 234
  case study: Mike Parker, 81–83

Branding channels and tools (*continued*)
  direct mail, 71–72
  inclusive and exclusive, 67–68
  indoor advertising, 72, 235
  Internet, 72–74, 235
  networking, 74–75, 235
  outdoor advertising, 76
  OYBP, 234–236
  point-of-purchase (POP) display, 77–78, 235–236
  print advertising, 78–79, 235
  private seminars, 86–88, 235
  professional referrals, 79–81, 185–189, 235
  public relations (PR), 83–85, 235
  public seminars, 88–89, 235
  publishing, 85–86, 235
  radio advertising, 86, 204, 235
  referrals, 69–70, 79–81, 234
  Rule of Five, 93–94
  seminars, 86–89, 235
  special events, 89–90, 235–236
  sponsorships, 90–91, 203, 214–216
  synergy, 94–95
  telemarketing, 91, 235
  television advertising, 91–92, 204, 235
  things you can do in a month, 89
  things you can do in a week, 76–77
  things you can do today, 70
  trade shows, 92–93, 235
Branding handbook, 242–243
Branding strategy creation (*See* One-Year Branding Plan [OYBP])
Branding timetable, 238–242, 245–246
Broadband, 150
Brochures, 126–136
  brand surgery, 135–136
  building rapport with, 128–129
  case study: Todd Walkow, 132–134
  cover and layout, 130–131
  design, 127–132
  ideal uses for, 134–135
  layout, 130–131
  leading attribute, 128
  mail copies, 198–199
  OYBP, 235–236
  personal story, 128–129
  photographs, 131
  printing, 135–136
  size of, 131–132
  things you can do in a week, 131
  things you can do today, 128
  trust development, 127
  writing, 129–130
  your story, 129–130
  (*See also* Postcards)
Budgeting, One-Year Branding Plan (OYBP), 223–227
Business cards, 111–112, 125
Business model, reinventing, 60–61
Buzz marketing channels, 68, 234

C-list clients, 35, 41
Cadillac Escalade, 18
Call to Action (Eisenberg), 18
Calvin Klein brand, 64
Canvassing channels, 68–69, 234
Carson, Ron, 33
Case studies
  Wally Amos, 24–26
  David Bach, 9–12
  Kathy Kaehler, 243–245
  Tony Little, 220–222
  Mike Parker, 81–83
  Carlton Pearson, 259–262
  Shiva Rea, 189–191
  David Riley, 206–208
  Melissa Rivers, 170–172
  Marty Rodriguez, 120–122
  Dr. Laura Schlessinger, 55–57
  Kendra Todd, 153–157
  Todd Walkow, 132–134
  Daniel Will-Harris, 103–105
  Wyland, 37–40
Change as needs change, and specialization, 65
Channels (*See* Branding channels and tools)
Clarity, as key to a winning brand, 27
Client advisory board, 101
Client referrals (*See* Referrals)
Client retention budget, 225–227
Client service, referrals, 187
Client-service manager, 248
Client service plan, 97–99
Client understanding, as specialization benefit, 50

Clients, ideal, 31–45
  A-list, ideal clients, 35–36, 41–42
  actions to double earnings, 32, 34
  B-list clients, 35, 41
  becoming exclusive, 36, 43
  better branding, 33–35
  bottom line benefits, 43–45
  brand surgery: selling and marketing, 34–35
  C-list clients, 35, 41
  case study: Wyland, 37–40
  as crucial, 33–35
  earnings, 31–33
  fewer, and better quality, 8–12
  identify, 35–36
  prequalification as specialization benefit, 50
  things you can do in a month, 43
  things you can do in a week, 37
  things you can do today, 32
Color in logo, 123
Column, writing your own column, 175–176
Come Away with Me (recording), 29
Comfort level, 7, 19–20
Commitment to brand, 16
Communication, 252
Company name
  brand identity, 12, 113–115
  Web sites, 148
Complaints, recovering from, 107–108
Complaints, recovering from client-service, 107–108
Consistency, 27–28, 262–263
Constant Contact, 162–163
Contact, on Web site, 148
Contact methods, referrals, 187
Content (*See* Writing and content)
Continuous improvement, creating customer delight, 108
Cost, from ideal clients, 44
Cover and layout, brochures, 130–131
Cramer, Jim, 63
Credibility, 137, 145
CRM customer relationship management (CRM), 253–254, 265
Customer expectations, 5, 102–103
Customer service (delight), 96–108

brand surgery: balancing personal and professional, 102
case study: Daniel Will-Harris, 103–105
continuous improvement, 108
develop client service plan, 97–99
know what your customers want, 100–101
overdeliver, 102–103
recovering from complaints, 107–108
secrets to creating, 97–103
tenets, 105–106
things you can do in a month, 106–107
things you can do in a week, 99–100
things you can do today, 97
underpromise, 102–103

Decision threshold as brand response, 21
Design
  brochures, 127–132
  to interest the ideal client, 59–60
  postcards, 137
  Web site, 153
Designer, graphical, 112, 119, 122, 124–125
Development services, Web sites, 152–153
Dial-up connections, 159
Differentiation, as specialization benefit, 50
Dilution, as specialization mistake, 64
Direct mail
  as channel, 71–72, 139
  e-mail, 161–162, 243
  mailing service resources, 266
  referrals, 198
  (*See also* Brochures; Postcards)
Diversification, as specialization mistake, 63
DKNY, 112
Download, 151

E-mail, 148, 161–162, 243
E-newsletters, 162–163
Earnings, increasing, 31–33
Eight-step program for Personal Branding, 22–23
Eisenberg, Bryan, 18
Emotional needs, and specialization, 65
Enjoyment, from ideal clients, 44–45
Escape clauses, referrals, 187

Evaluation, referrals, 80
Every Day (magazine), 62
Everything is branding, 13–14
Exclusive branding channels, 67–68
Expectations, customer, 5, 102–103
Expert status establishment, 176–177
    (*See also* Specialization)
Extras for Web sites, 148–150

Fear, and focus on the ideal client, 33–34
Fees, from ideal clients, 43
Finances, 43–45, 223–227
Findability, company name for, 113
First 30 days of One-Year Branding Plan
    (OYBP), 245–246
First-mover advantage, 65
Flash, 151
Focus on strength, as specialization bene-
    fit, 50
Follow-up
    networking and referrals, 195
    postcards, 142–143
    referrals, 81
Formal networking, 183–185
Freedemographics.com, 54
Freelance vendor resources, 265
Future Now, 18

Gestalt, 21
Gift resources, 266
Goals
    of advertising, 203
    reasons for Personal Brand, 6–7
    Web sites, 146–147
Google AdWords, 158
Google Calendar, 240–241
Google Maps, 158–159, 214
Graphical designer, 112, 119, 122, 124–125
Graphical icon, 112, 119

Handbook, branding, 242–243
Home page, on Web site, 147
Homes and Land, 209
Hosting, 151
Hours worked, from ideal clients, 44
How it works (*See* Process of Personal
    Branding)
Hyperlink, 151

Icon, 112, 119
Ideal brochure/postcard use, 134–135,
    141–143
Ideal clients (*See* Clients, ideal)
Identity of brand (*See* Brand identity)
Incentives, referrals, 187
Inclusive branding channels, 67
Income, from ideal clients, 43–44
Indoor advertising channels, 72, 235
Informal networking, 183, 192–194
Internet, as branding channel, 72–74, 235
    (*See also* Web site)
Internet marketing resources, 268
Iron John (Bly), 65
Irrational branding, 15
ISP, 151

Jobs, Steve, 255
Jones, Norah, 29

Launch One-Year Branding Plan (OYBP),
    237–249
Layout of brochures, 130–131
Leading attribute, 128, 233–234
Leads, 80, 145
    (*See also* Clients, ideal; Referrals)
Lifestyle, from ideal clients, 45
Lifestyle Market Analyst, 54
Logo, 112, 115–116, 122–124

Mad Money (TV program), 63
Magazine and newspaper advertising, 203,
    208–211
Mail (*See* Direct mail)
Mailing service resources, 266
Maintaining and defending Personal
    Brand, 250–263
    adjusting rapidly, 255–257
    be your brand, 263
    brand crisis, 257–259
    brand surgery, 253
    case study: Carlton Pearson, 259–262
    communication, 252
    consistency, 262–263
    customer relationship management
        (CRM), 253–254
    staying current, 251–252
    things you can do in a month, 257

things you can do in a week, 254–255
things you can do today, 251
Market research, 100–101
Marketing support, referrals, 187
Marketresearch.com, 54
Meetings, referrals, 80
Memorable, company name as, 113
Mistakes, 62–65, 107–108
Month (*See* Things you can do in a
    month)

Names
    for the company, 12, 113–115
    Web sites, 148
Networking, 182–200
    benefits of, 183
    brand surgery, 193
    case study: Shiva Rea, 189–191
    formal, 183–185
    informal, 183, 192–194
    joining, 194
    professional referral network (PRN),
        185–189
    referrals (*See* Referrals)
    smart networking, 194–196
    things you can do in a month, 196
    things you can do in a week, 188
    things you can do today, 183–184
Networking channels, 74–75, 235
Newspaper and magazine advertising,
    203, 208–211
Novelty, and specialization, 65

Office manager, 248
One-Year Branding Plan (OYBP), 219–249
    brand surgery, 230, 241
    branding channels, 234–236
    branding handbook, 242–243
    branding timetable, 238–242, 245–246
    budgeting, 223–227
    building your personal brand, 230–234
    case studies
      Kathy Kaehler, 243–245
      Tony Little, 220–222
    defined, 219–220
    first 30 days, 245–246
    leading attribute, 233–234
    let your current clients know, 247

perception, 228–231
    Rule of Five, 236
    specialization statement, 61–62,
        232–233
    staffing, 247–249
    target market, choosing, 231–232
    things you can do in a month, 234
    things you can do in a week, 227–228,
        242
    things you can do today, 224, 238
Online local business directories, 203,
    214
Outdoor advertising, 76, 203, 211–213,
    235
Overdelivering customer service, 102–103
OYBP (*See* One-Year Branding Plan
    [OYBP])

Parker, Mike, 81–83
Partnering, and specialization, 65
Partnerships and brand identity, 116
PDF, 151
Perception, 6–7, 228–231
Personal assistant, 248
Personal Brand
    advertising, 201–216
    attract and retain elite clients, 31–45
    brand identity, 111–125
    branding strategy creation, 219–236
    brochure and postcard, 126–143
    channels for, 67–95
    customer delight, creating, 96–108
    defined, 4–6
    maintaining and defending, 250–263
    naming the business, 12, 113–115
    networking and referrals, 182–200
    OYBP, 219–249
    process of Personal Branding, 17–30
    public relations (PR), 164–181
    reasons for, 3–16
    resources, 264–268
    specialization, 49–66
    Web resources, 264–268
    Web site, 144–163
Personal brochure and postcard (*See*
    Brochures; Postcards)
Personal referrals, 197
Personal story in brochures, 128–129

Personality (leading attribute), 233–234
Personnel page, on Web site, 147
Phone directory advertising, 78, 201, 203, 205, 208, 213–214
Photographer resources, 266–267
Photographs in brochures, 131
Plan (*See* One-Year Branding Plan [OYBP])
Point-of-purchase (POP) display channels, 77–78, 235–236
Postcards, 136–143
    design, 137
    direct mailing, 140–141
    essential elements, 138
    ideal uses of, 141–143
    OYBP, 235–236
    printing, 139
    response channels, 138–139
    size of, 136
    things you can do in a month, 140
    writing, 137–138
    (*See also* Brochures)
PR (*See* Public relations [PR])
Prequalification of clients, as specialization benefit, 50
Press releases and articles, 168–174
Presumed expertise, as specialization benefit, 50
Print advertising channels, 78–79, 235
Print publications, 168–178
Printing, 16, 135–136, 139
Printing resources, 267
Private seminar channels, 86–88, 235
PRN (professional referral network), 185–189
Process of Personal Branding, 17–30
    authenticity, 29
    brand response, 20–21
    brand surgery: budget, 28
    case study: Wally Amos, 24–26
    comfort, doing business with, 19–20
    eight-step program, 22–23
    keys to a winning brand, 27–28
    things you can do in a month, 23–24
    things you can do in a week, 21–22
    things you can do today, 18–19
    visibility *vs.* ability, 29–30
Products list, on Web site, 147–148

Professional referral channels, 79–81, 235
Professional referral network (PRN), 185–189
Programming, Web site, 153
Promise, Personal Brand as, 5
Prospects, 7
    (*See also* Clients, ideal)
Public relations (PR)
    basic steps, 167
    brand surgery, 168
    case study: Melissa Rivers, 170–172
    channels for, 83–85, 235
    community outreach, 179–181
    defined, 164–165
    expert status establishment, 176–177
    importance of, 165–166
    press releases and articles, 168–174
    print publications, 168–178
    radio, 178–179
    things you can do in a month, 178
    things you can do in a week, 174–175
    things you can do today, 166–167
    types of, 168–178
    your own column, 175–176
Public seminar channels, 88–89, 235
Publishing channels, 85–86, 235

Radio, 86, 178–179, 204, 235
Randi, James "The Amazing," 63
Ray, Rachael, 62–63
Rea, Shiva, 189–191
Reasons for Personal Brand, 3–16
    attract and retain quality clients, 8–12
    brand surgery: your company brand, 9
    case study: David Bach, 9–12
    commitment to brands, 16
    effects of branding, 16
    everything is branding, 13–14
    fewer, and better quality, 8–12
    goals, 6–7
    irrational branding, 15
    organic growth, 15
    Personal Brand, defined, 4–6
    things to do in a month, 14
    things to do in a week, 7
    things to do today, 4
    time for branding, 15

Recovering from client-service
    complaints, 107–108
Referral response team, 188
Referrals
    asking for, 197–198
    building system, 198–200
    channels, 69–70, 234
    client service, referrals, 187
    company name for, 113
    from ideal clients, 44
    personal, 197
    professional, 79–81, 235
    professional referral network (PRN),
        185–189
Registered Rep, 33
Relationships, 5–6, 145
Renewal clauses, referrals, 187
Resources, 264–268
Response, brand, 20–21
Response channels, 138–139
Rewards, referrals, 187
Ries, Al and Laura, 123
Right of first refusal, referrals, 187
Risks of specialization, 52–53
Rivers, Melissa, 170–172
Rodriguez, Marty, 120–122
Rule of Five, branding channels, 93–94,
    236

Sans serif typeface for logo, 123–124
Santa Barbara Independent, 209
Schlessinger, Dr. Laura, 55–57
Search engine optimization (SEO),
    157–158
Selling your business, and ideal clients,
    44
Seminars, as branding channel, 86–89,
    235
SEO (search engine optimization),
    157–158
Serif typeface for logo, 123–124
Server, 151
Service list, on Web site, 147–148
Service resources, business, 264–265
Shopping cart, 151
Signage as outdoor advertising, 76, 203,
    211–213, 235
Signage resources, 267–268

Six-Weeks Marketing Blitz, 141–142
Size
    of brochures, 131–132
    of logo, 124
    of postcards, 136
Slogan, 112, 117–118
Smart networking, 194–196
Special event channels, 89–90, 235–236
Specialization, 49–66
    to attract and retain quality clients, 8–9
    benefits of, 50–51
    brand surgery: business relationships,
        61
    case study: Dr. Laura Schlessinger,
        55–57
    design service for ideal client, 59–60
    identify target market, 52–59
    importance of, 49–50
    improving, 65
    as key to a winning brand, 27
    mistakes, 62–65
    Personal Brand control of perception,
        6–7
    reinvent business model, 60–61
    risks of, 52–53
    specialization statement, 61–62,
        232–233
    steps in, 53–61
    things you can do in a month, 64
    things you can do in a week, 59
    things you can do today, 51
Specialization statement, 61–62, 232–233
Sponsorships, 90–91, 203, 214–216
Staffing, 247–249
Synergy channels, 94–95

Target market, 52–59, 231–232
Telemarketing channels, 91, 235
Television advertising, 91–92, 204, 235
Terminology for Web sites, 150–151
Things you can do in a month
    advertising, 213
    brand identity, 124–125
    branding channels, 89
    clients, attract and retain quality, 43
    creating customer delight, 106–107
    maintaining your brand, 257
    networking, 196

Things you can do (*continued*)
OYBP, 234
postcards, 140
process of Personal Branding, 23–24
public relations (PR), 178
reasons for Personal Brand, 14
specialization, 64
Web sites, 160
Things you can do in a week
advertising, 204–205
brand identity, 118
branding channels, 76–77
brochures, 131
clients, attract and retain quality, 37
creating customer delight, 99–100
maintaining your brand, 254–255
networking, 188
OYBP, 227–228, 242
process of Personal Branding, 21–22
public relations (PR), 174–175
reasons for Personal Brand, 7
specialization, 59
Web sites, 150
Things you can do today
advertising, 202
brand identity, 113
branding channels, 70
brochures, 128
clients, attract and retain quality, 32
creating customer delight, 97
maintaining your brand, 251
networking, 183–184
OYBP, 224, 238
process of Personal Branding, 18–19
public relations (PR), 166–167
reasons for Personal Brand, 4
specialization, 51
Web sites, 146
Throughput, 151
Time
for branding, 15
month (*See* Things you can do in a
month)
today (*See* Things you can do today)
week (*See* Things you can do in a week)
year (*See* One-Year Branding Plan
[OYBP])
Timed campaigns, postcards, 142

Timetable, branding, 238–242, 245–246
Today (*See* Things you can do today)
Todd, Kendra, 153–157
Trade shows channels, 92–93, 235
Traffic, Web, 151
Twelve-month branding campaign,
141
The 23 Immutable Laws of Branding
(Ries), 123
Typeface for logo, 123–124

Underpromising customer service,
102–103
Understanding as brand response, 21
URL, 151
USA Today, 7
User interface, 151

Virtual assistant resources, 268
Visibility *vs.* ability, 29–30

Walkow, Todd, 132–134
Walt Disney theme parks, 103
Warm calling, 91, 142
Web site, 144–163
bells and whistles (extras), 148–150
blogs, 160–161
brand surgery: Web site, 152
as branding channel, 72–74
case study: Kendra Todd, 153–157
design, 153
developer resources, 268
development services, 152–153
direct e-mail, 161–162
drive traffic to, 157–159
e-mail, 148, 161–162, 243
e-newsletters, 162–163
essential pages, 147–148
goals of, 146–147
Internet, as branding channel, 72–74,
235
Internet marketing resources, 268
OYBP, 235–236
reasons for, 145
referrals, 189
resources for, 264–268
terminology, 150–151
things you can do in a month, 160

things you can do in a week, 150
things you can do today, 146
Week (*See* Things you can do in a week)
Wi-Fi, 151
Wieden + Kennedy, 15
Will-Harris, Daniel, 103–105
Winfry, Oprah, 12, 15
Wozniak, Steve, 255
Writing and content
    brochures, 129–130
    column, writing your own, 175–176

postcards, 137–138
Web site, 153
Wyland, 37–40

Yahoo Calendar, 240–241
Year (*See* One-Year Branding Plan
    [OYBP])
Yellow Pages ads, 78, 201, 205, 208,
    213–214
You, Personal Brand as, 4–5
Your story in brochures, 129–130

ABOUT THE AUTHORS

Peter Montoya is a renowned speaker, trainer, and media expert on personal branding. He is widely regarded as the leading teacher on the concept, potential, and application of personal branding as a strategy for transforming an independent professional practice into a successful business that delivers profits and personal fulfillment, and that generates a self-fueling stream of high-quality clients.

Peter has entertained and educated more than 100,000 professionals and business owners around the United States and Canada. He has appeared on Fox News, MSNBC, CNN, and ABC, and has been featured in print and online media, including *USA Today*, the *Los Angeles Times*, the *Chicago Tribune, New York Newsday*, the BBC, AFP, Reuter's, and CBS Marketwatch.

Tim Vandehey is an established freelance ghostwriter and book collaborator, editor, and book doctor who has written or edited more than 20 nonfiction books.